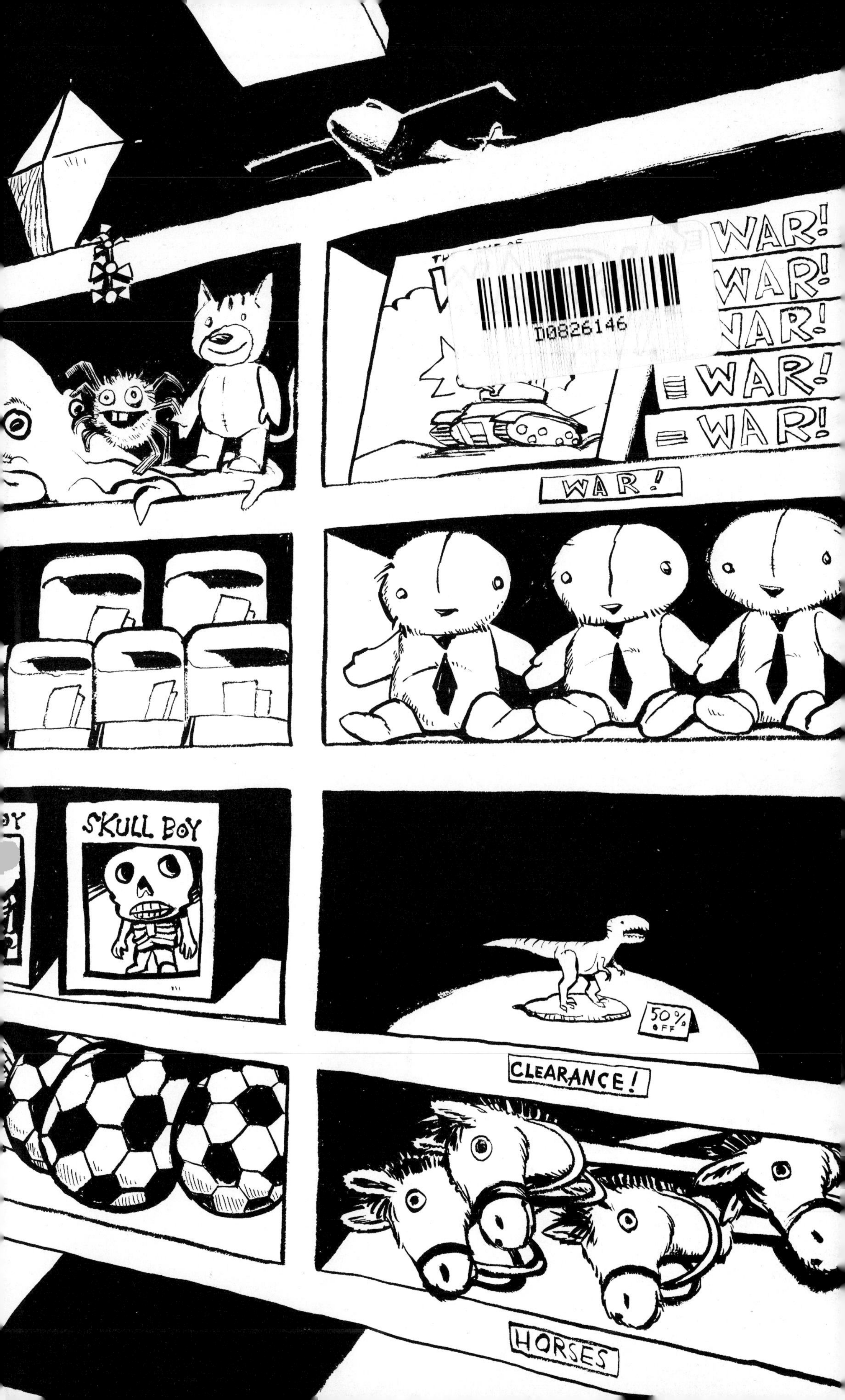

WAR!
WAR!
WAR!
WAR!
WAR!
WAR!
SKULL BOY
50% OFF
CLEARANCE!
HORSES

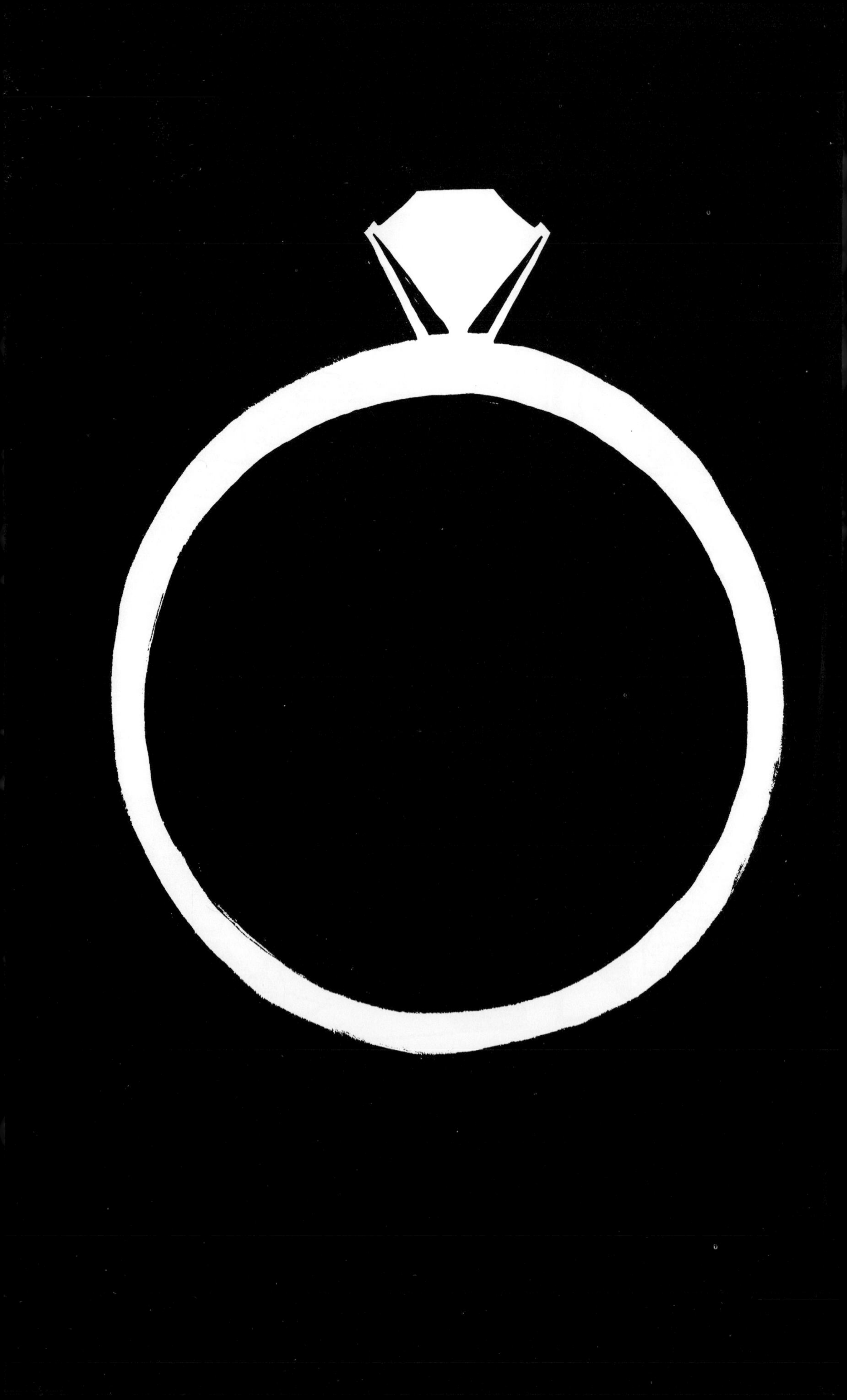

image® COMICS PRESENTS

TOMMYSAURUS REX ™

by
Doug TenNapel

FOR IMAGE COMICS:

Erik Larsen - *Publisher*
Todd McFarlane - *President*
Marc Silvestri - *CEO*
Jim Valentino - *Vice-President*

Eric Stephenson - *Managing Editor*
Brett Evans - *Production Manager*
Cindie Espinoza - *Controller*

B. Clay Moore - *Public Relations & Marketing Coordinator*
Allen Hui - *Web Developer*
Jon Malin - *Production Assistant*
Tim Hegarty - *Booktrade/International Rights*

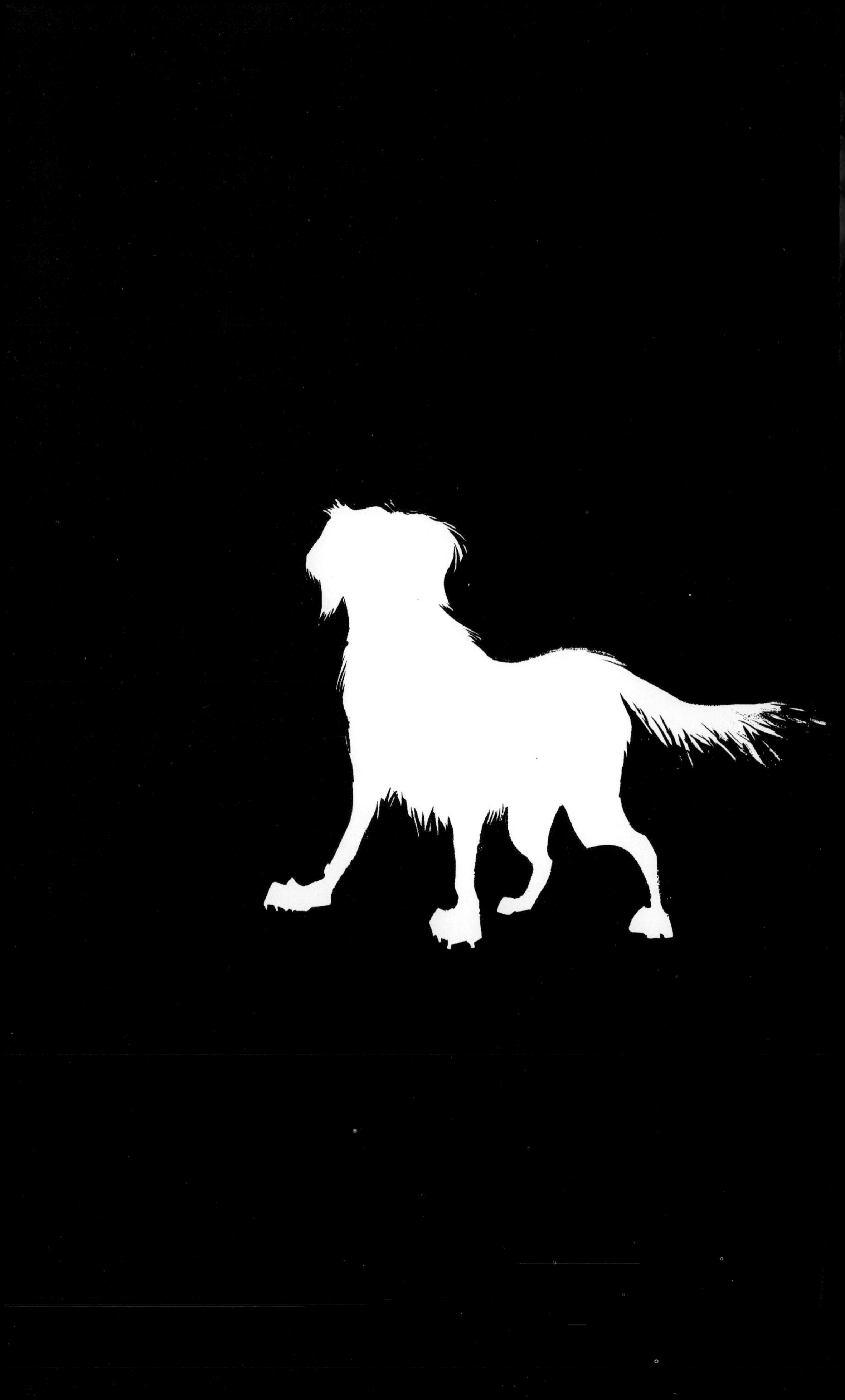

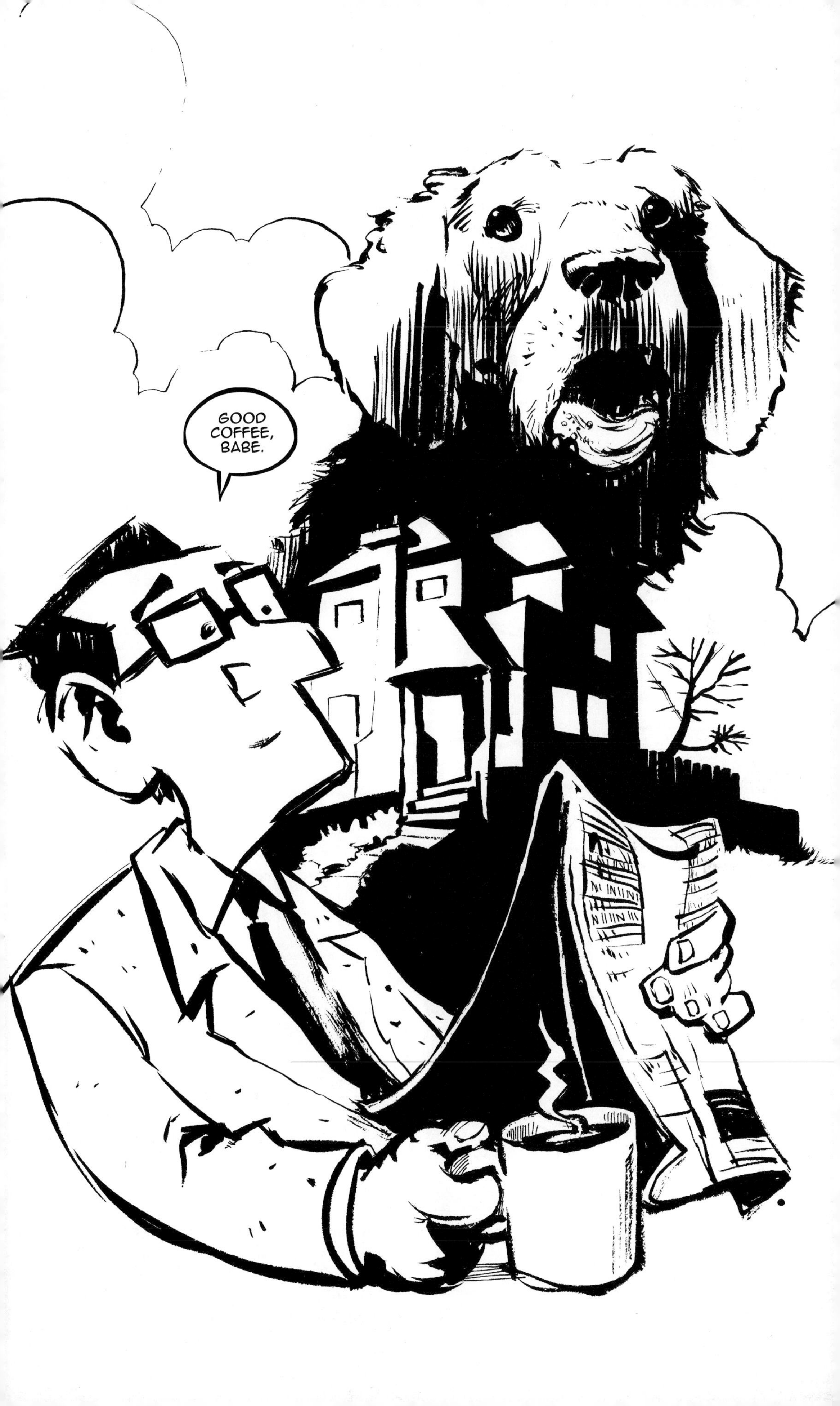
GOOD COFFEE, BABE.

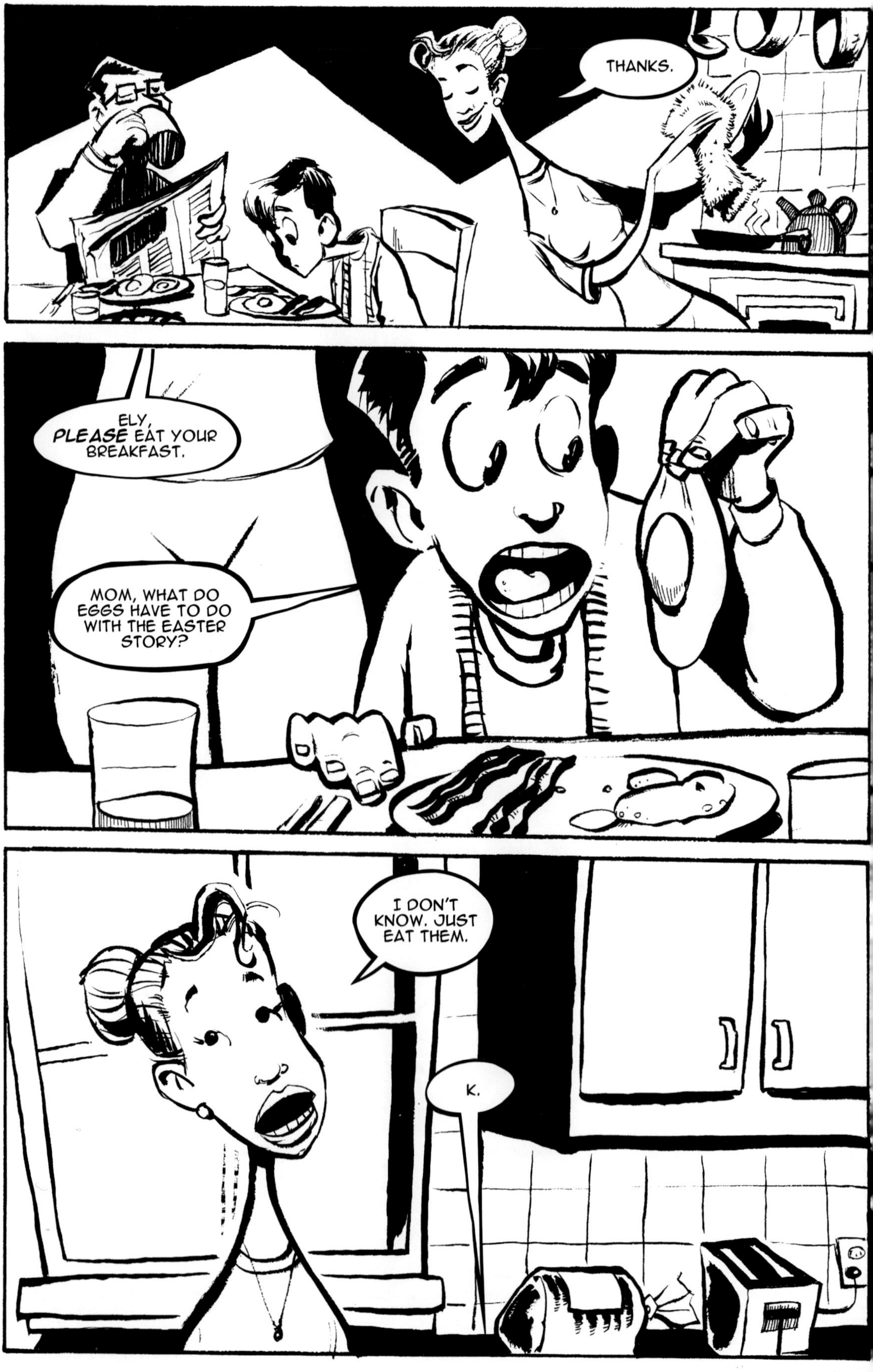
THANKS.
ELY, PLEASE EAT YOUR BREAKFAST.
MOM, WHAT DO EGGS HAVE TO DO WITH THE EASTER STORY?
I DON'T KNOW. JUST EAT THEM.
K.

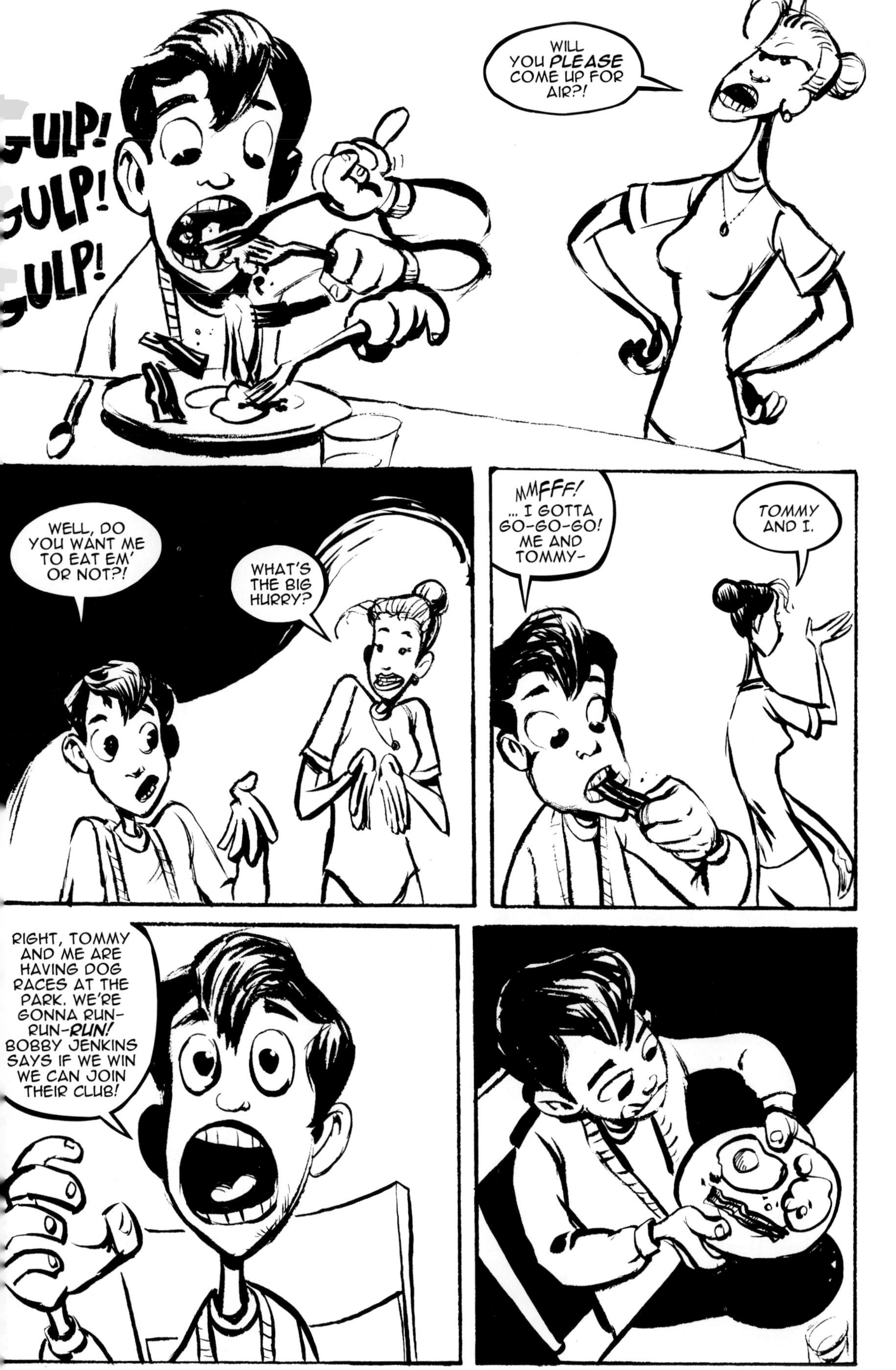
GULP! GULP! GULP!
WILL YOU PLEASE COME UP FOR AIR?!
WELL, DO YOU WANT ME TO EAT EM' OR NOT?!
WHAT'S THE BIG HURRY?
MMFFF! ... I GOTTA GO-GO-GO! ME AND TOMMY-
TOMMY AND I.
RIGHT, TOMMY AND ME ARE HAVING DOG RACES AT THE PARK. WE'RE GONNA RUN-RUN-RUN! BOBBY JENKINS SAYS IF WE WIN WE CAN JOIN THEIR CLUB!

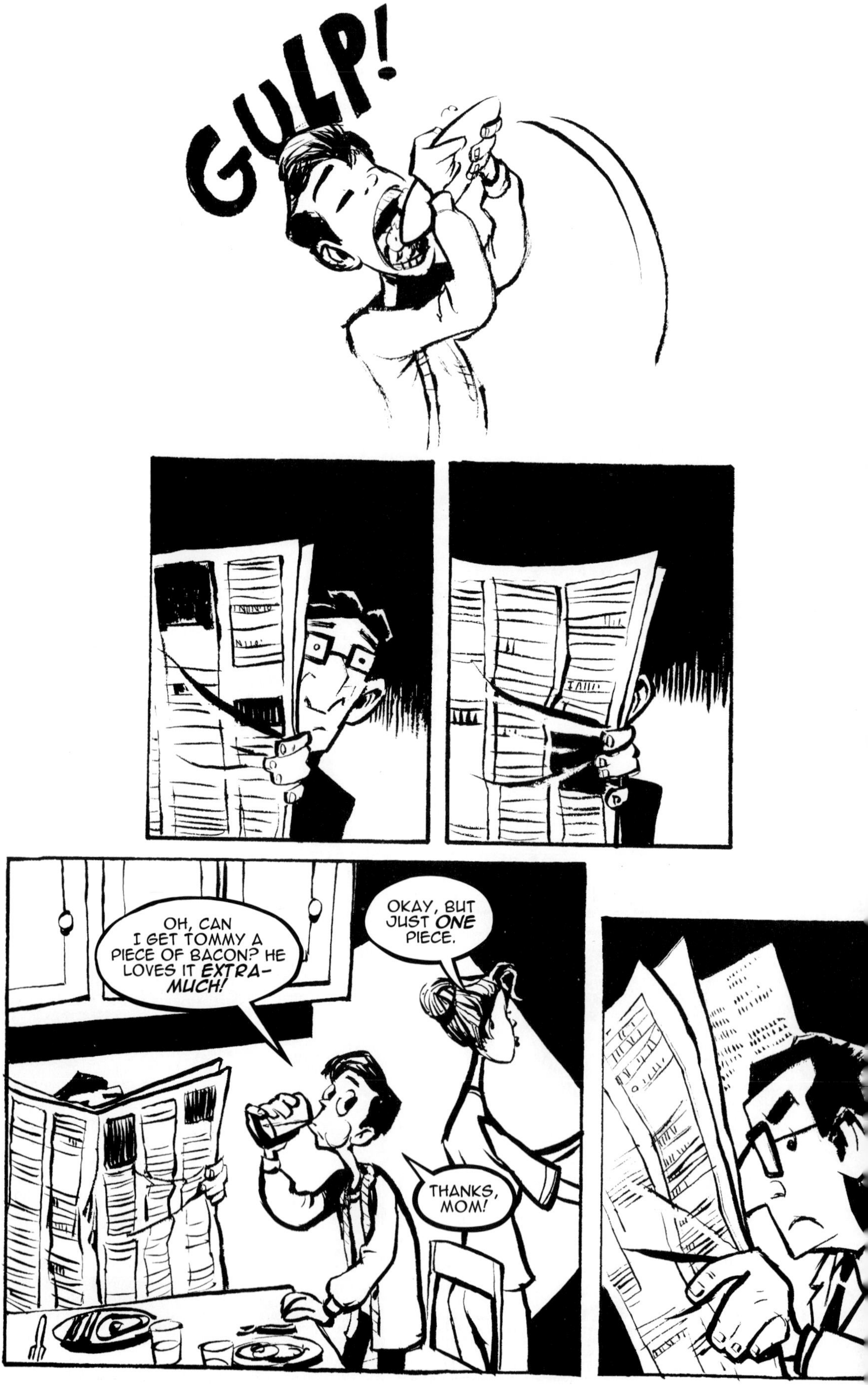
GULP!
OH, CAN I GET TOMMY A PIECE OF BACON? HE LOVES IT EXTRA-MUCH!
OKAY, BUT JUST ONE PIECE.
THANKS, MOM!

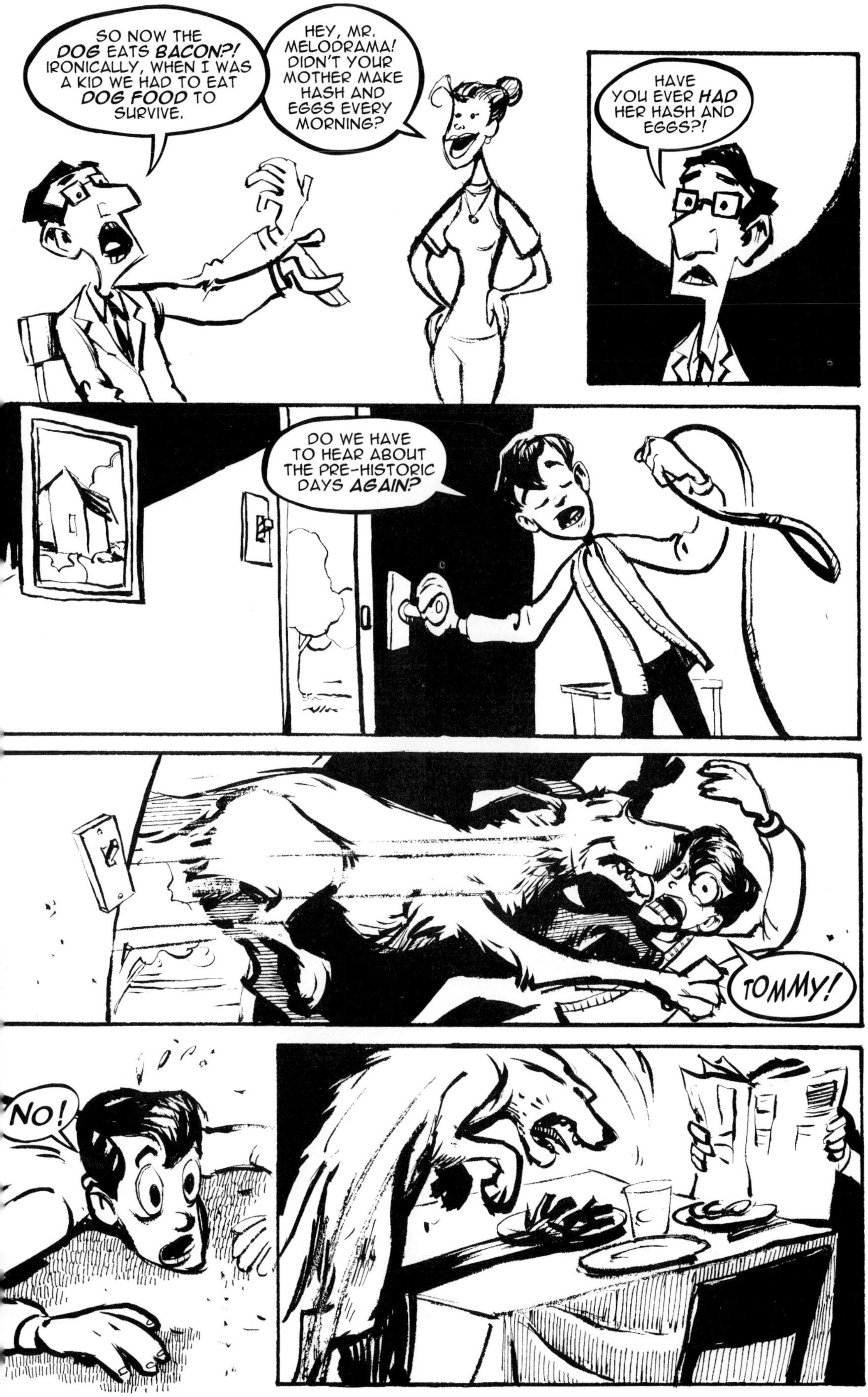
SO NOW THE DOG EATS BACON?! IRONICALLY, WHEN I WAS A KID WE HAD TO EAT DOG FOOD TO SURVIVE.
HEY, MR. MELODRAMA! DIDN'T YOUR MOTHER MAKE HASH AND EGGS EVERY MORNING?
HAVE YOU EVER HAD HER HASH AND EGGS?!
DO WE HAVE TO HEAR ABOUT THE PRE-HISTORIC DAYS AGAIN?
TOMMY!
NO!

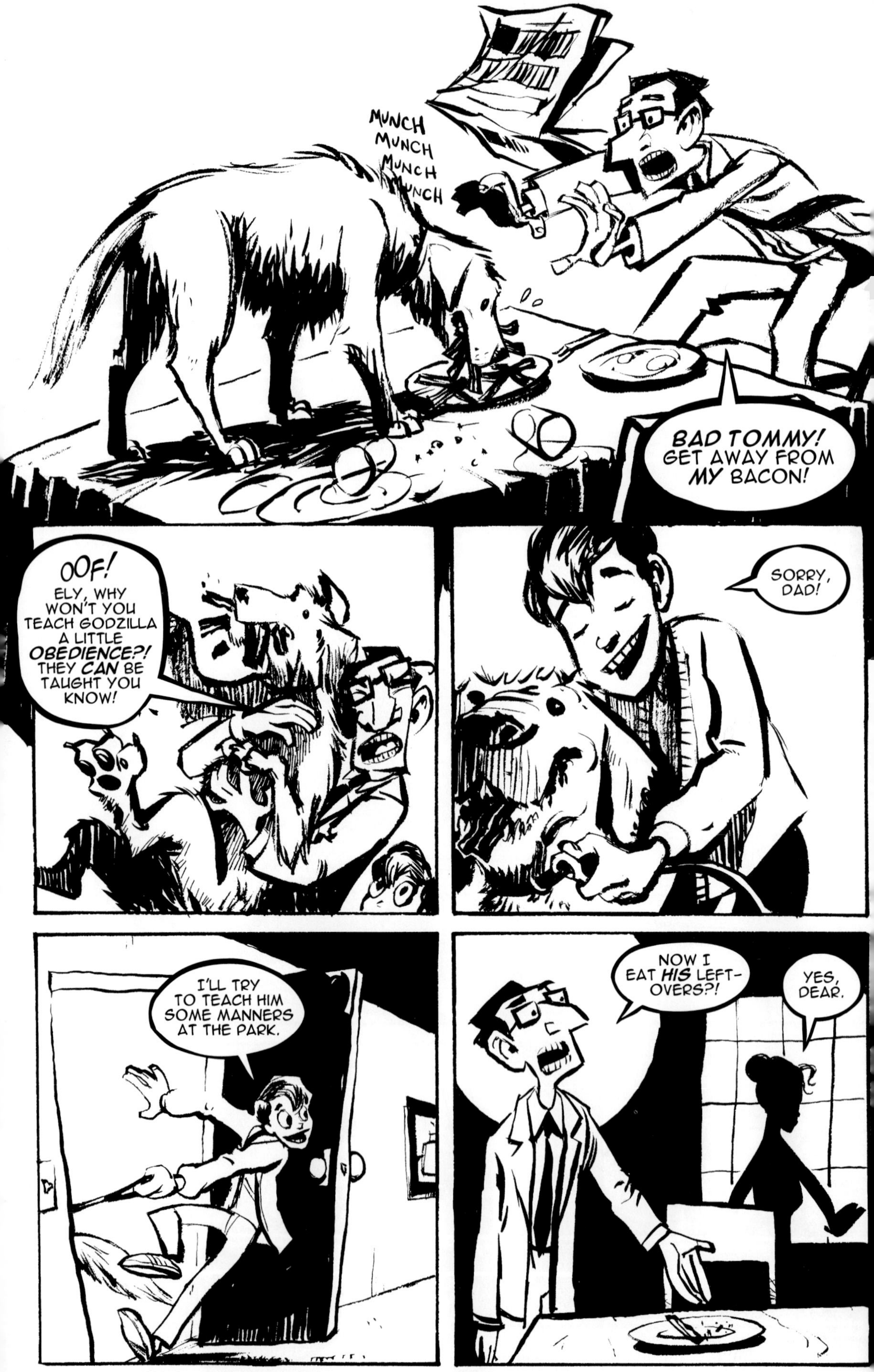
MUNCH
MUNCH
MUNCH
MUNCH
BAD TOMMY! GET AWAY FROM MY BACON!
OOF! ELY, WHY WON'T YOU TEACH GODZILLA A LITTLE OBEDIENCE?! THEY CAN BE TAUGHT YOU KNOW!
SORRY, DAD!
I'LL TRY TO TEACH HIM SOME MANNERS AT THE PARK.
NOW I EAT HIS LEFT-OVERS?!
YES, DEAR.

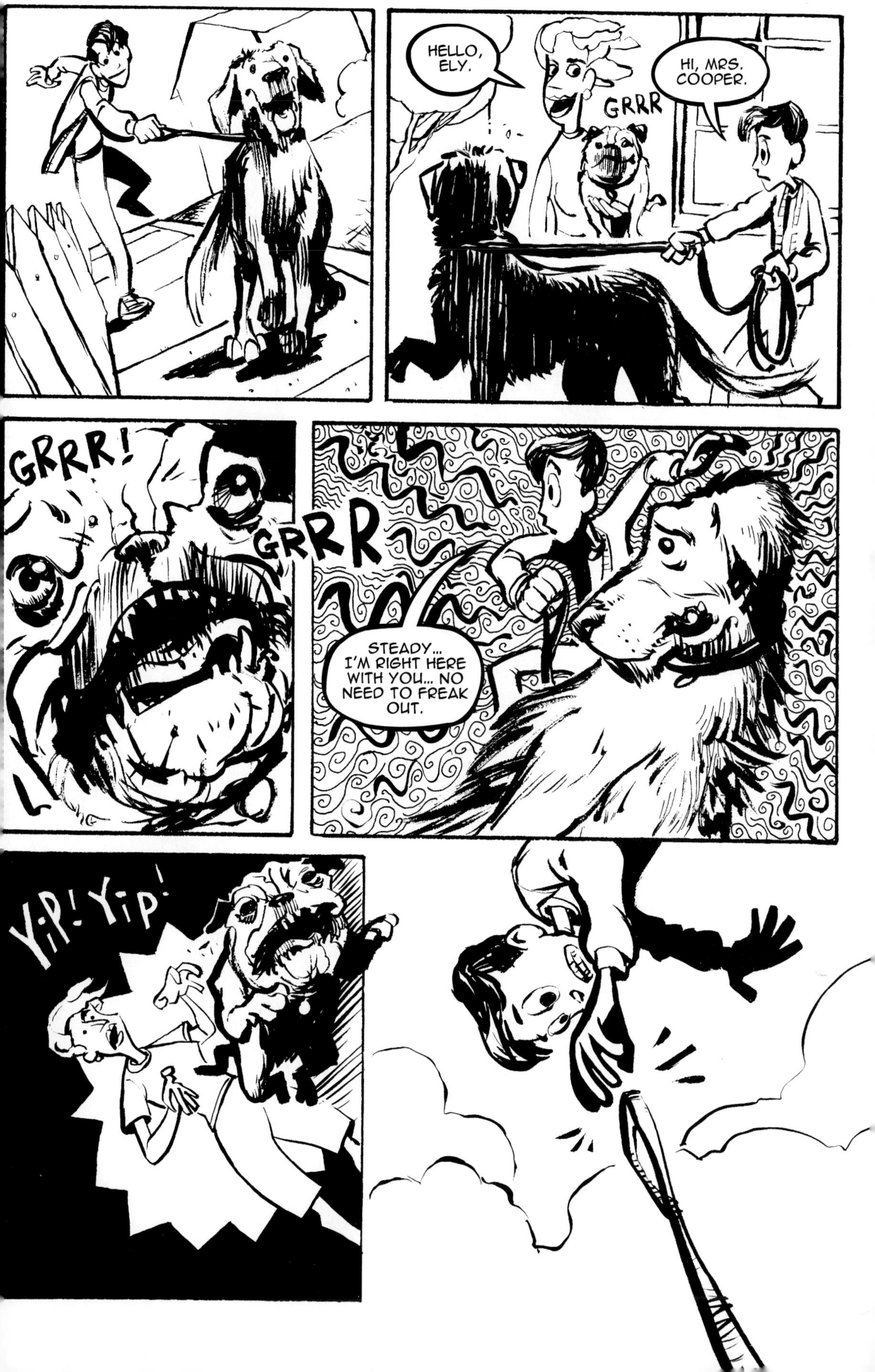
HELLO, ELY.
HI, MRS. COOPER.
GRRR
GRRR!
GRRR
STEADY... I'M RIGHT HERE WITH YOU... NO NEED TO FREAK OUT.
YIP! YIP!

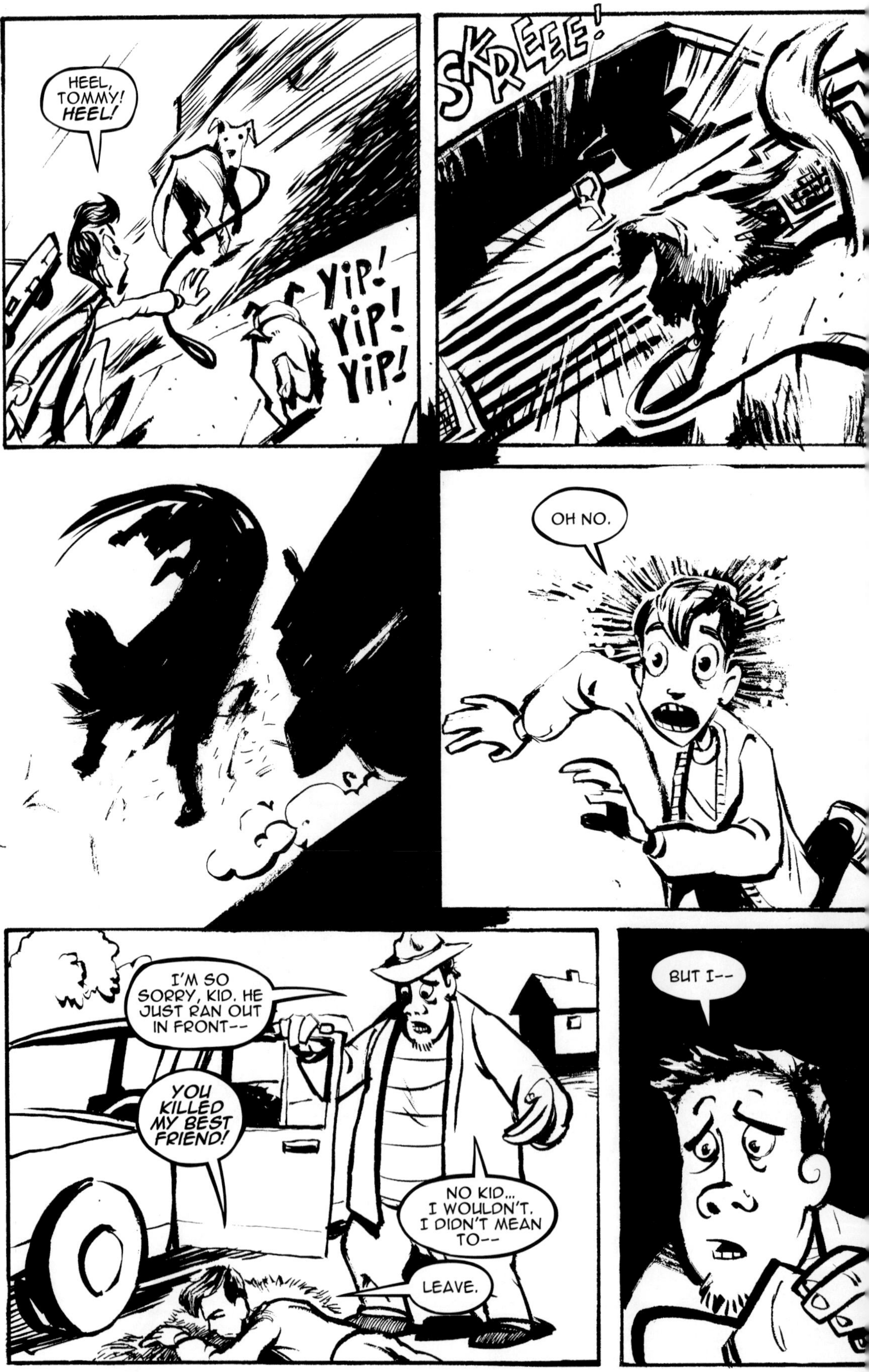
HEEL, TOMMY! HEEL!
YIP! YIP! YIP!
SKREEEE!
OH NO.
I'M SO SORRY, KID. HE JUST RAN OUT IN FRONT--
YOU KILLED MY BEST FRIEND!
NO KID... I WOULDN'T. I DIDN'T MEAN TO--
LEAVE.
BUT I--

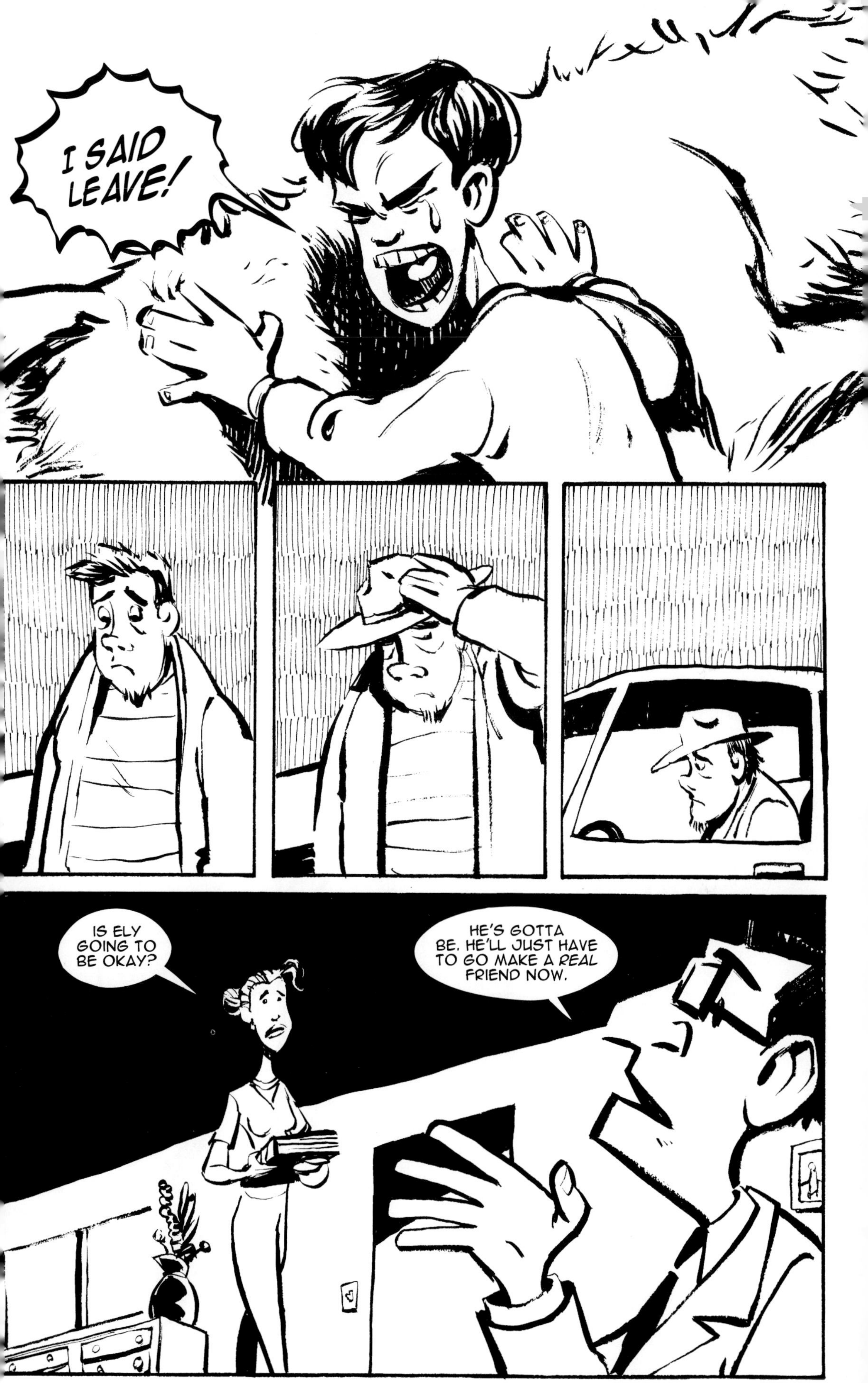
I SAID LEAVE!
IS ELY GOING TO BE OKAY?
HE'S GOTTA BE. HE'LL JUST HAVE TO GO MAKE A *REAL* FRIEND NOW.

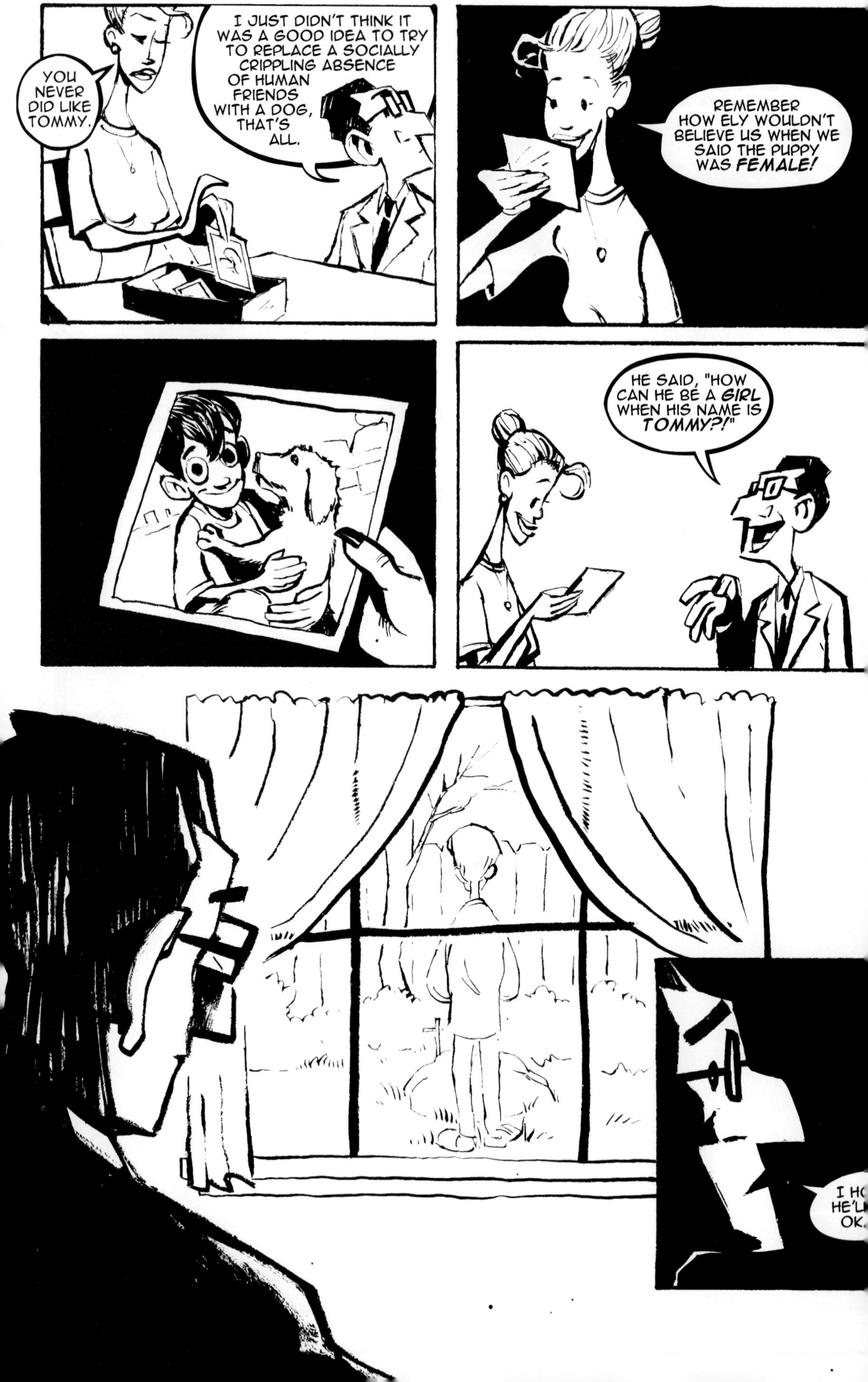
YOU NEVER DID LIKE TOMMY.
I JUST DIDN'T THINK IT WAS A GOOD IDEA TO TRY TO REPLACE A SOCIALLY CRIPPLING ABSENCE OF HUMAN FRIENDS WITH A DOG, THAT'S ALL.
REMEMBER HOW ELY WOULDN'T BELIEVE US WHEN WE SAID THE PUPPY WAS *FEMALE!*
HE SAID, "HOW CAN HE BE A *GIRL* WHEN HIS NAME IS *TOMMY?!*"
I H HE'L OK.

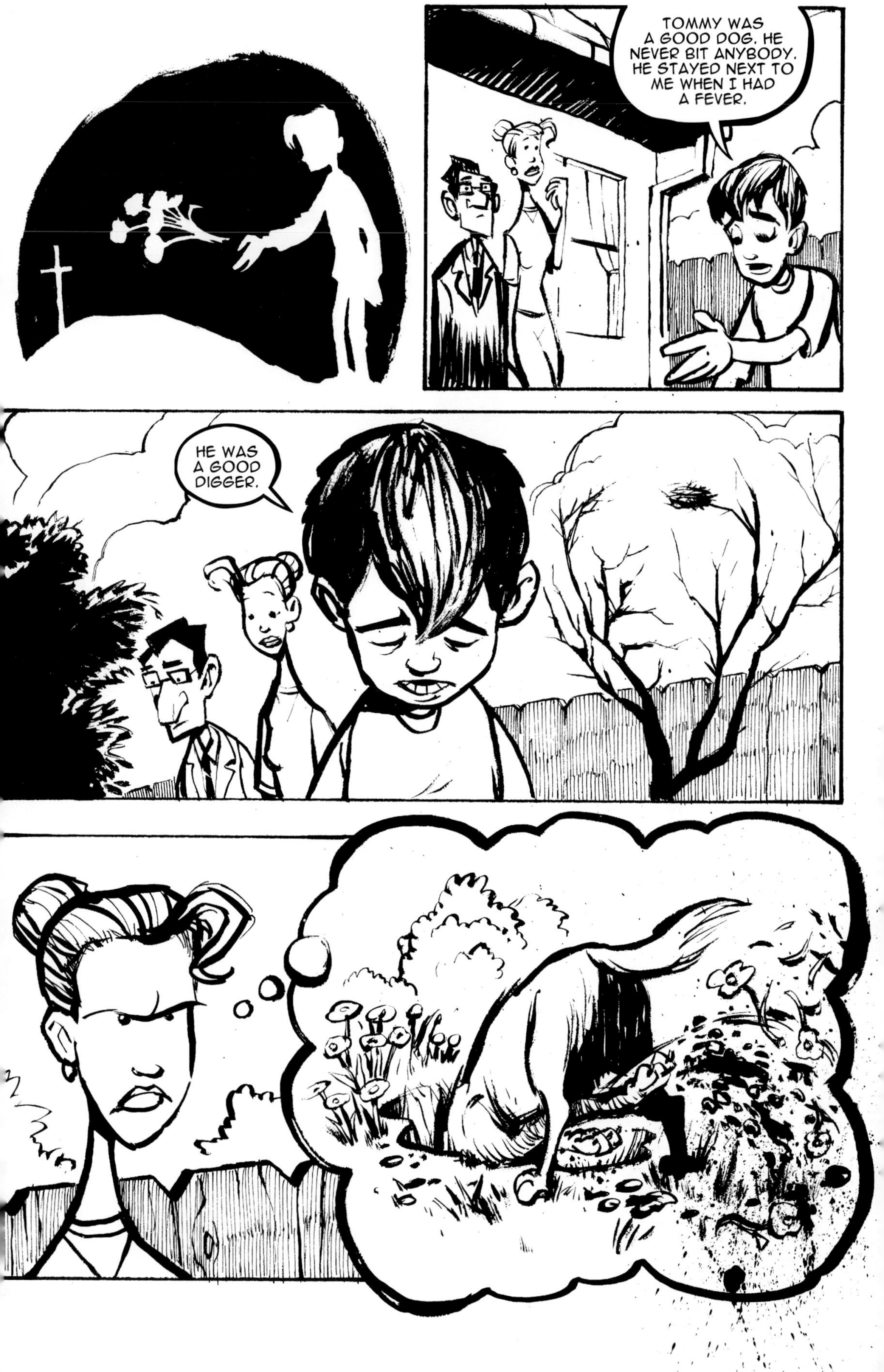
TOMMY WAS A GOOD DOG. HE NEVER BIT ANYBODY. HE STAYED NEXT TO ME WHEN I HAD A FEVER.
HE WAS A GOOD DIGGER.

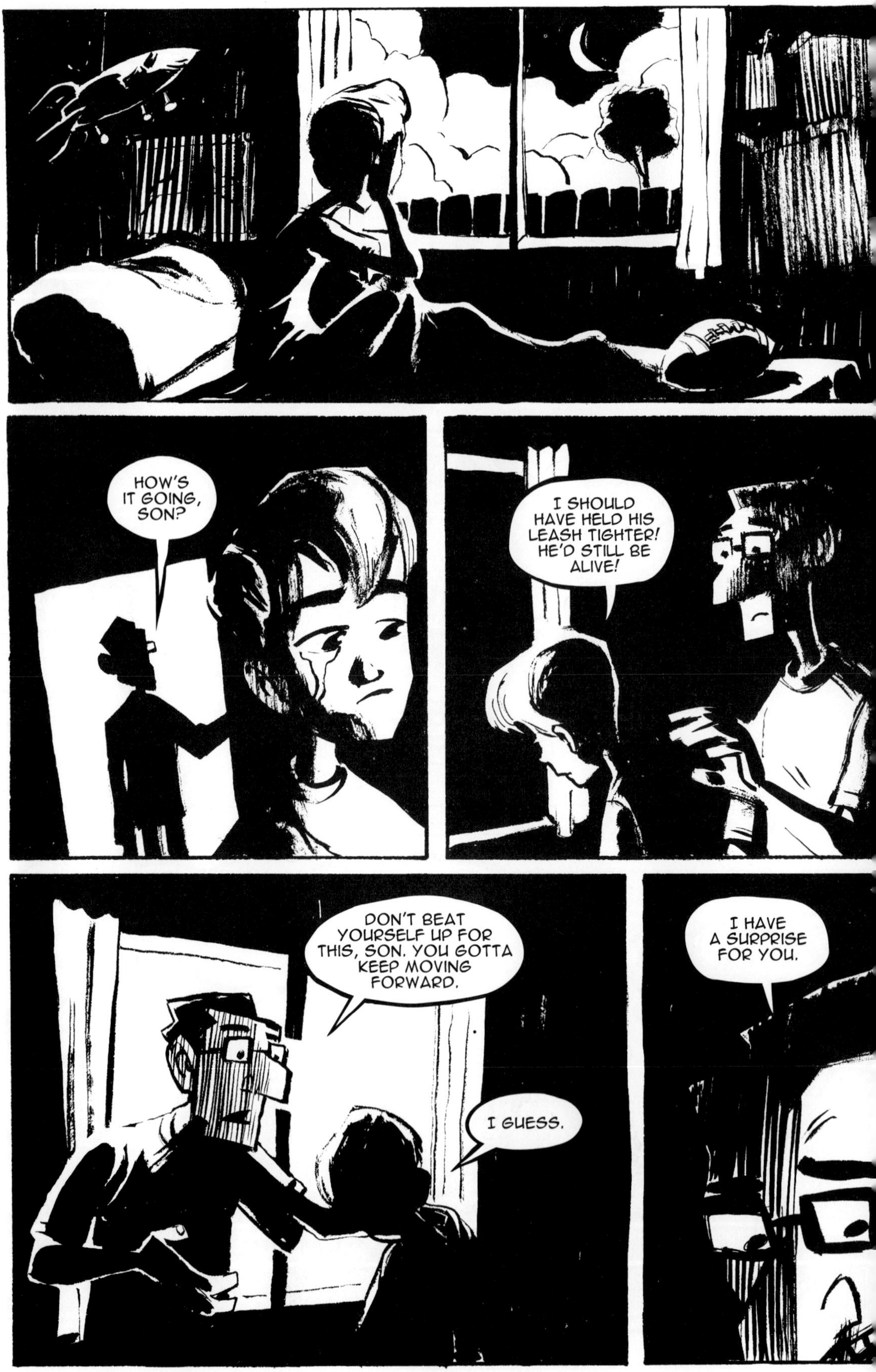
HOW'S IT GOING, SON?
I SHOULD HAVE HELD HIS LEASH TIGHTER! HE'D STILL BE ALIVE!
DON'T BEAT YOURSELF UP FOR THIS, SON. YOU GOTTA KEEP MOVING FORWARD.
I GUESS.
I HAVE A SURPRISE FOR YOU.

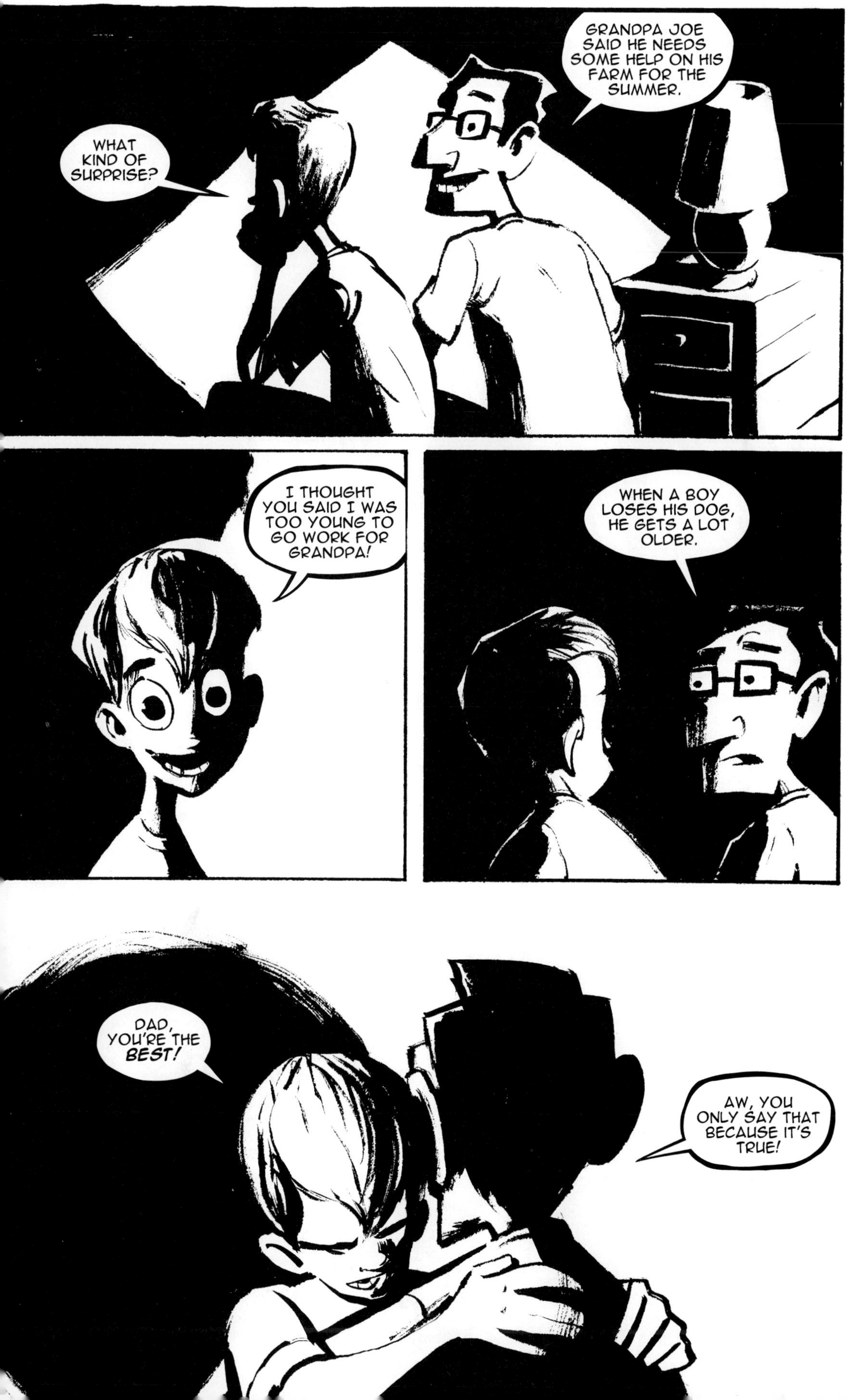
GRANDPA JOE SAID HE NEEDS SOME HELP ON HIS FARM FOR THE SUMMER.
WHAT KIND OF SURPRISE?
I THOUGHT YOU SAID I WAS TOO YOUNG TO GO WORK FOR GRANDPA!
WHEN A BOY LOSES HIS DOG, HE GETS A LOT OLDER.
DAD, YOU'RE THE *BEST!*
AW, YOU ONLY SAY THAT BECAUSE IT'S TRUE!

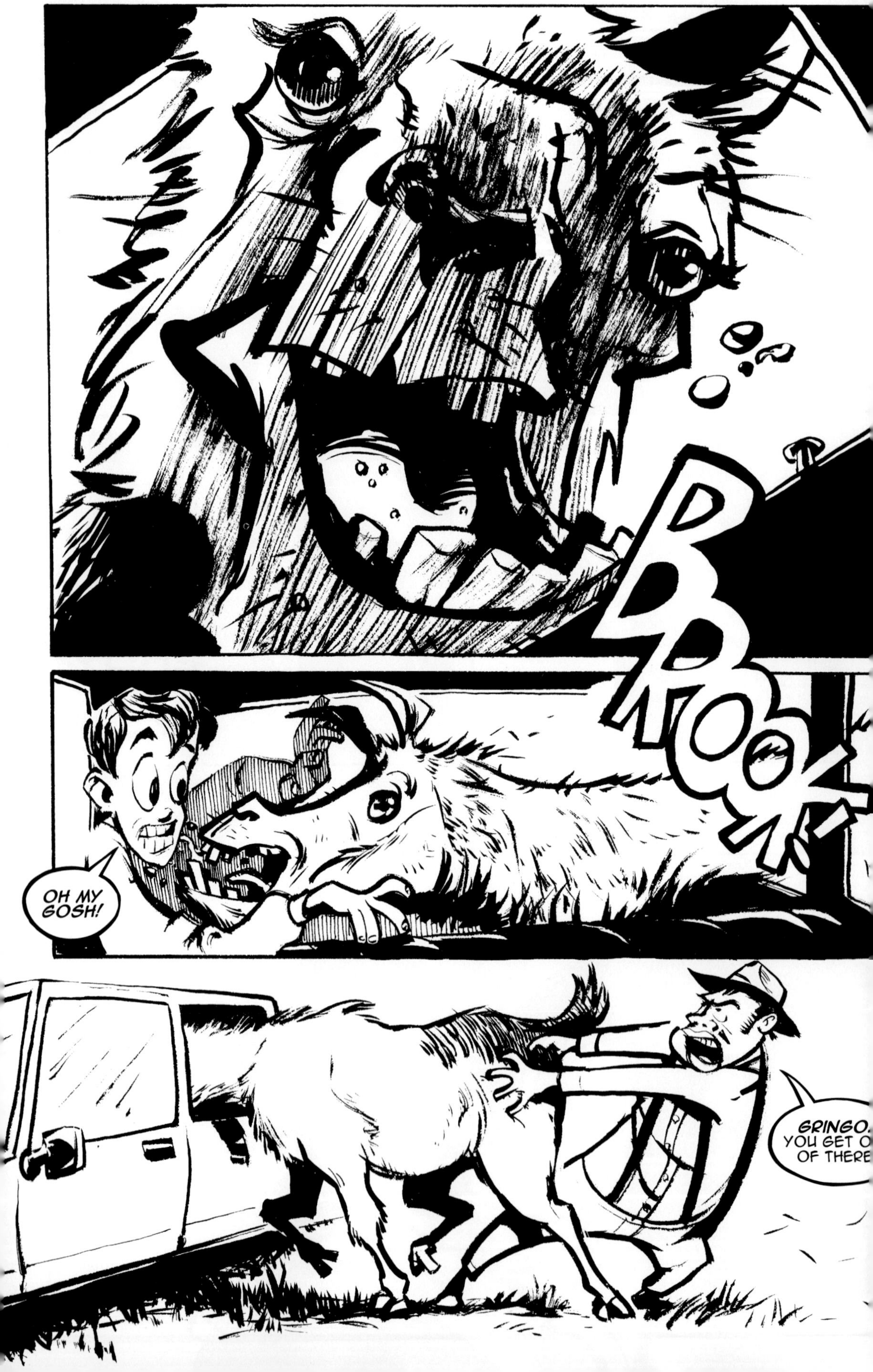
BROOK!
OH MY GOSH!
GRINGO. YOU GET O OF THERE

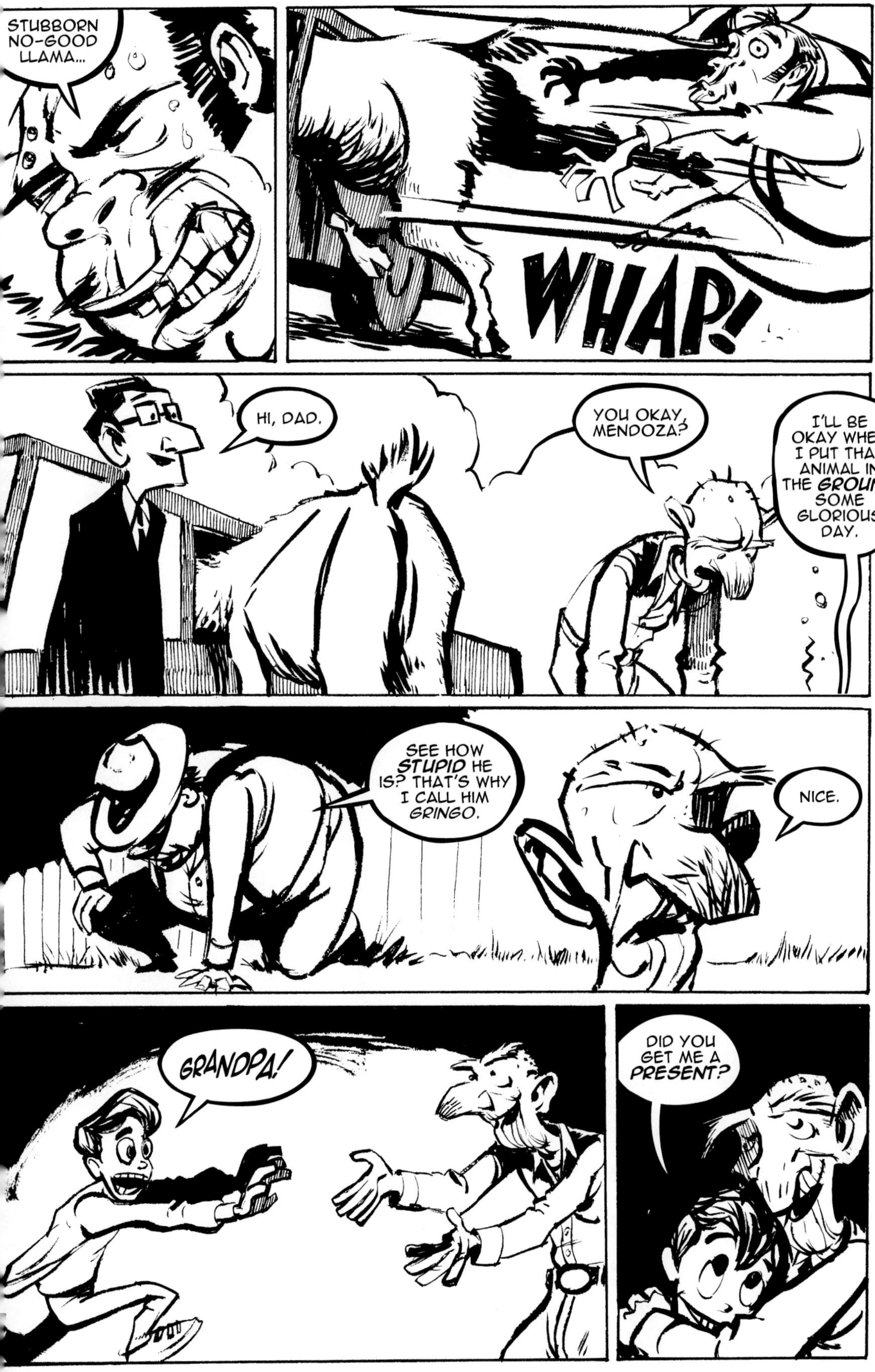
STUBBORN NO-GOOD LLAMA...
WHAP!
HI, DAD.
YOU OKAY, MENDOZA?
I'LL BE OKAY WHEN I PUT THAT ANIMAL IN THE GROUND SOME GLORIOUS DAY.
SEE HOW STUPID HE IS? THAT'S WHY I CALL HIM GRINGO.
NICE.
GRANDPA!
DID YOU GET ME A PRESENT?

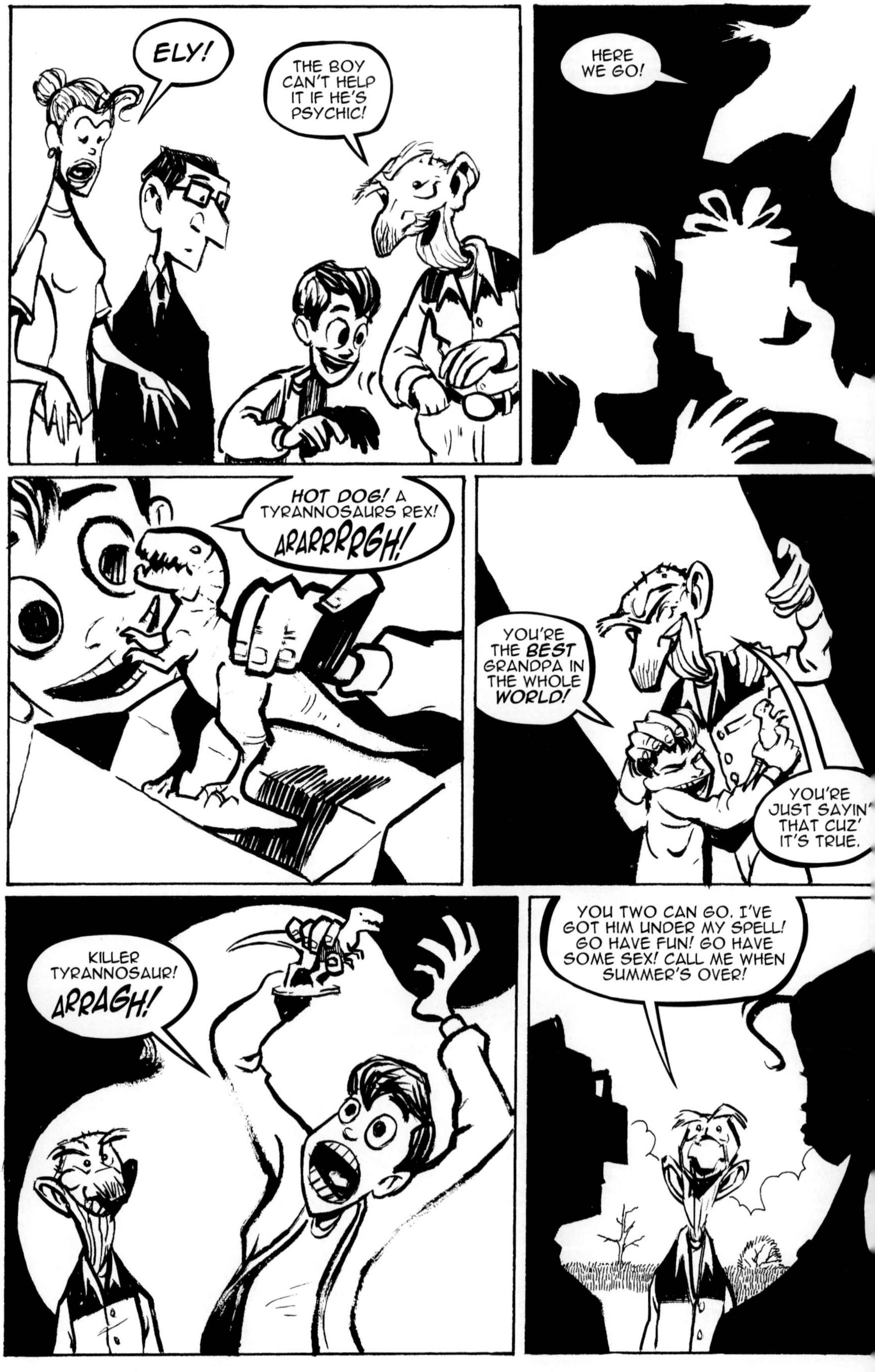
ELY!
THE BOY CAN'T HELP IT IF HE'S PSYCHIC!
HERE WE GO!
HOT DOG! A TYRANNOSAURS REX! ARARRRRGH!
YOU'RE THE BEST GRANDPA IN THE WHOLE WORLD!
YOU'RE JUST SAYIN' THAT CUZ' IT'S TRUE.
KILLER TYRANNOSAUR! ARRAGH!
YOU TWO CAN GO. I'VE GOT HIM UNDER MY SPELL! GO HAVE FUN! GO HAVE SOME SEX! CALL ME WHEN SUMMER'S OVER!

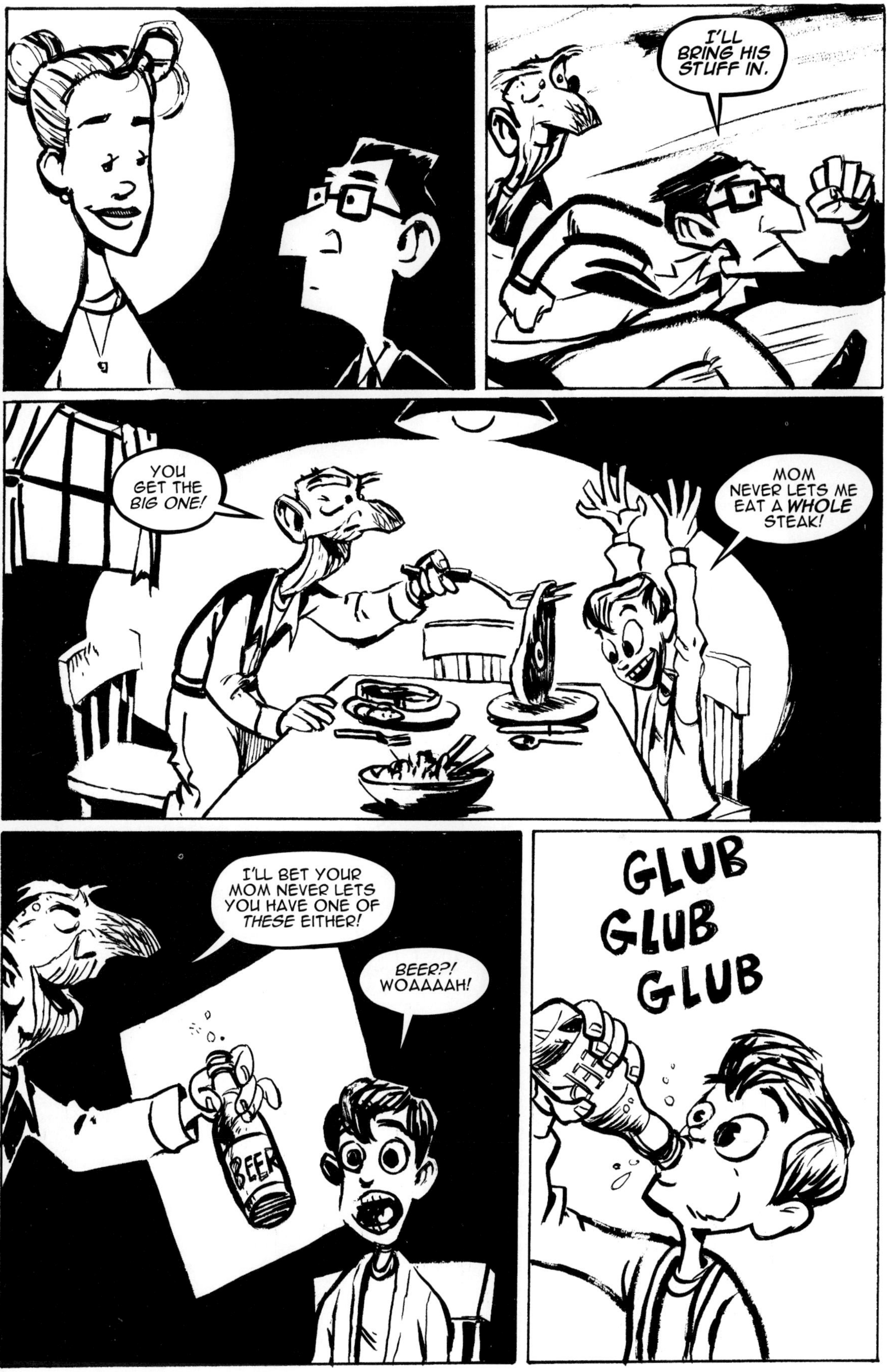
I'LL BRING HIS STUFF IN.
YOU GET THE BIG ONE!
MOM NEVER LETS ME EAT A WHOLE STEAK!
I'LL BET YOUR MOM NEVER LETS YOU HAVE ONE OF THESE EITHER!
BEER?! WOAAAAH!
BEER
GLUB GLUB GLUB

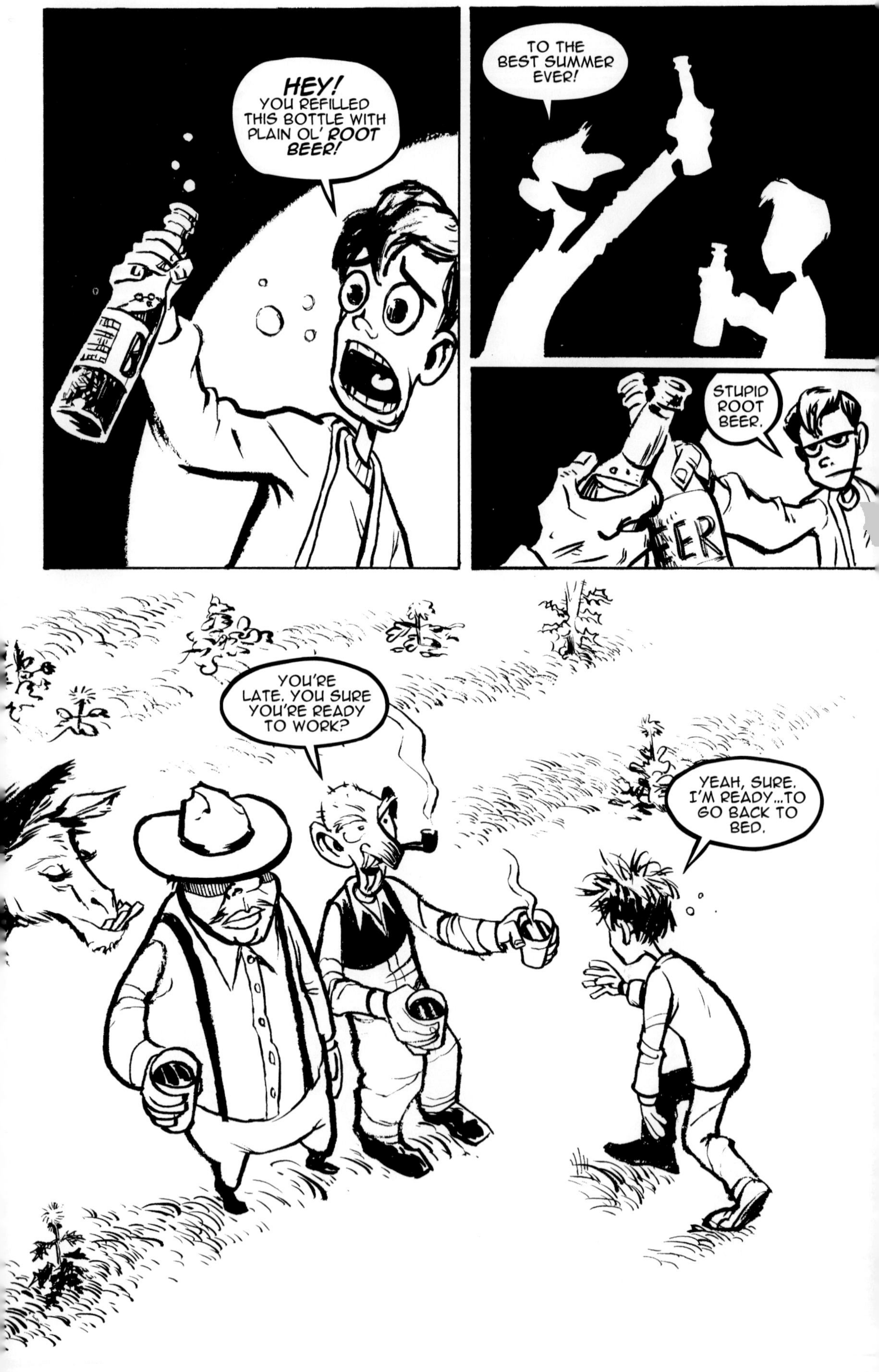
HEY! YOU REFILLED THIS BOTTLE WITH PLAIN OL' ROOT BEER!
TO THE BEST SUMMER EVER!
STUPID ROOT BEER.
EER
YOU'RE LATE. YOU SURE YOU'RE READY TO WORK?
YEAH, SURE. I'M READY...TO GO BACK TO BED.

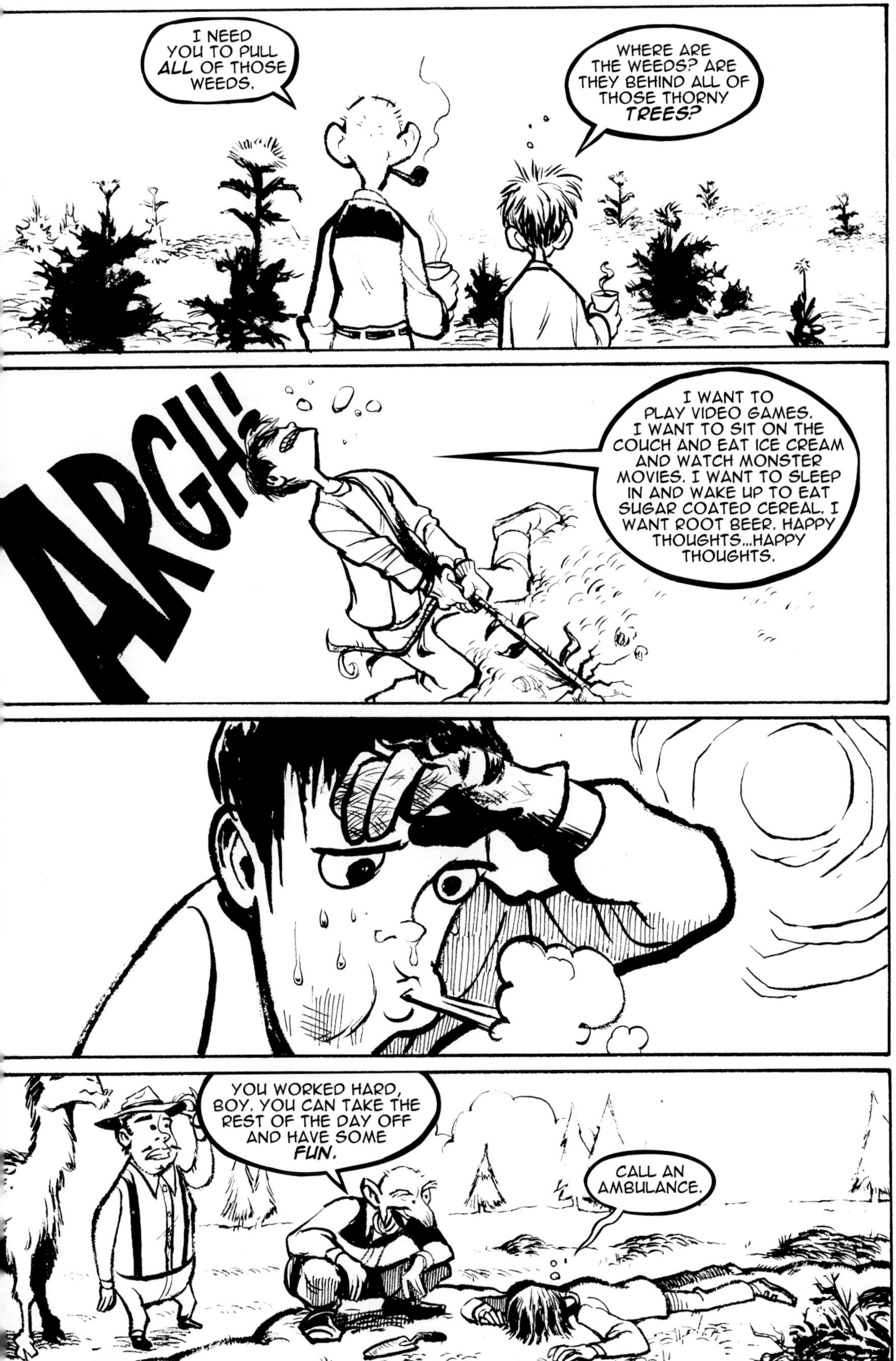
I NEED YOU TO PULL ALL OF THOSE WEEDS.
WHERE ARE THE WEEDS? ARE THEY BEHIND ALL OF THOSE THORNY TREES?
ARGH!
I WANT TO PLAY VIDEO GAMES. I WANT TO SIT ON THE COUCH AND EAT ICE CREAM AND WATCH MONSTER MOVIES. I WANT TO SLEEP IN AND WAKE UP TO EAT SUGAR COATED CEREAL. I WANT ROOT BEER. HAPPY THOUGHTS...HAPPY THOUGHTS.
YOU WORKED HARD, BOY. YOU CAN TAKE THE REST OF THE DAY OFF AND HAVE SOME FUN.
CALL AN AMBULANCE.

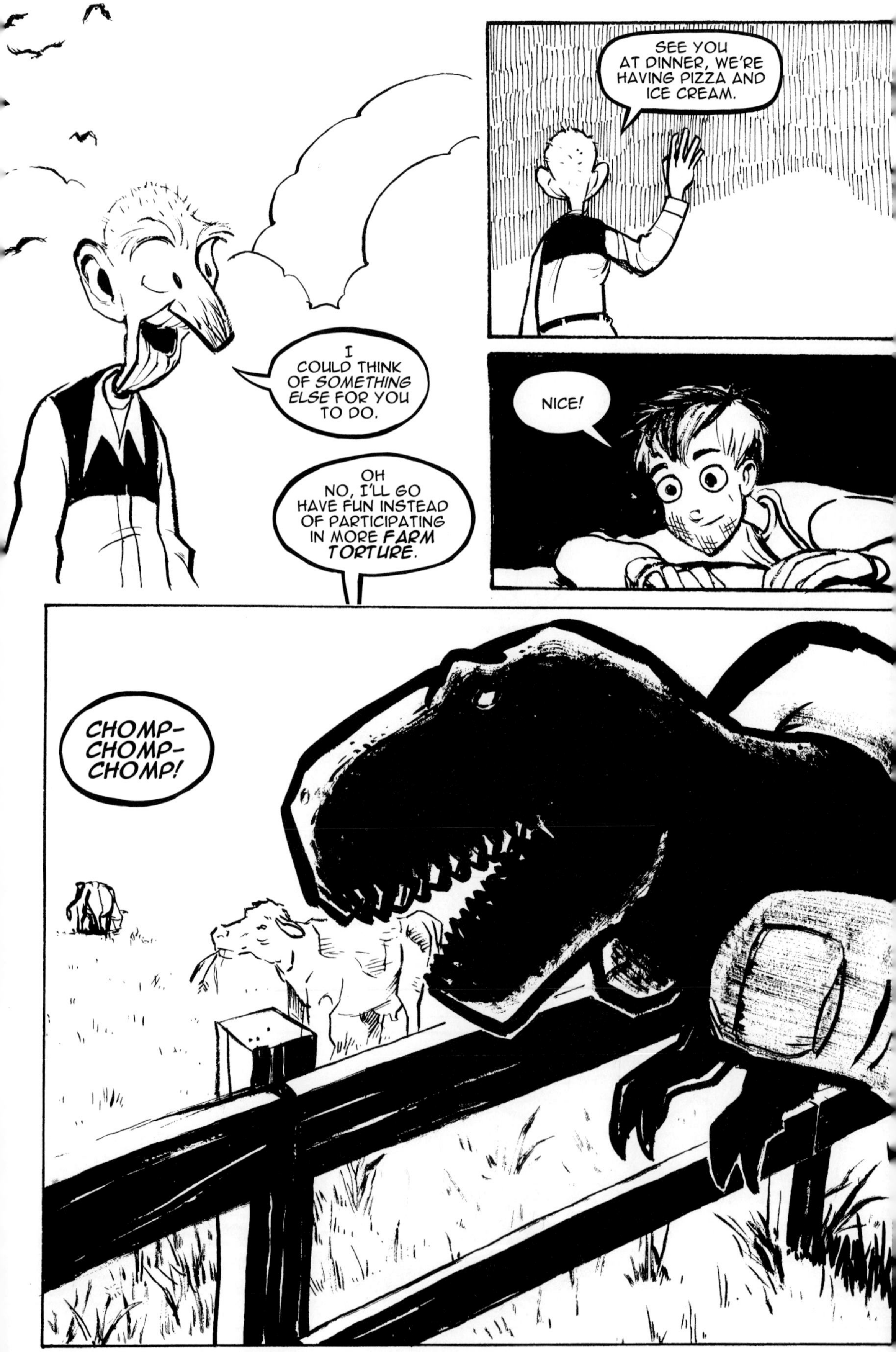
SEE YOU AT DINNER, WE'RE HAVING PIZZA AND ICE CREAM.
I COULD THINK OF SOMETHING ELSE FOR YOU TO DO.
NICE!
OH NO, I'LL GO HAVE FUN INSTEAD OF PARTICIPATING IN MORE FARM TORTURE.
CHOMP-CHOMP-CHOMP!

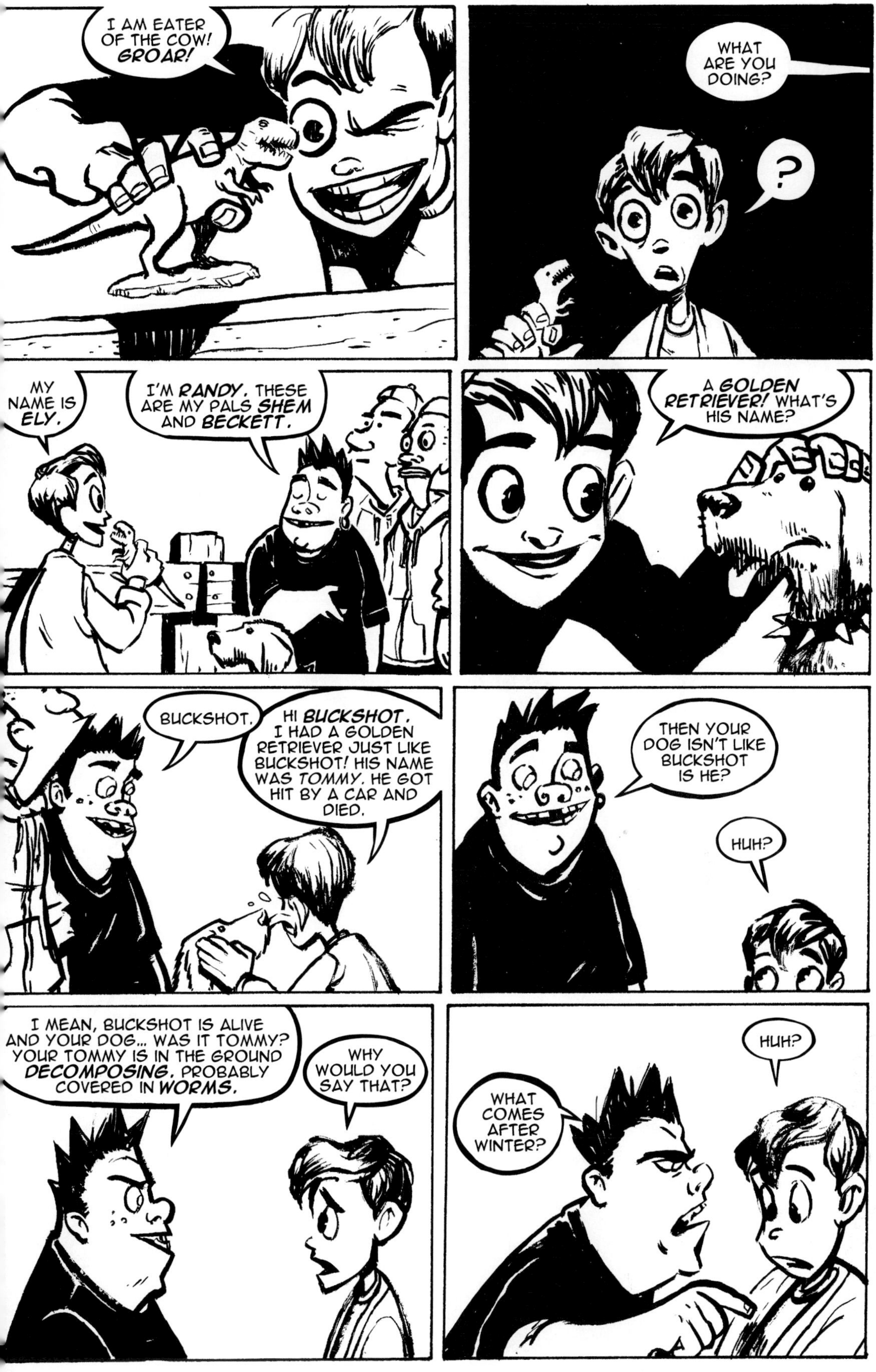
I AM EATER OF THE COW! GROAR!
WHAT ARE YOU DOING?
?
MY NAME IS ELY.
I'M RANDY. THESE ARE MY PALS SHEM AND BECKETT.
A GOLDEN RETRIEVER! WHAT'S HIS NAME?
BUCKSHOT.
HI BUCKSHOT. I HAD A GOLDEN RETRIEVER JUST LIKE BUCKSHOT! HIS NAME WAS TOMMY. HE GOT HIT BY A CAR AND DIED.
THEN YOUR DOG ISN'T LIKE BUCKSHOT IS HE?
HUH?
I MEAN, BUCKSHOT IS ALIVE AND YOUR DOG... WAS IT TOMMY? YOUR TOMMY IS IN THE GROUND DECOMPOSING, PROBABLY COVERED IN WORMS.
WHY WOULD YOU SAY THAT?
HUH?
WHAT COMES AFTER WINTER?

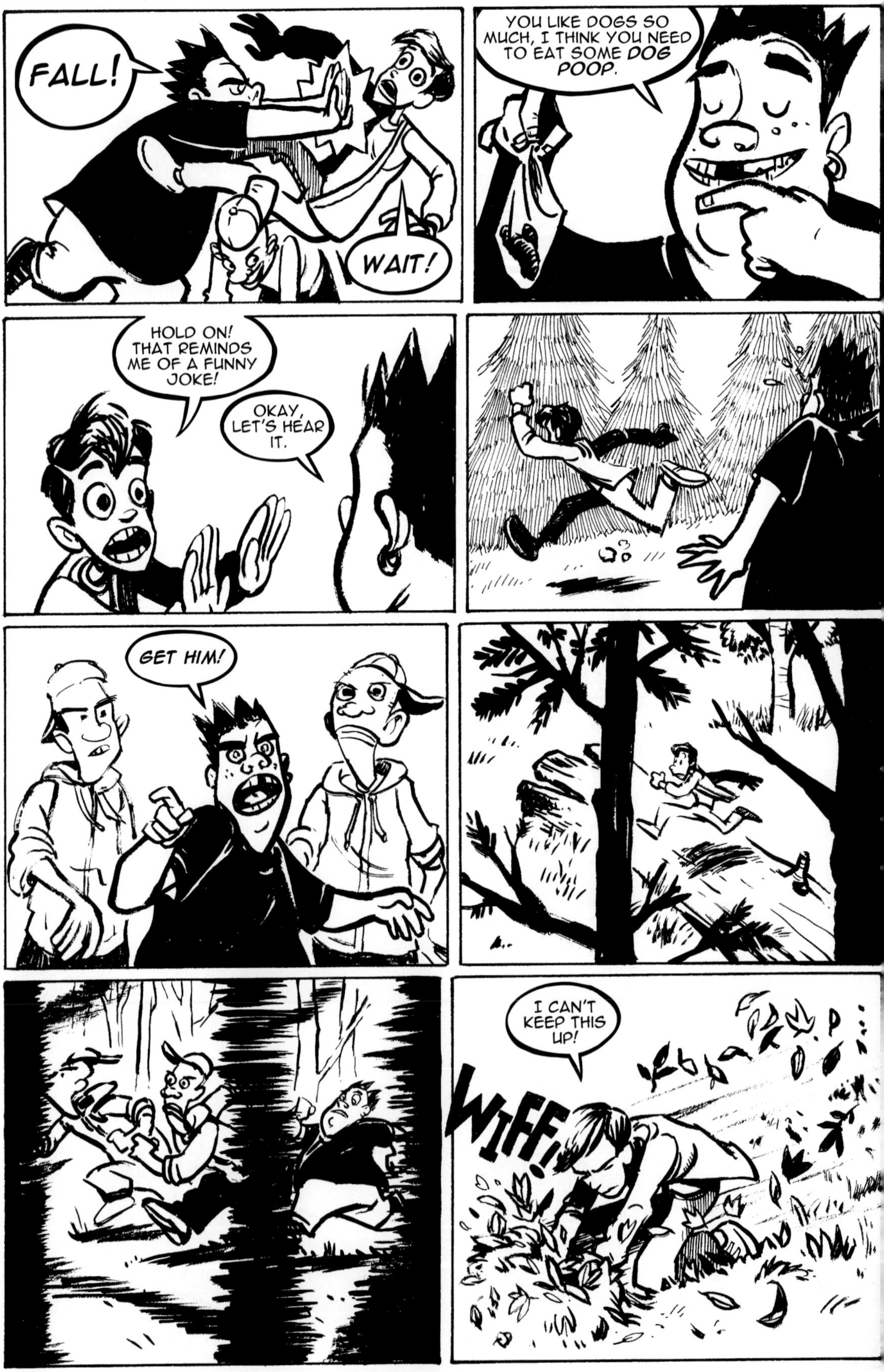
FALL!
WAIT!
YOU LIKE DOGS SO MUCH, I THINK YOU NEED TO EAT SOME *DOG POOP*.
HOLD ON! THAT REMINDS ME OF A FUNNY JOKE!
OKAY, LET'S HEAR IT.
GET HIM!
I CAN'T KEEP THIS UP!
WIFF!

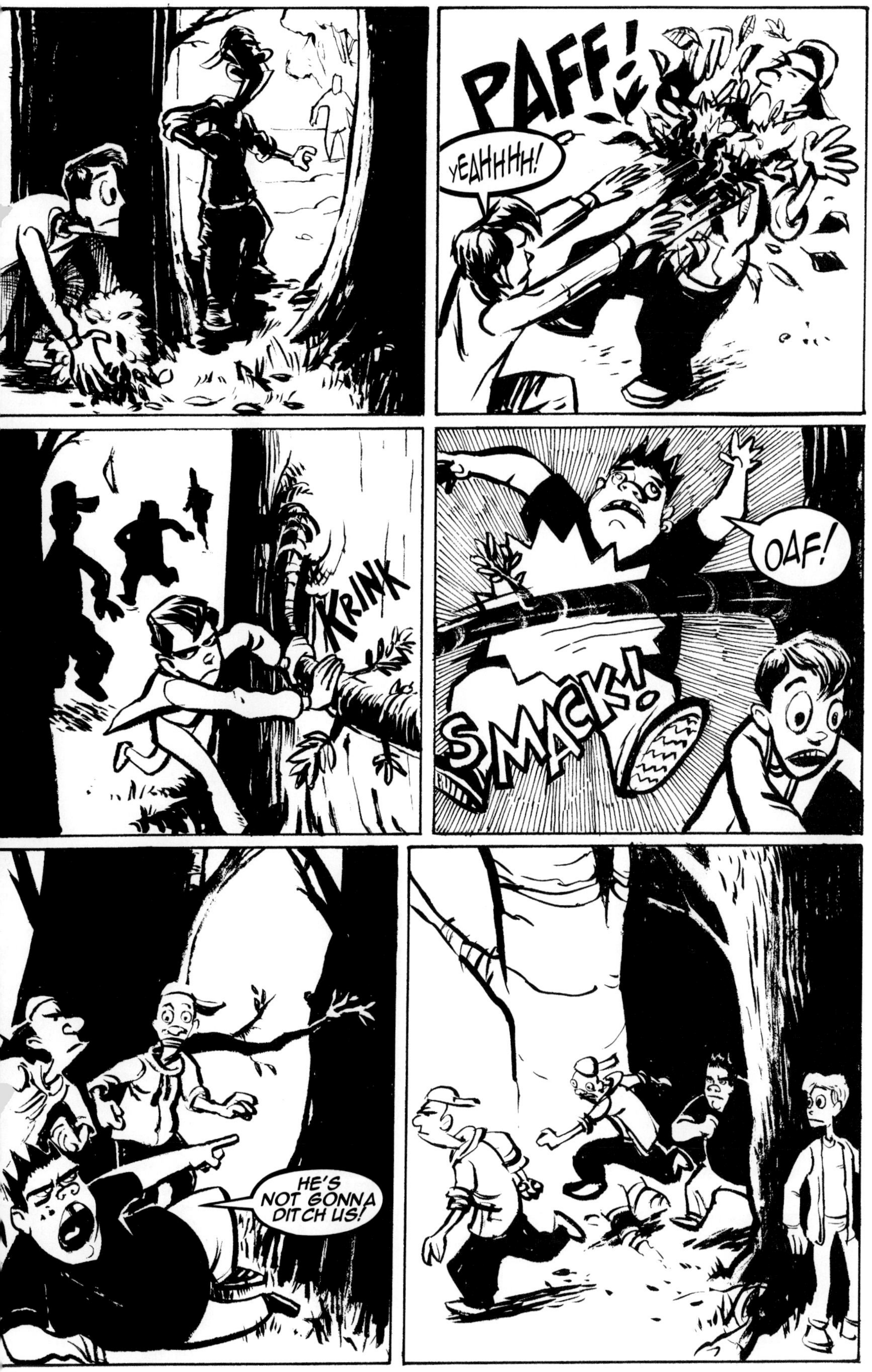
PAFF!
YEAHHHH!
KRINK
OAF!
SMACK!
HE'S NOT GONNA DITCH US!

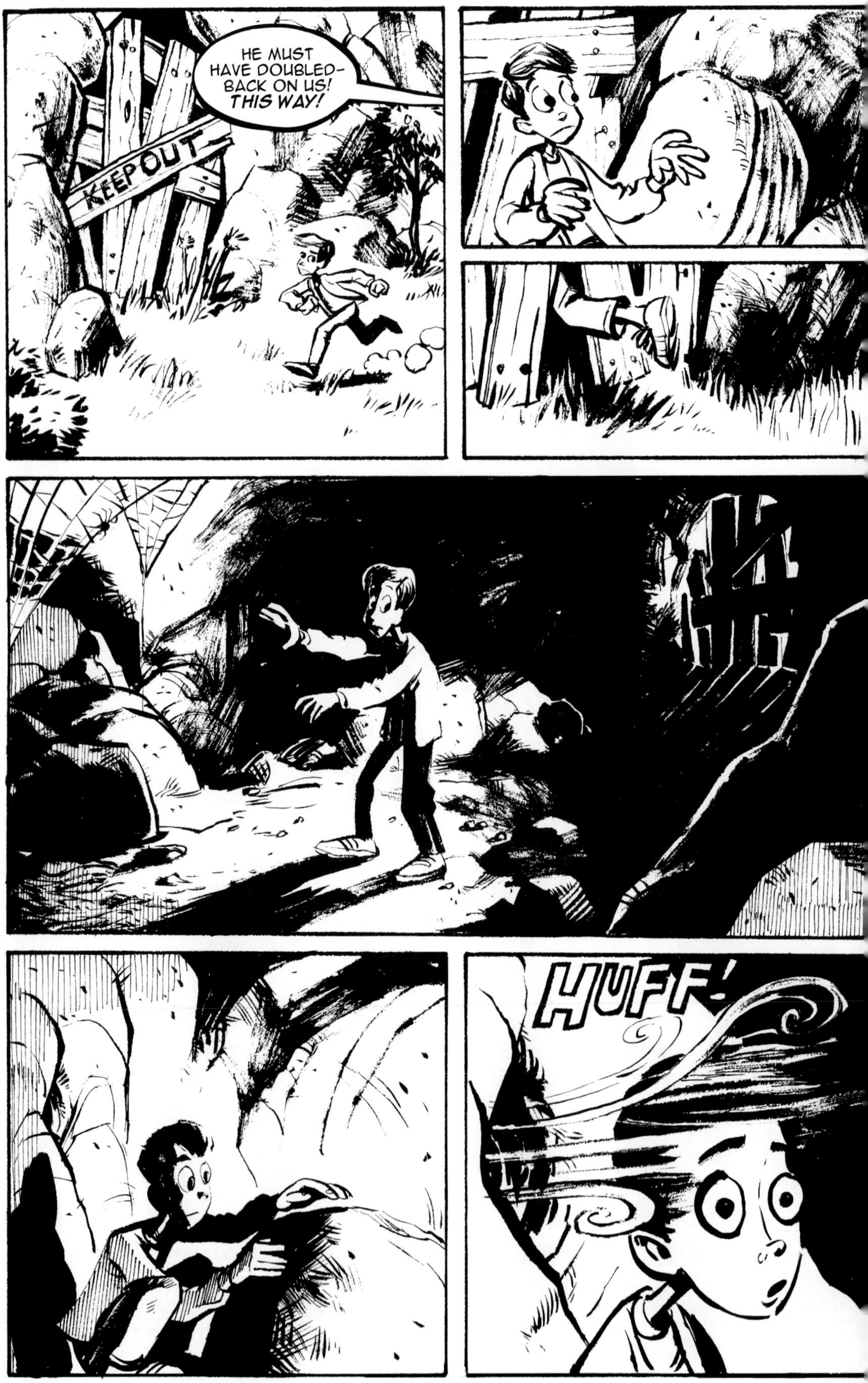
KEEP OUT
HE MUST HAVE DOUBLED-BACK ON US! THIS WAY!
HUFF!

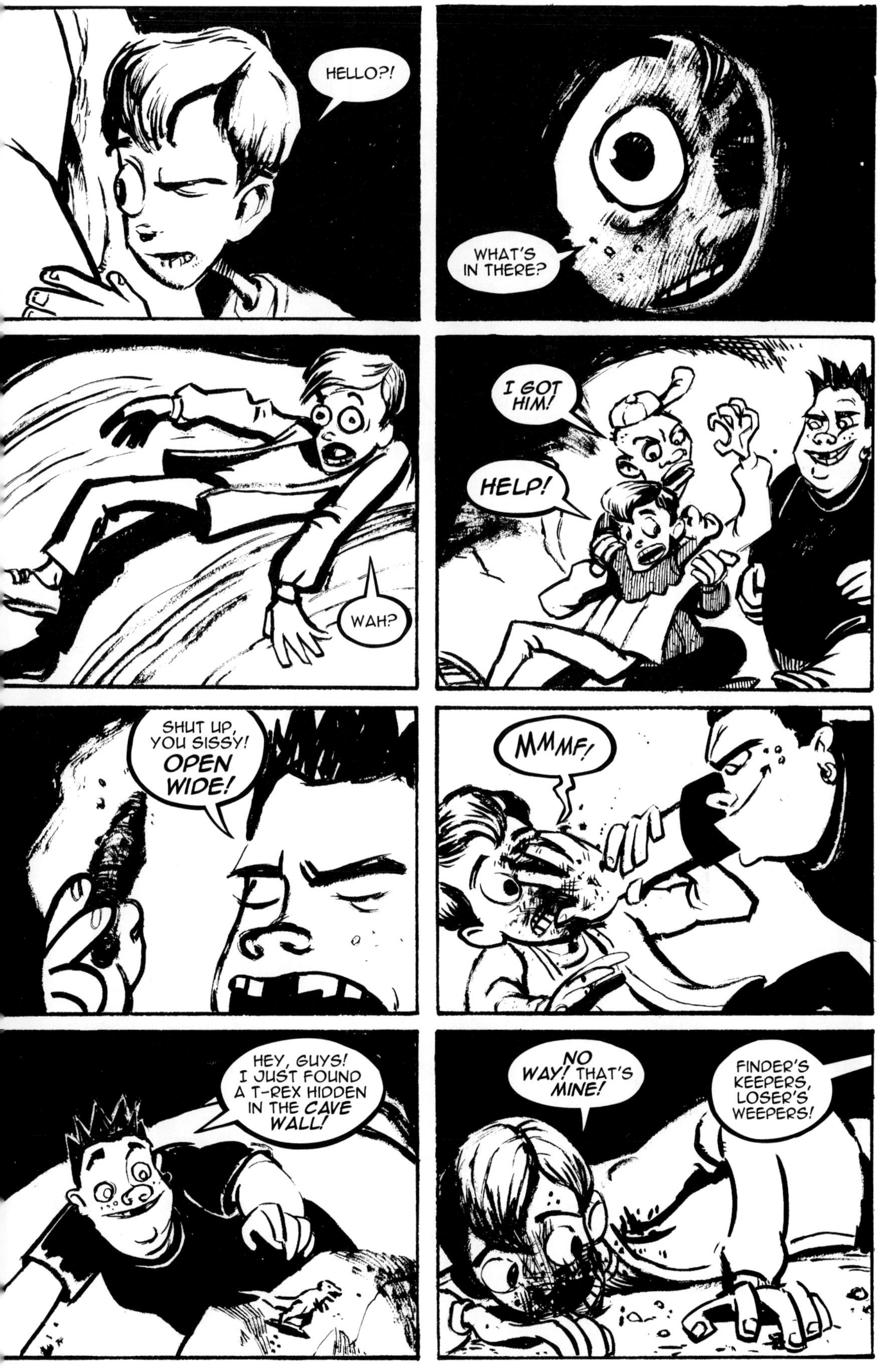
HELLO?!
WHAT'S IN THERE?
WAH?
I GOT HIM!
HELP!
SHUT UP, YOU SISSY! OPEN WIDE!
MMMF!
HEY, GUYS! I JUST FOUND A T-REX HIDDEN IN THE CAVE WALL!
NO WAY! THAT'S MINE!
FINDER'S KEEPERS, LOSER'S WEEPERS!

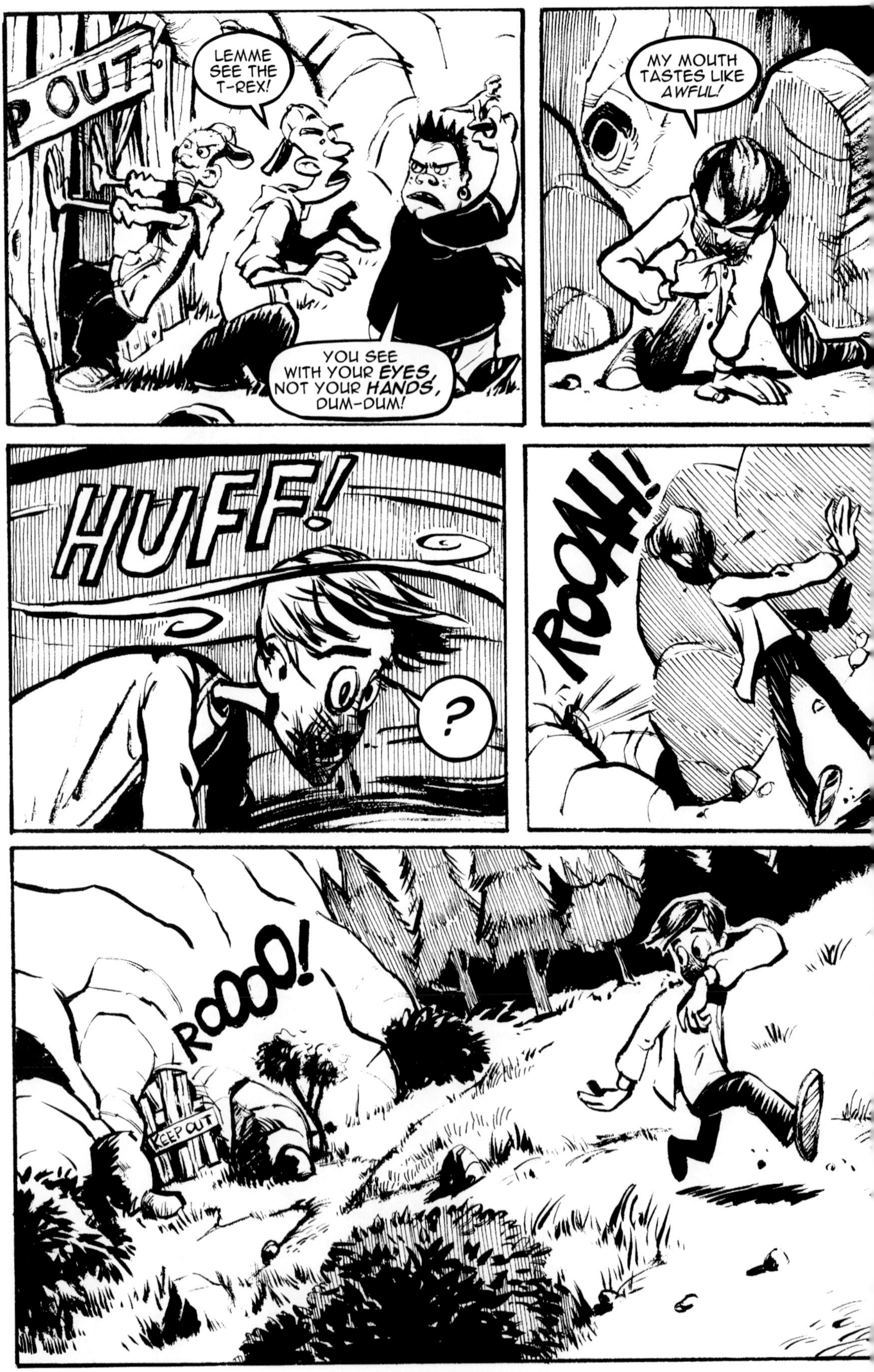
P OUT
LEMME SEE THE T-REX!
YOU SEE WITH YOUR EYES, NOT YOUR HANDS, DUM-DUM!
MY MOUTH TASTES LIKE AWFUL!
HUFF!
?
ROOAH!
ROOOO!
KEEP OUT

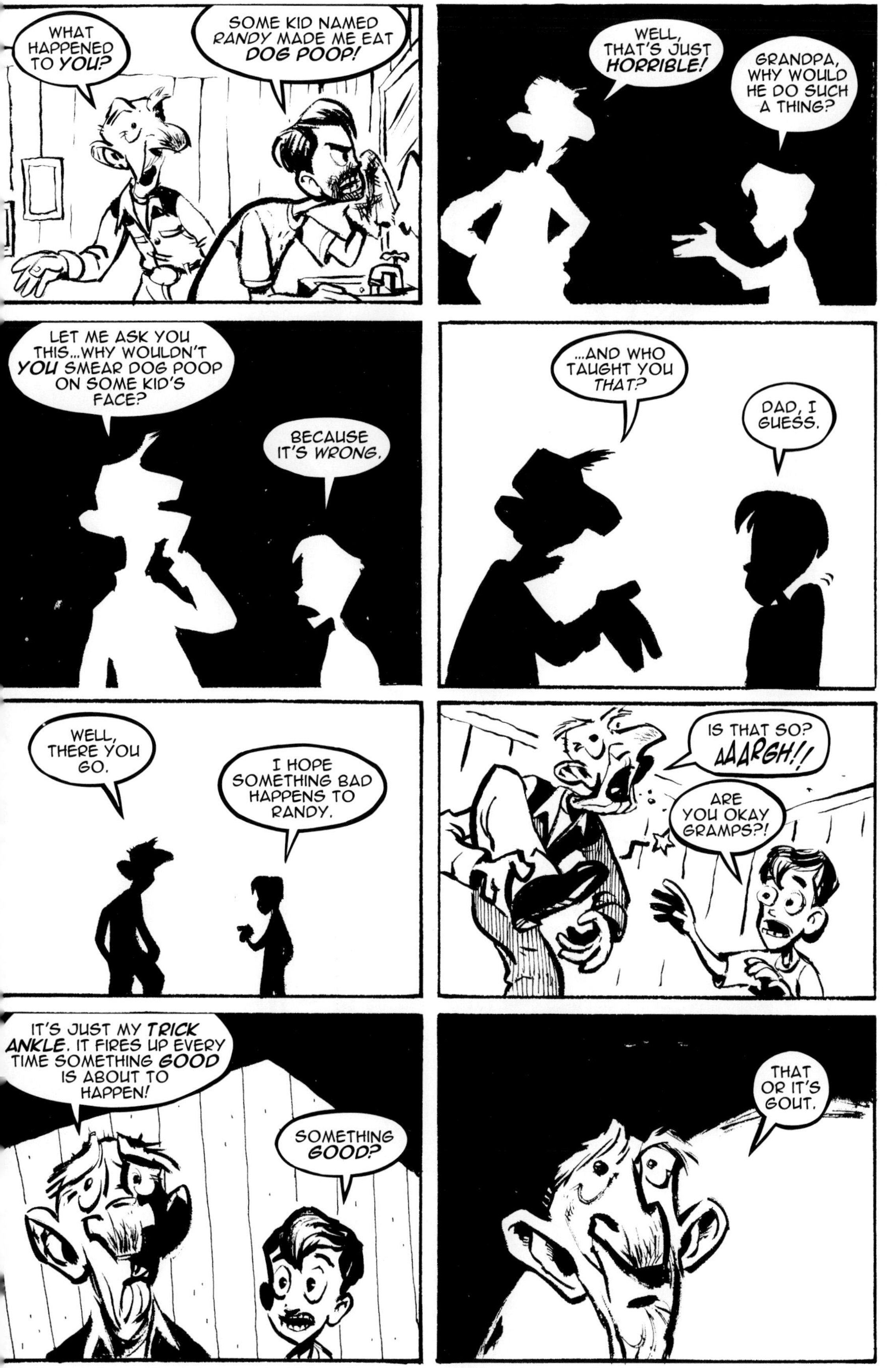

WHAT HAPPENED TO YOU?
SOME KID NAMED RANDY MADE ME EAT DOG POOP!
WELL, THAT'S JUST HORRIBLE!
GRANDPA, WHY WOULD HE DO SUCH A THING?
LET ME ASK YOU THIS...WHY WOULDN'T YOU SMEAR DOG POOP ON SOME KID'S FACE?
BECAUSE IT'S WRONG.
...AND WHO TAUGHT YOU THAT?
DAD, I GUESS.
WELL, THERE YOU GO.
I HOPE SOMETHING BAD HAPPENS TO RANDY.
IS THAT SO? AAARGH!!
ARE YOU OKAY GRAMPS?!
IT'S JUST MY TRICK ANKLE. IT FIRES UP EVERY TIME SOMETHING GOOD IS ABOUT TO HAPPEN!
SOMETHING GOOD?
THAT OR IT'S GOUT.

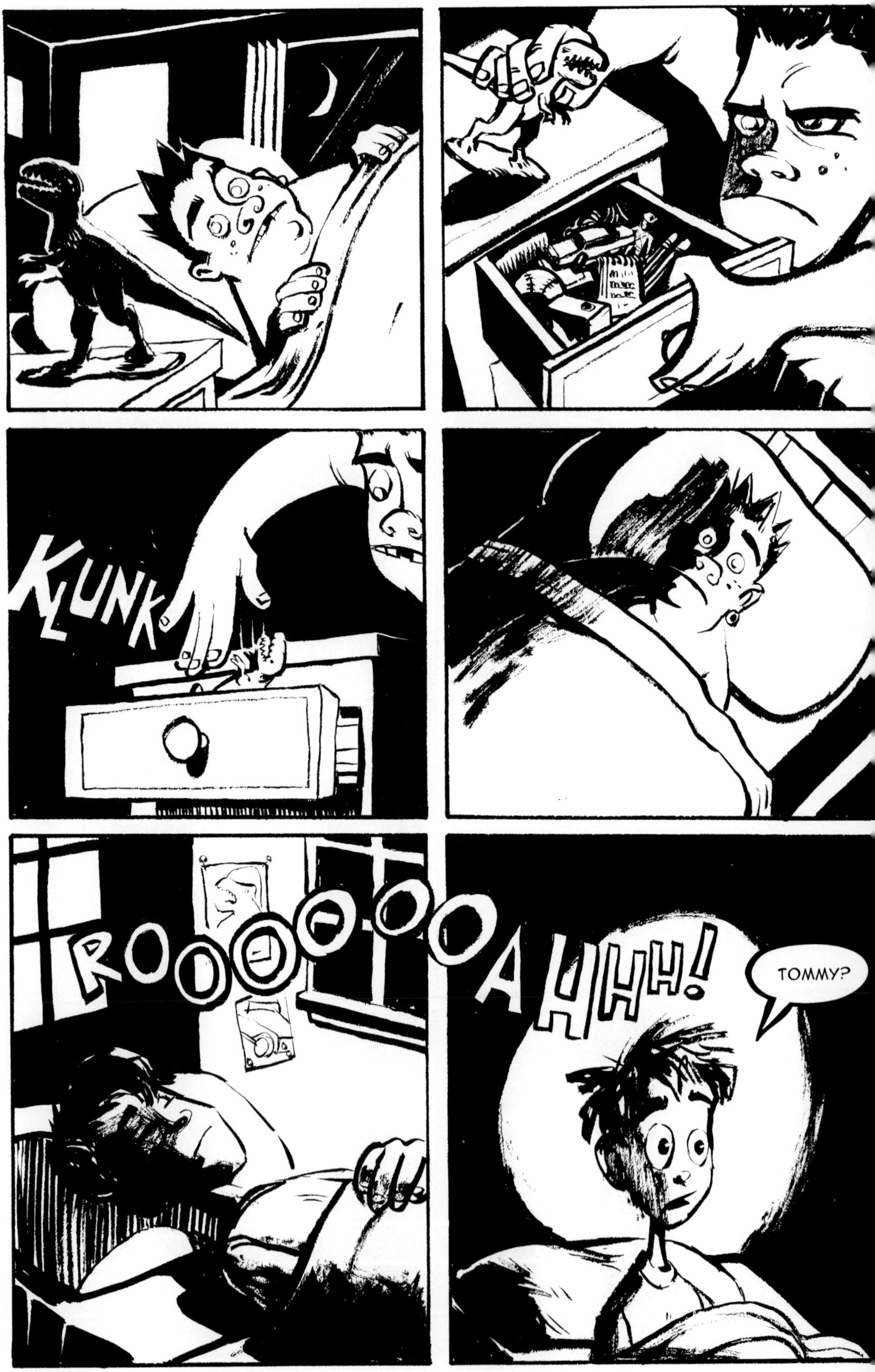
KLUNK
ROOOOOOOAHHH!
TOMMY?

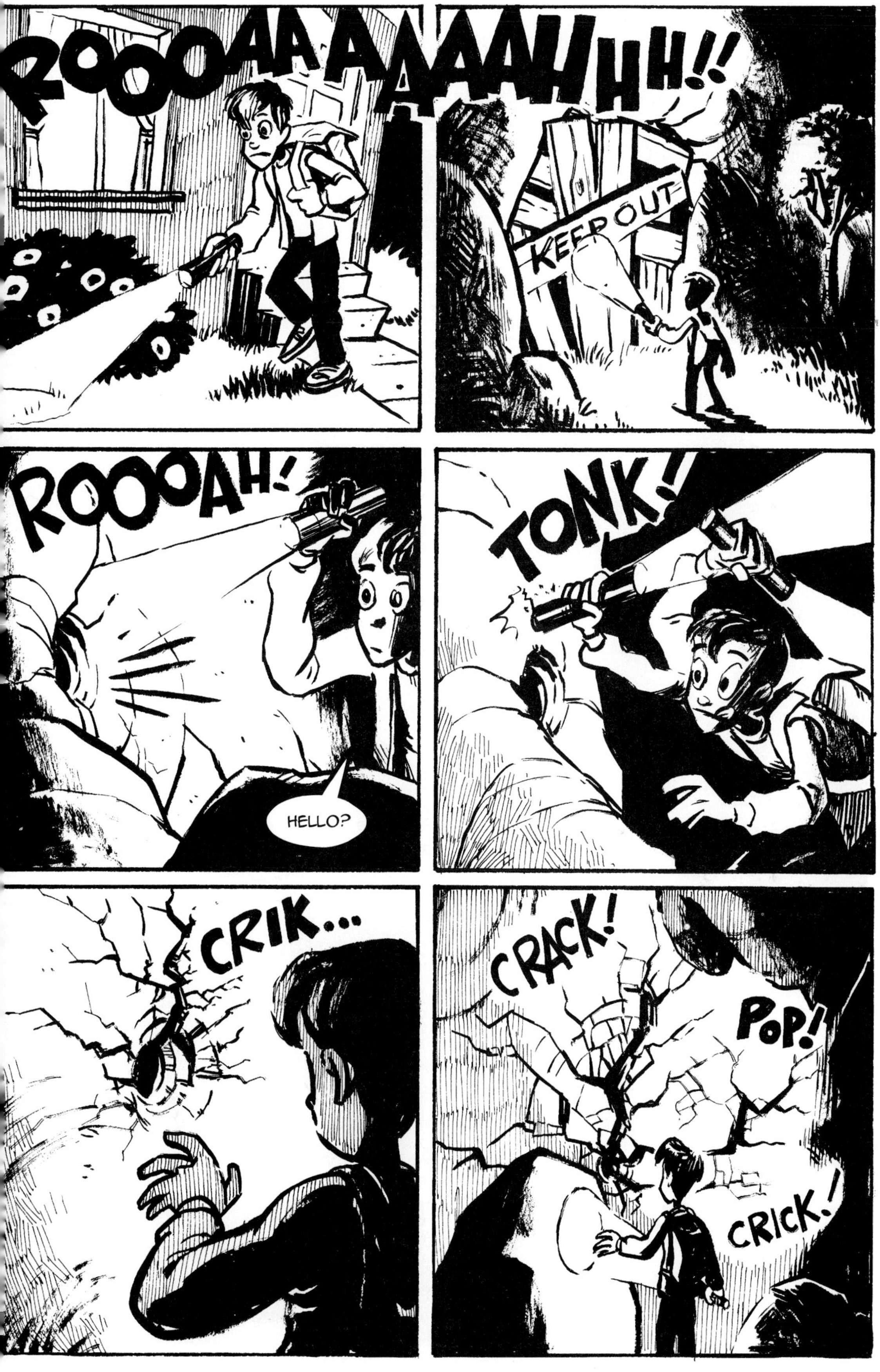
ROOOAAAAAAHHH!!
KEEP OUT
ROOOAH!
HELLO?
TONK!
CRIK...
CRACK!
POP!
CRICK!

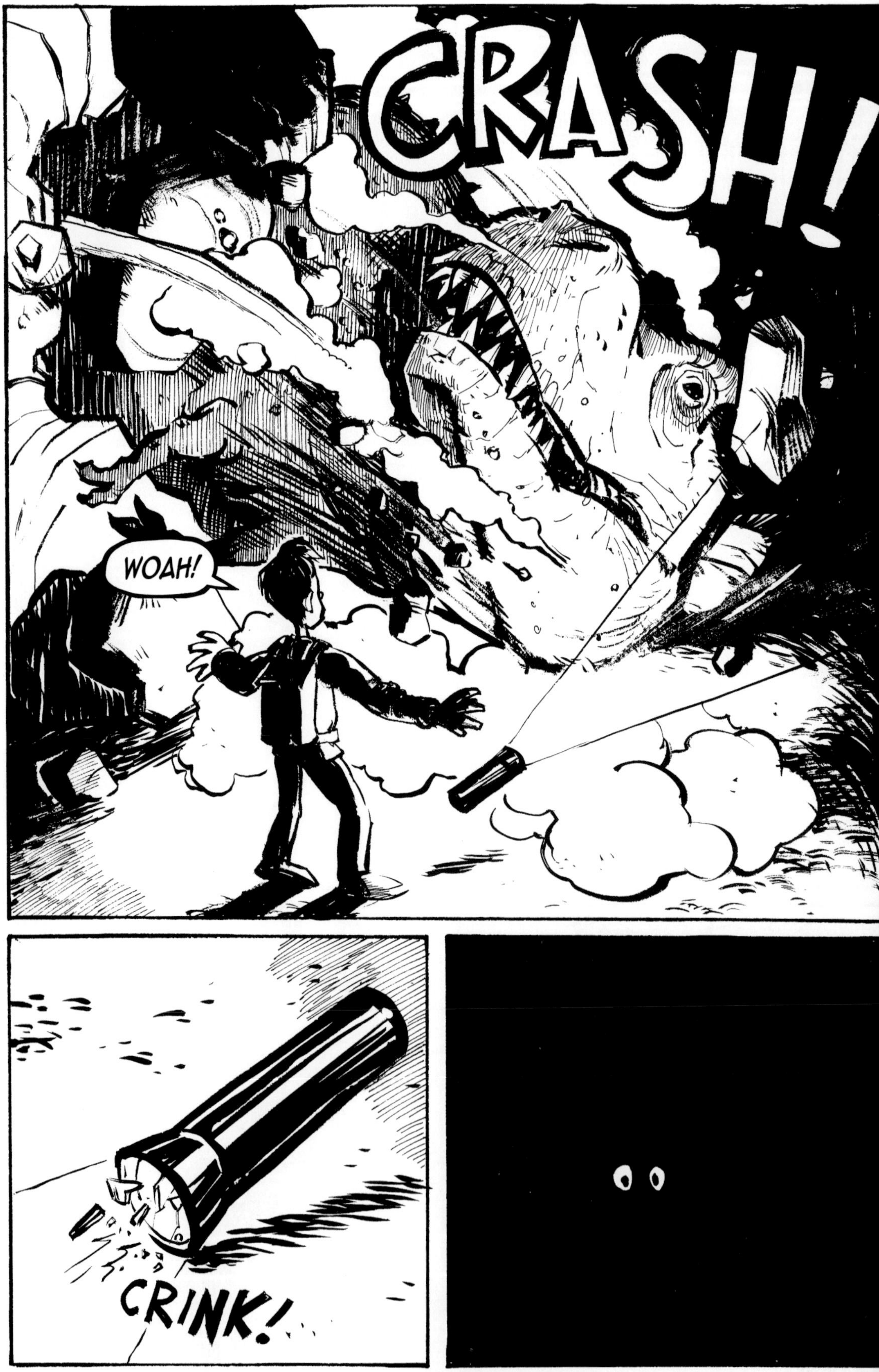
CRASH!
WOAH!
CRINK!

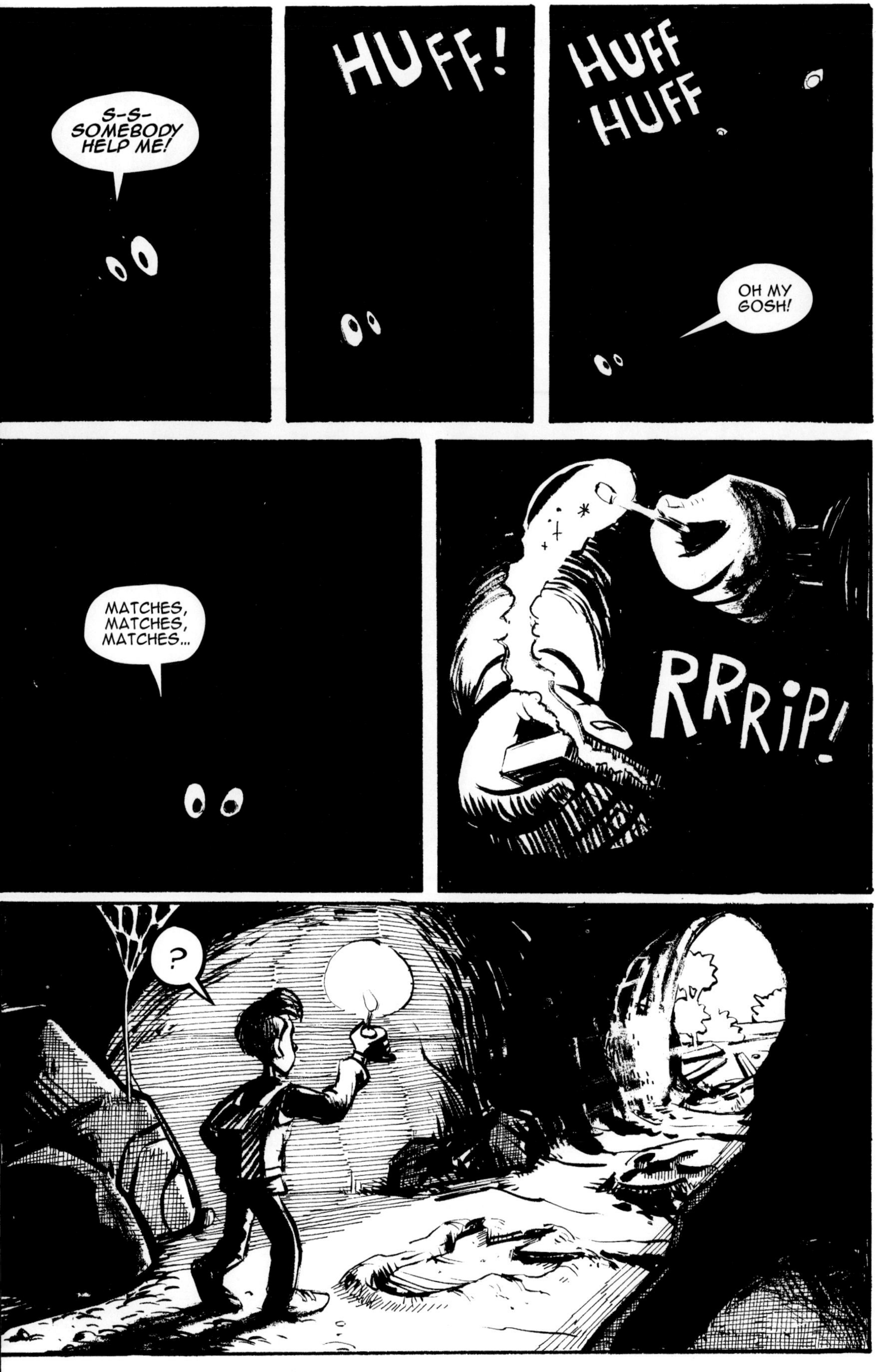
S-S-SOMEBODY HELP ME!
HUFF!
HUFF HUFF
OH MY GOSH!
MATCHES, MATCHES, MATCHES...
RRRIP!
?

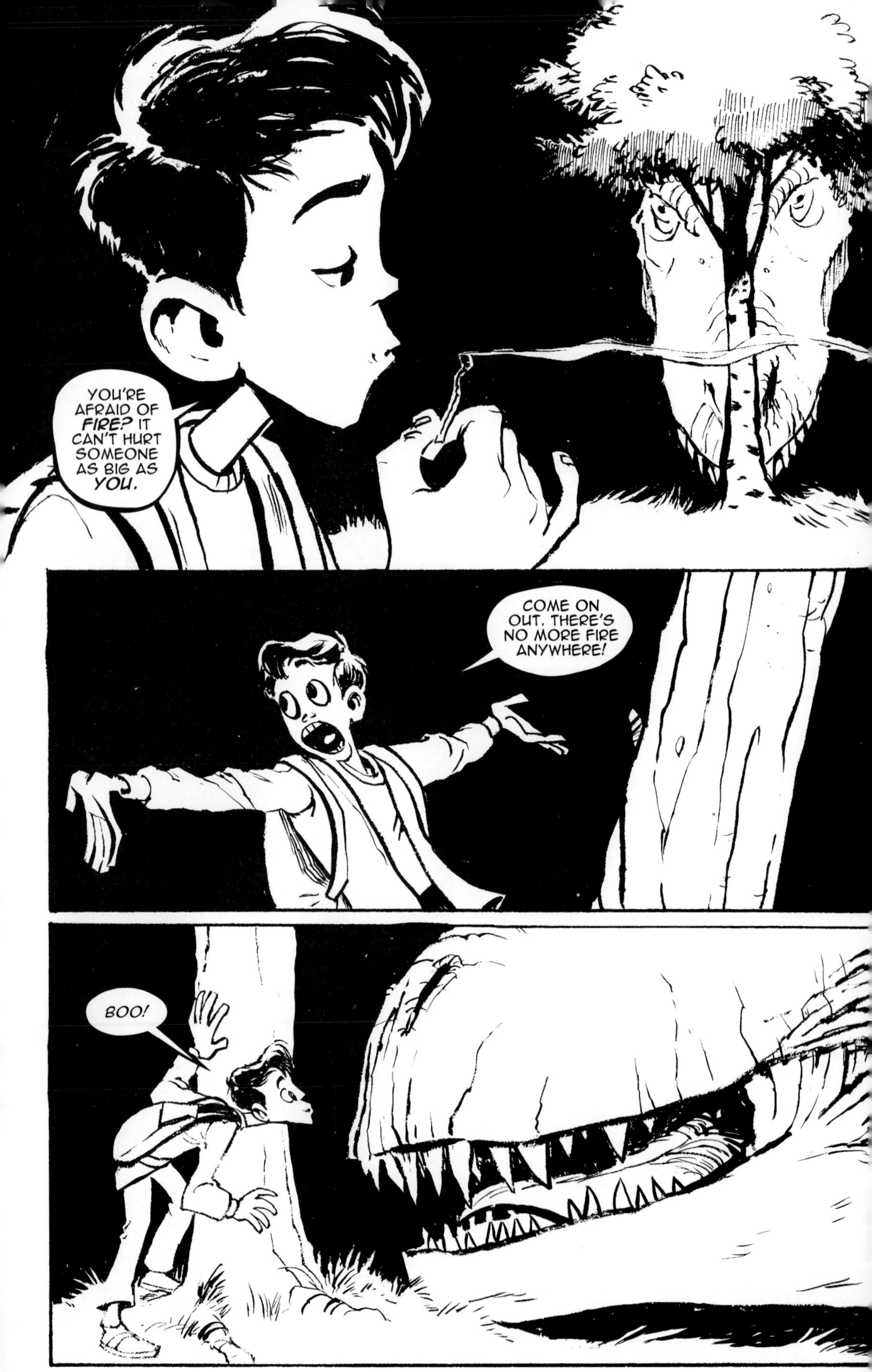
YOU'RE AFRAID OF FIRE? IT CAN'T HURT SOMEONE AS BIG AS YOU.
COME ON OUT. THERE'S NO MORE FIRE ANYWHERE!
BOO!

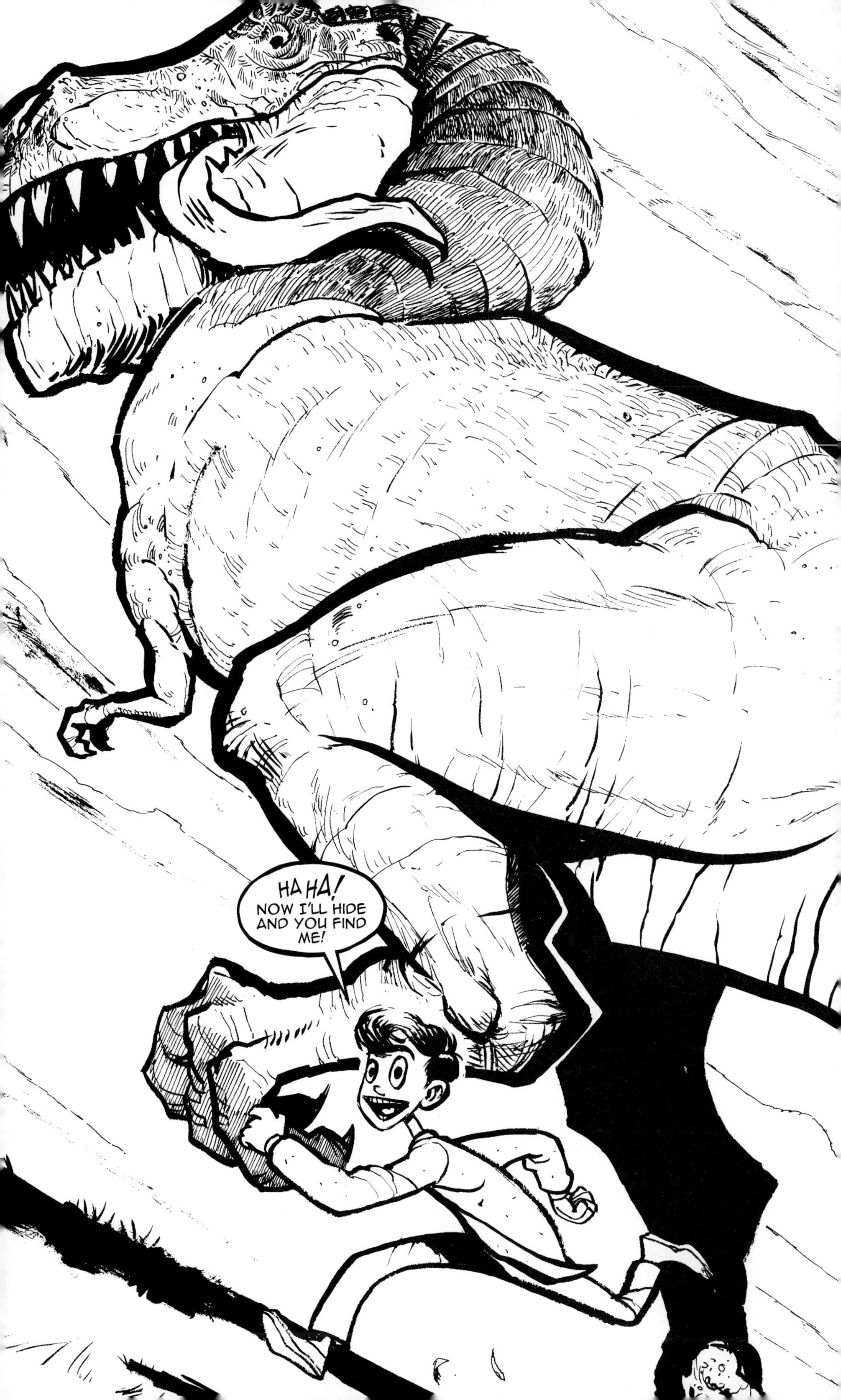
HA HA! NOW I'LL HIDE AND YOU FIND ME!

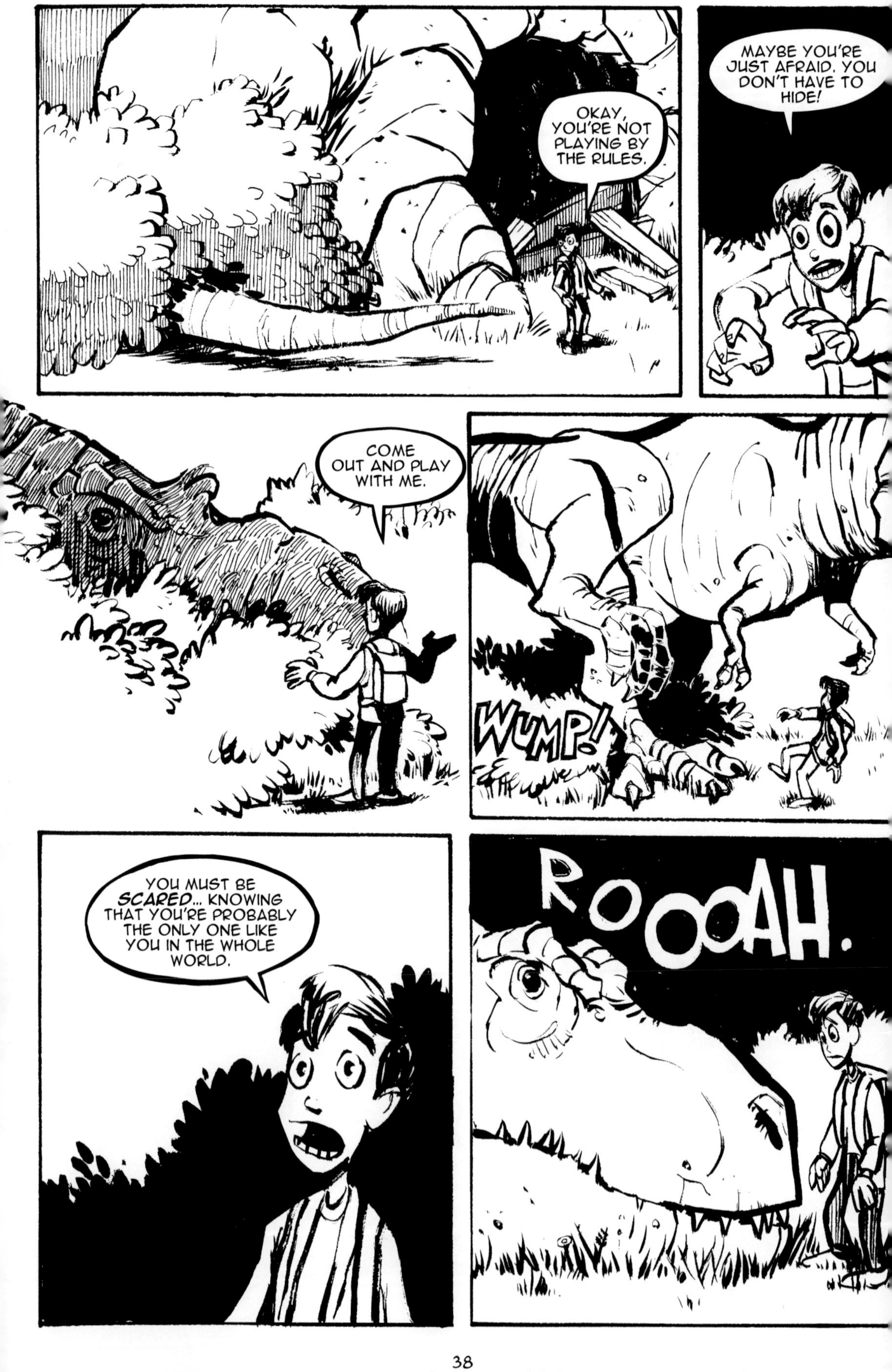
OKAY, YOU'RE NOT PLAYING BY THE RULES.
MAYBE YOU'RE JUST AFRAID. YOU DON'T HAVE TO HIDE!
COME OUT AND PLAY WITH ME.
WUMP!
YOU MUST BE SCARED... KNOWING THAT YOU'RE PROBABLY THE ONLY ONE LIKE YOU IN THE WHOLE WORLD.
ROOOAH.

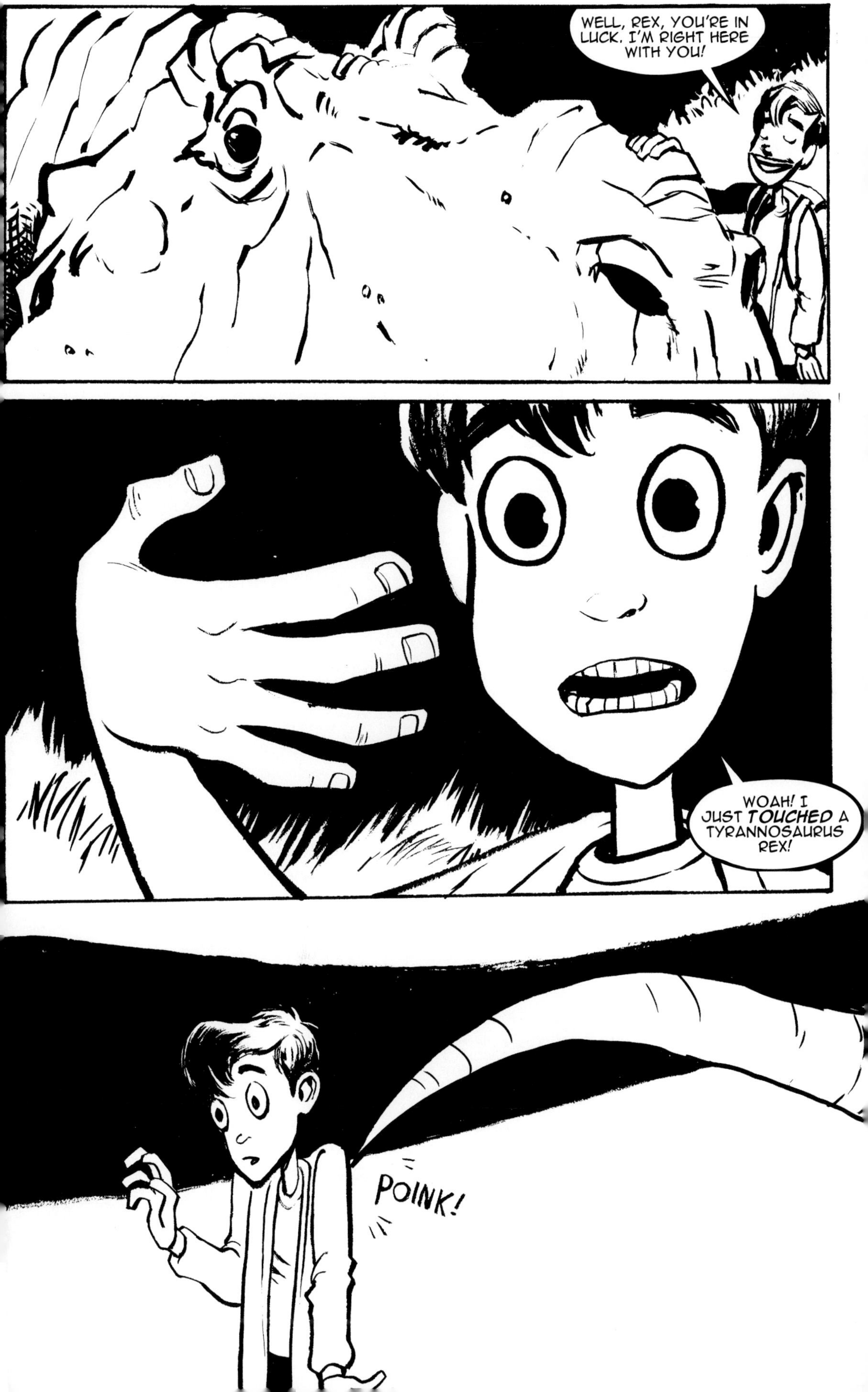
WELL, REX, YOU'RE IN LUCK. I'M RIGHT HERE WITH YOU!
WOAH! I JUST *TOUCHED* A TYRANNOSAURUS REX!
POINK!

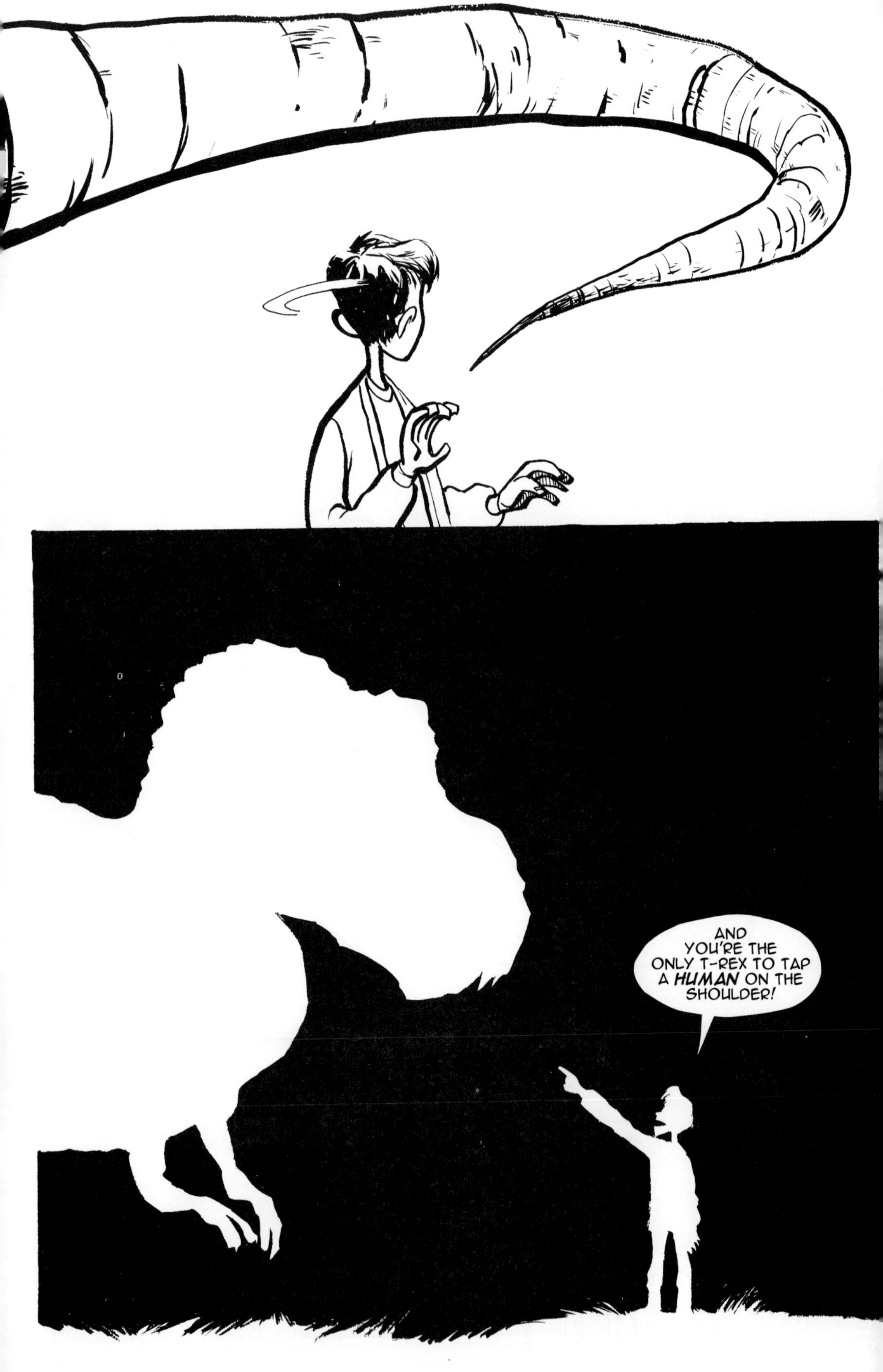
AND YOU'RE THE ONLY T-REX TO TAP A HUMAN ON THE SHOULDER!

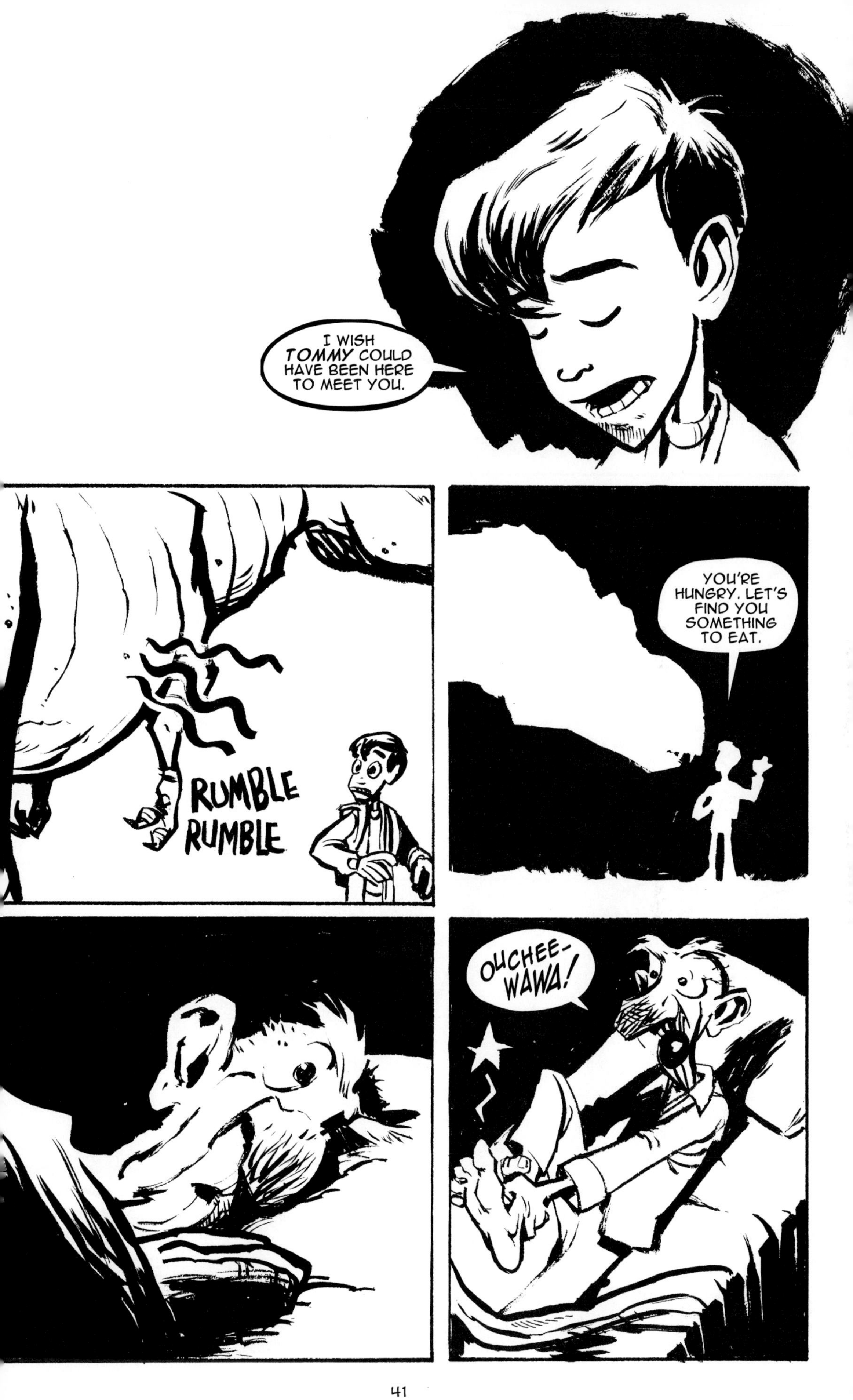
I WISH TOMMY COULD HAVE BEEN HERE TO MEET YOU.
RUMBLE RUMBLE
YOU'RE HUNGRY. LET'S FIND YOU SOMETHING TO EAT.
OUCHEE-WAWA!

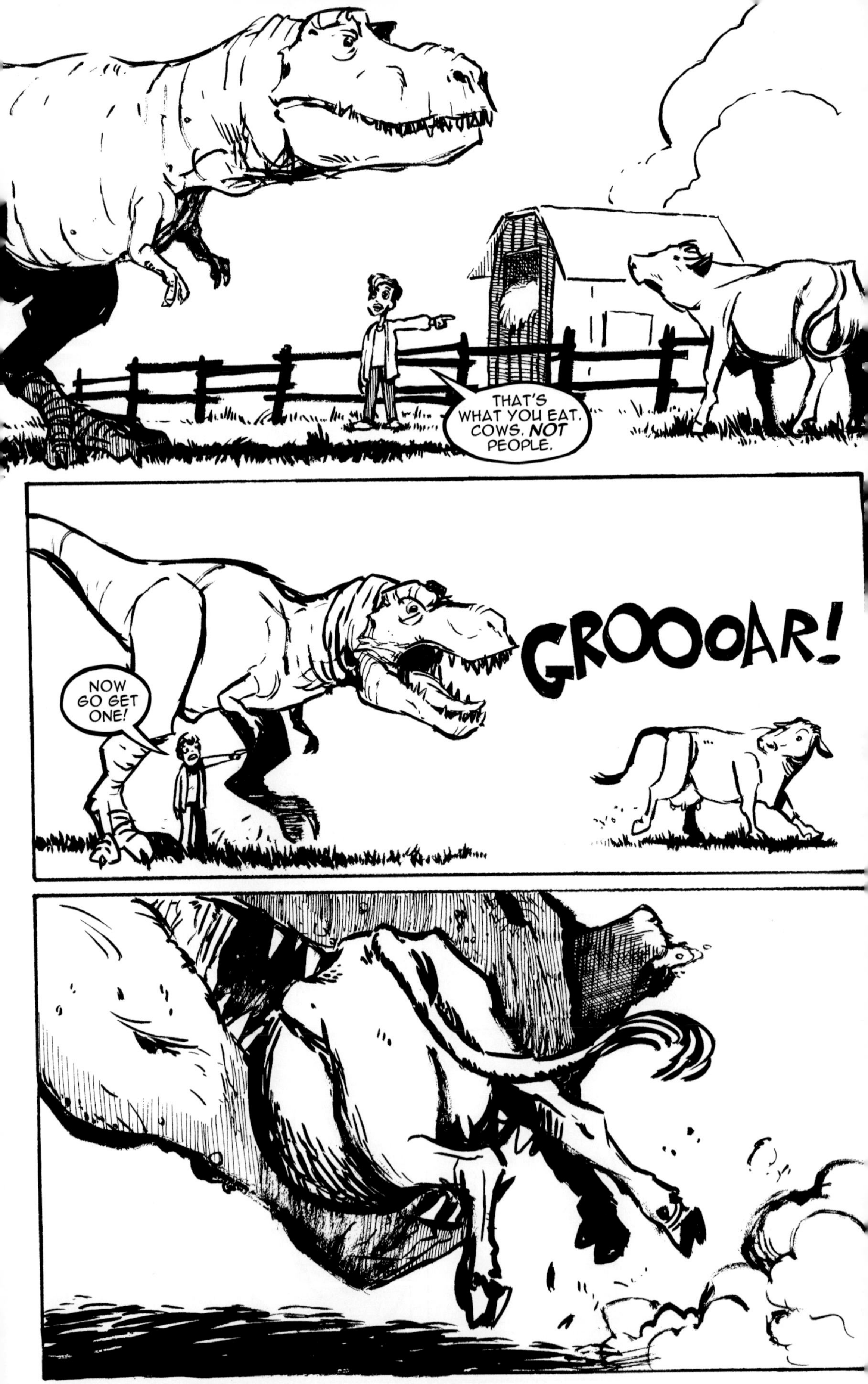

THAT'S WHAT YOU EAT. COWS. **NOT** PEOPLE.
NOW GO GET ONE!
GROOOAR!

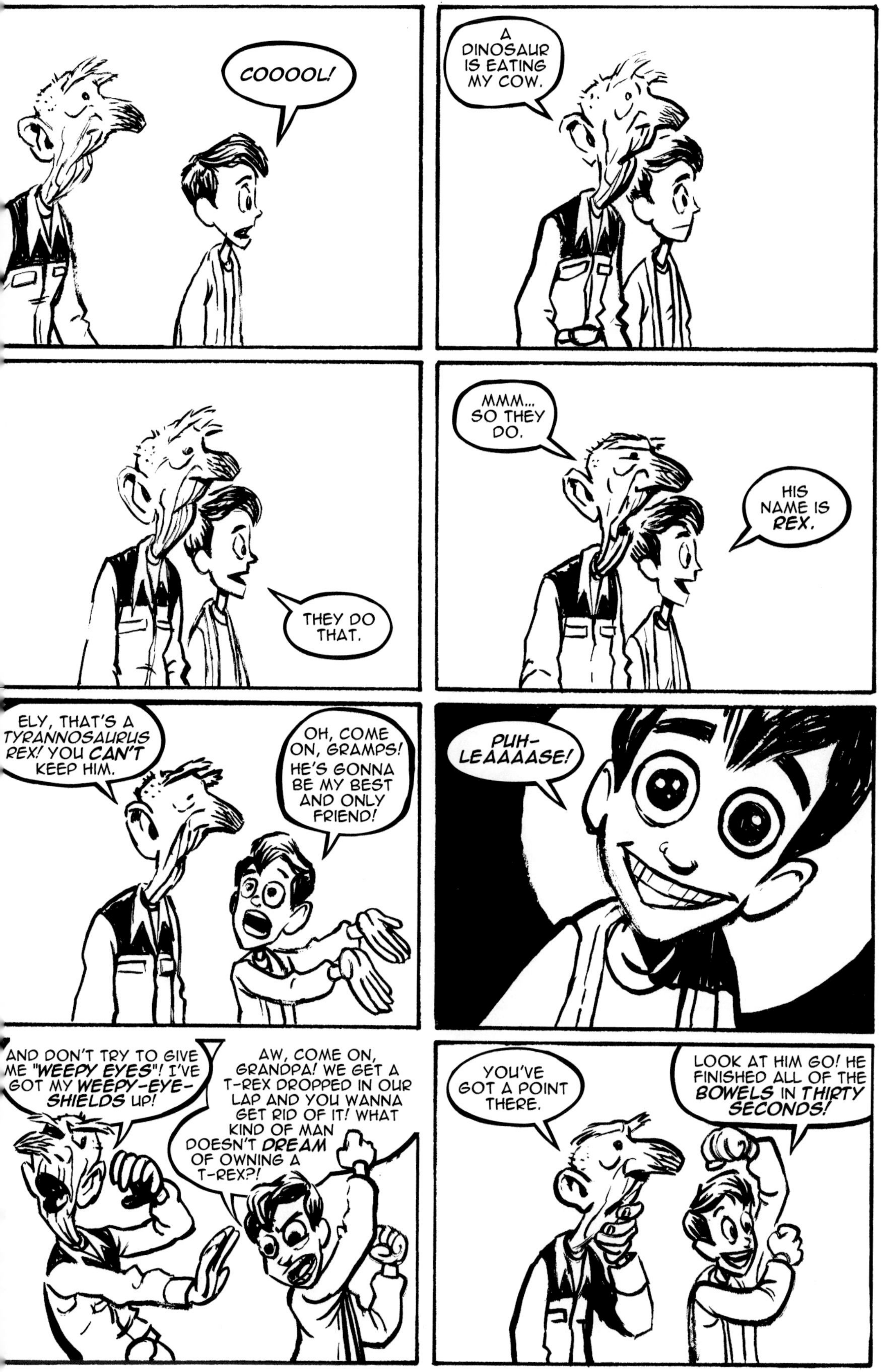
COOOOL!
A DINOSAUR IS EATING MY COW.
THEY DO THAT.
MMM... SO THEY DO.
HIS NAME IS REX.
ELY, THAT'S A TYRANNOSAURUS REX! YOU CAN'T KEEP HIM.
OH, COME ON, GRAMPS! HE'S GONNA BE MY BEST AND ONLY FRIEND!
PUH-LEAAAASE!
AND DON'T TRY TO GIVE ME "WEEPY EYES"! I'VE GOT MY WEEPY-EYE-SHIELDS UP!
AW, COME ON, GRANDPA! WE GET A T-REX DROPPED IN OUR LAP AND YOU WANNA GET RID OF IT! WHAT KIND OF MAN DOESN'T DREAM OF OWNING A T-REX?!
YOU'VE GOT A POINT THERE.
LOOK AT HIM GO! HE FINISHED ALL OF THE BOWELS IN THIRTY SECONDS!

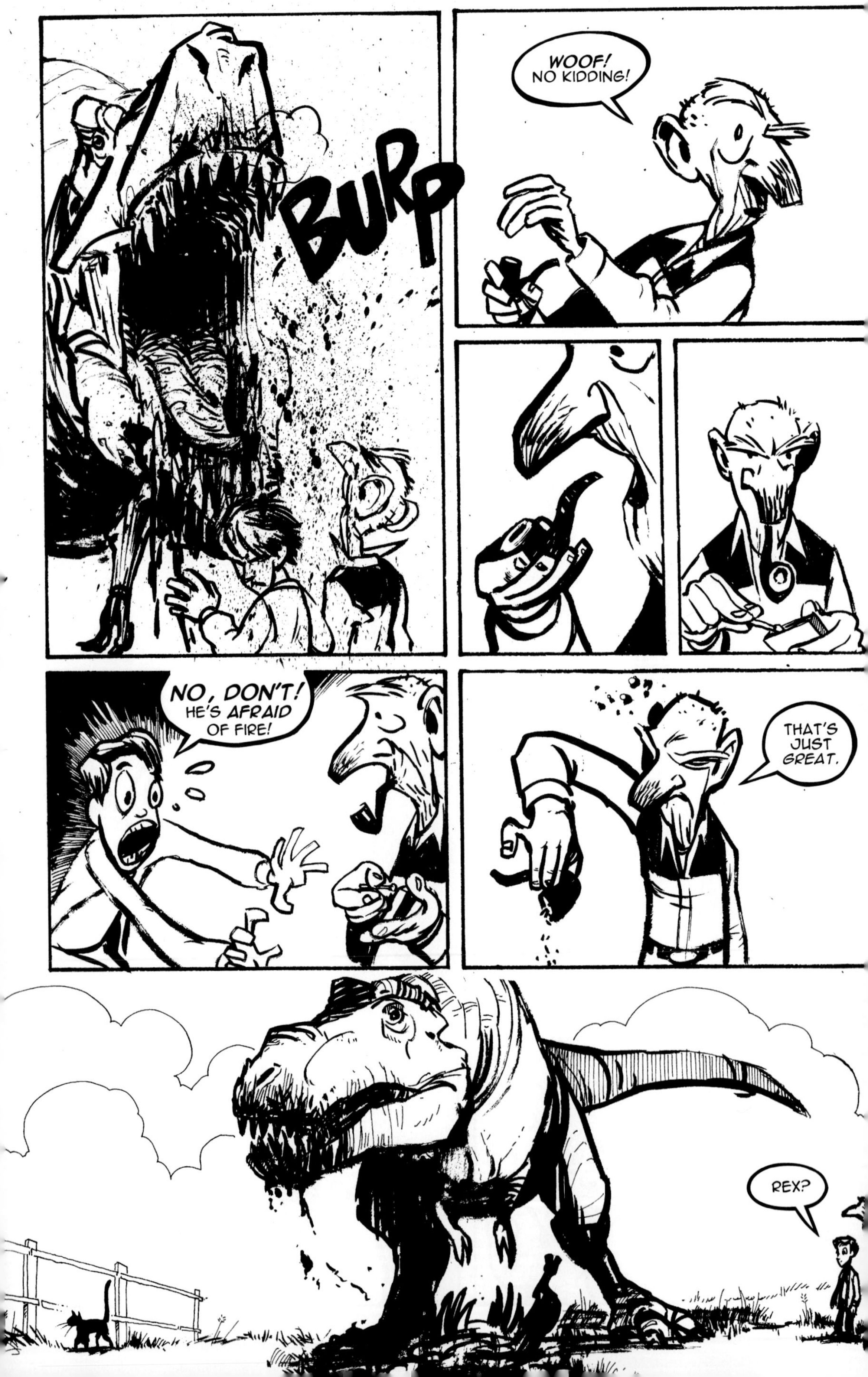
BURP
WOOF! NO KIDDING!
NO, DON'T! HE'S AFRAID OF FIRE!
THAT'S JUST GREAT.
REX?

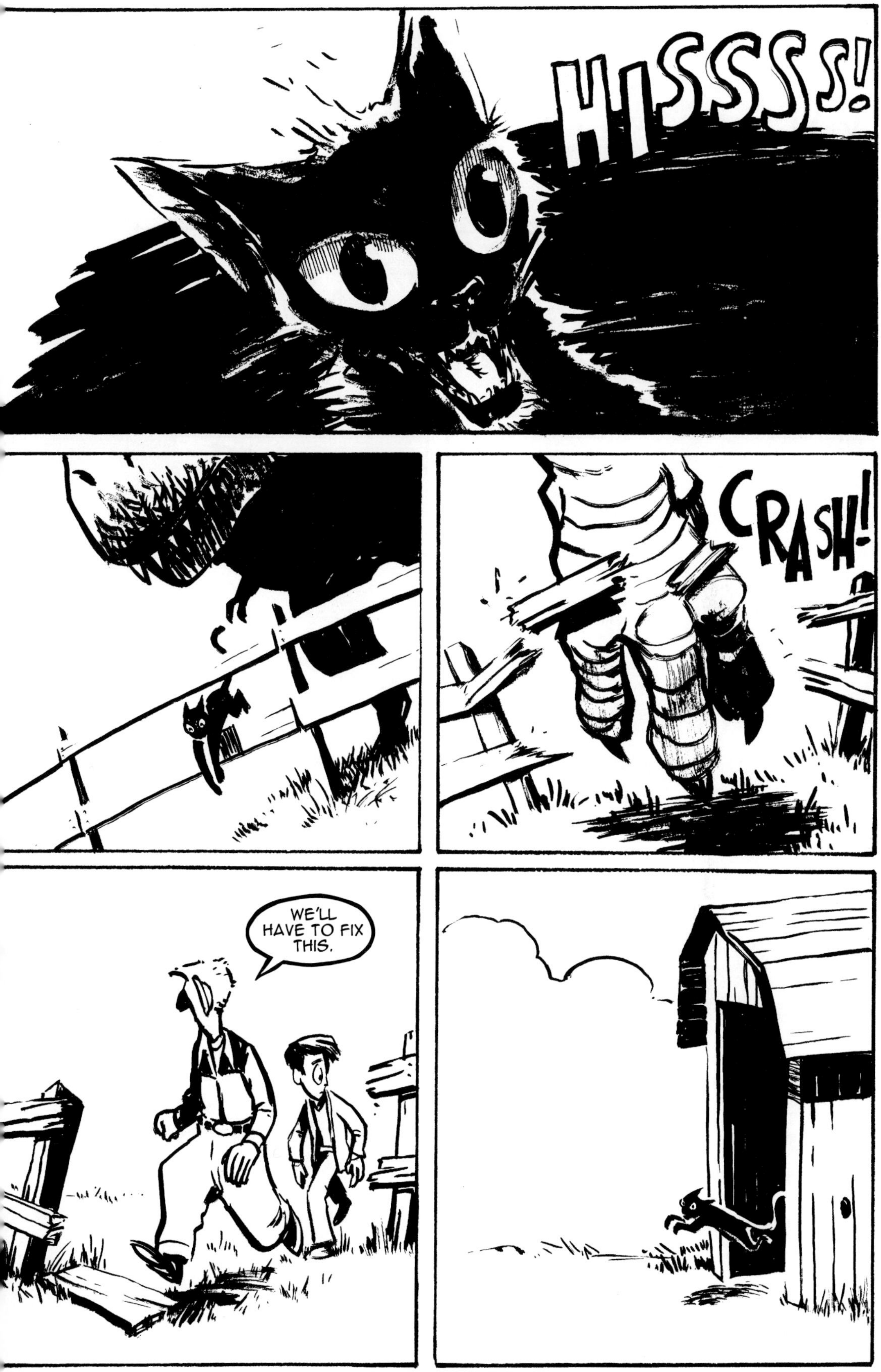
HISSSS!
CRASH!
WE'LL HAVE TO FIX THIS.

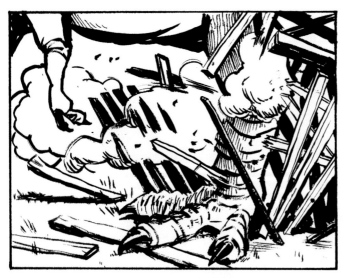

WE- WE-
WE'LL HAVE
TO FIX THAT
TOO!

CRASH!

OH NO.

THAT
YOUR T-REX,
JOE?

MORNIN'.

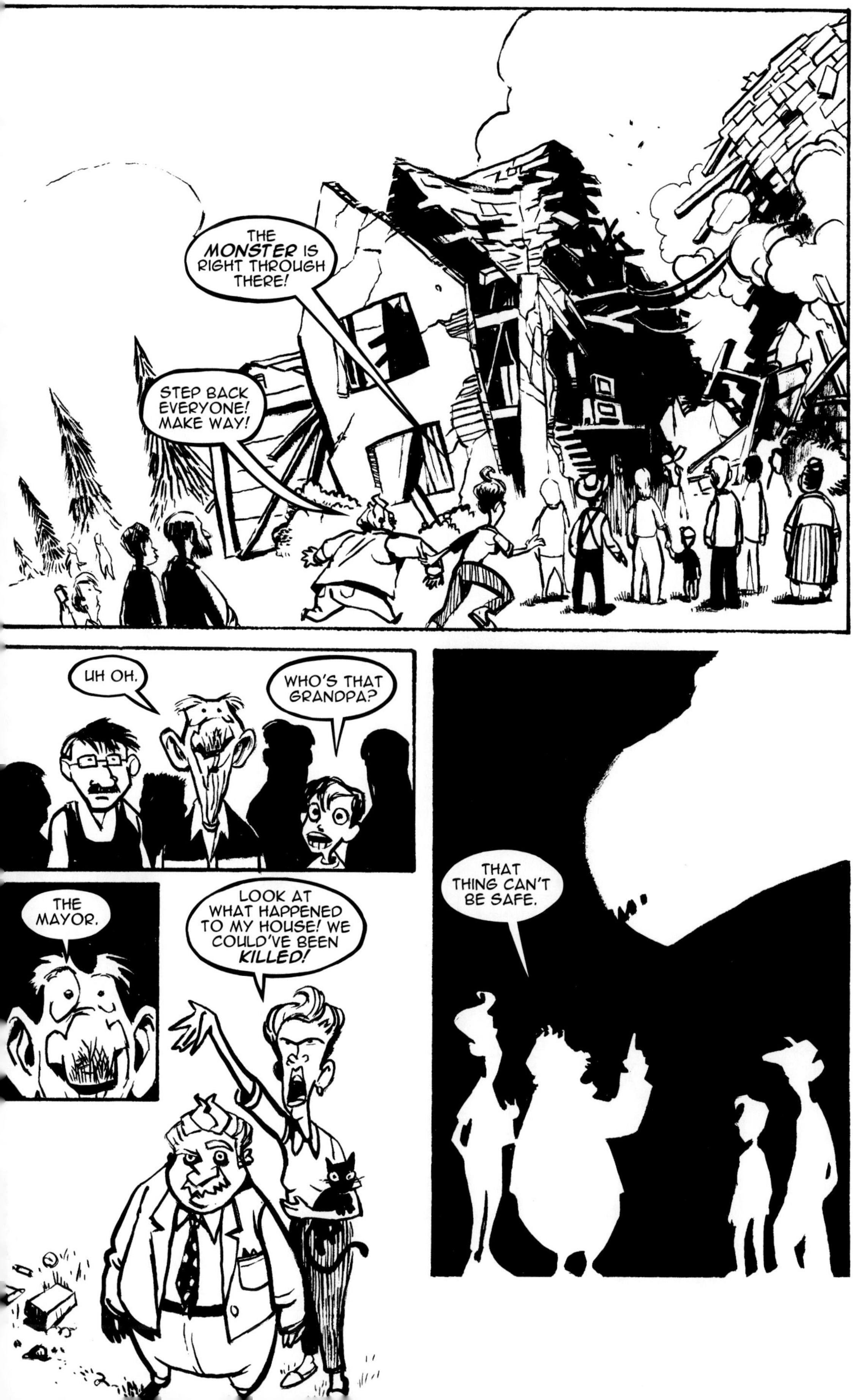
THE *MONSTER* IS RIGHT THROUGH THERE!
STEP BACK EVERYONE! MAKE WAY!
UH OH.
WHO'S THAT GRANDPA?
THE MAYOR.
LOOK AT WHAT HAPPENED TO MY HOUSE! WE COULD'VE BEEN *KILLED!*
THAT THING CAN'T BE SAFE.

48

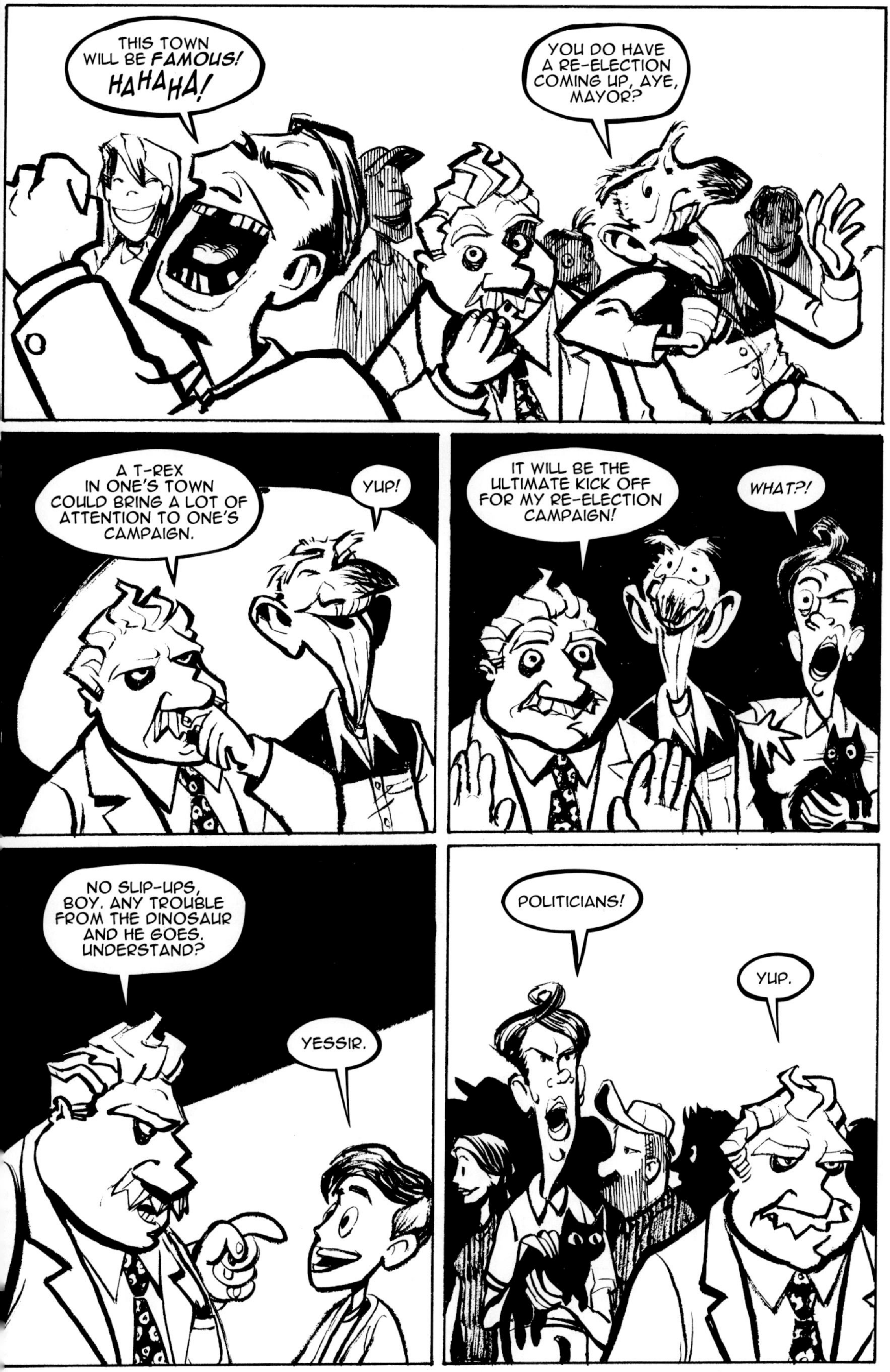
THIS TOWN WILL BE FAMOUS! HAHAHA!
YOU DO HAVE A RE-ELECTION COMING UP, AYE, MAYOR?
A T-REX IN ONE'S TOWN COULD BRING A LOT OF ATTENTION TO ONE'S CAMPAIGN.
YUP!
IT WILL BE THE ULTIMATE KICK OFF FOR MY RE-ELECTION CAMPAIGN!
WHAT?!
NO SLIP-UPS, BOY. ANY TROUBLE FROM THE DINOSAUR AND HE GOES. UNDERSTAND?
YESSIR.
POLITICIANS!
YUP.

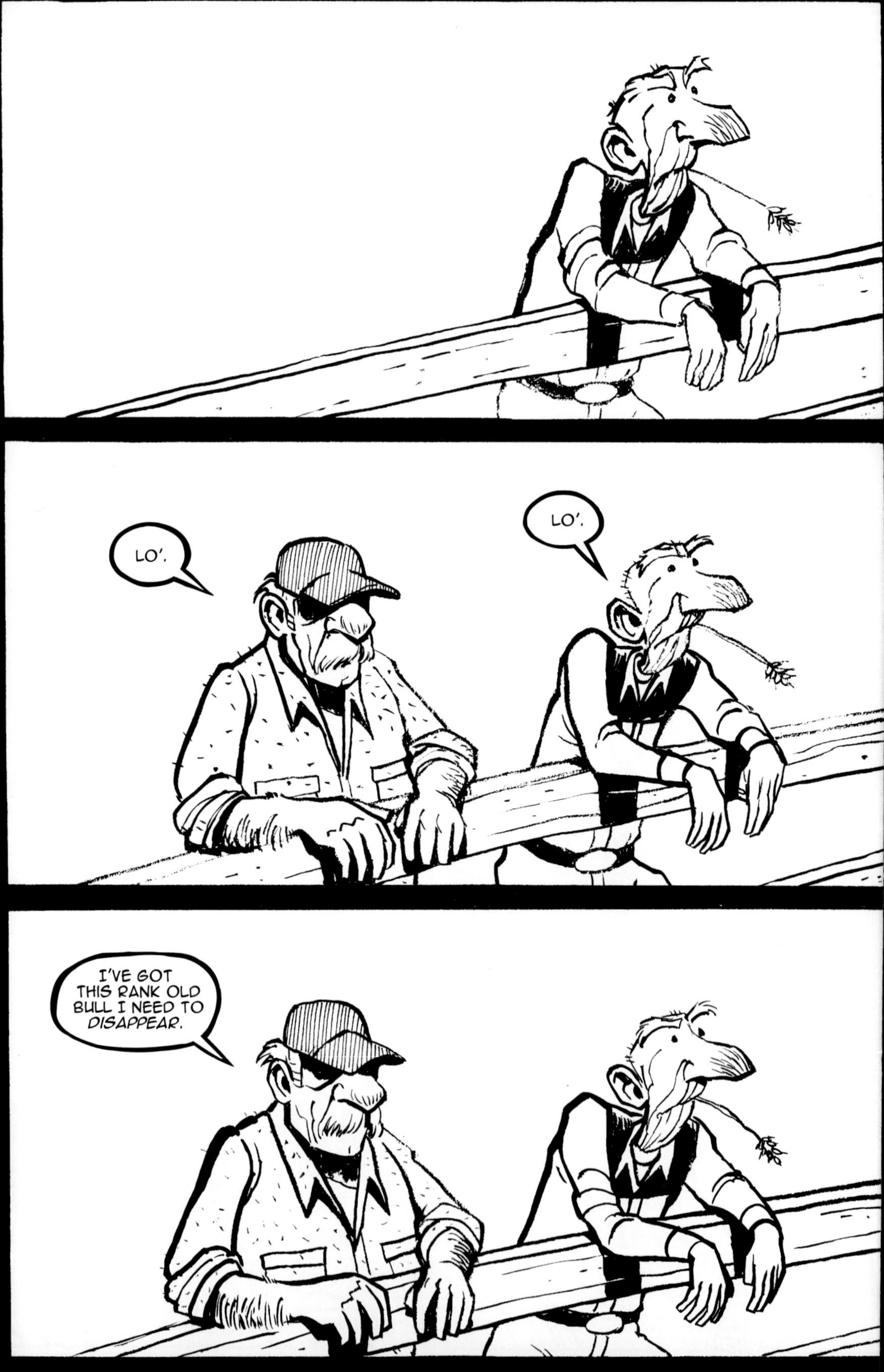
LO'.
LO'.
I'VE GOT THIS RANK OLD BULL I NEED TO *DISAPPEAR*.

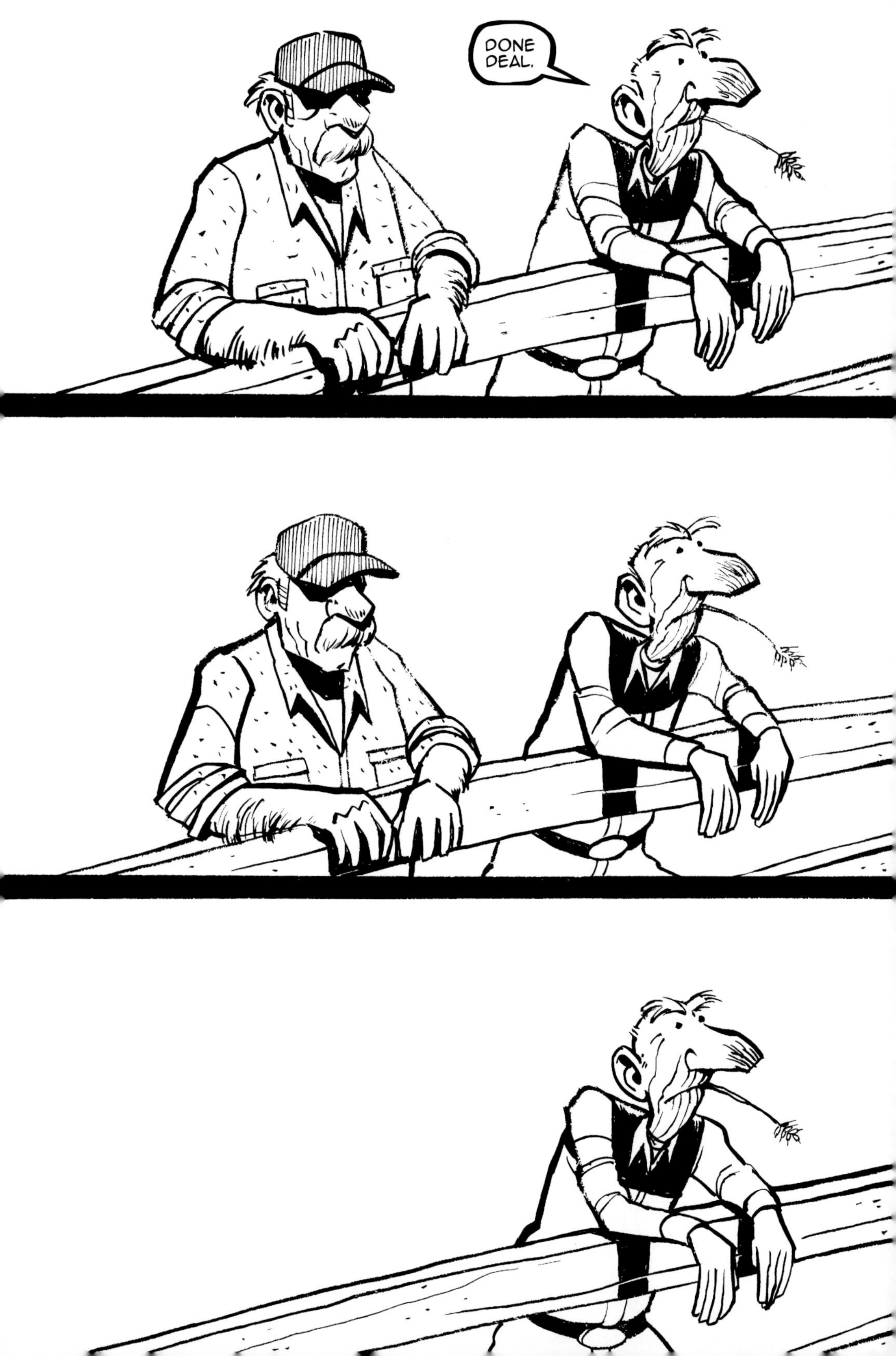
DONE DEAL.

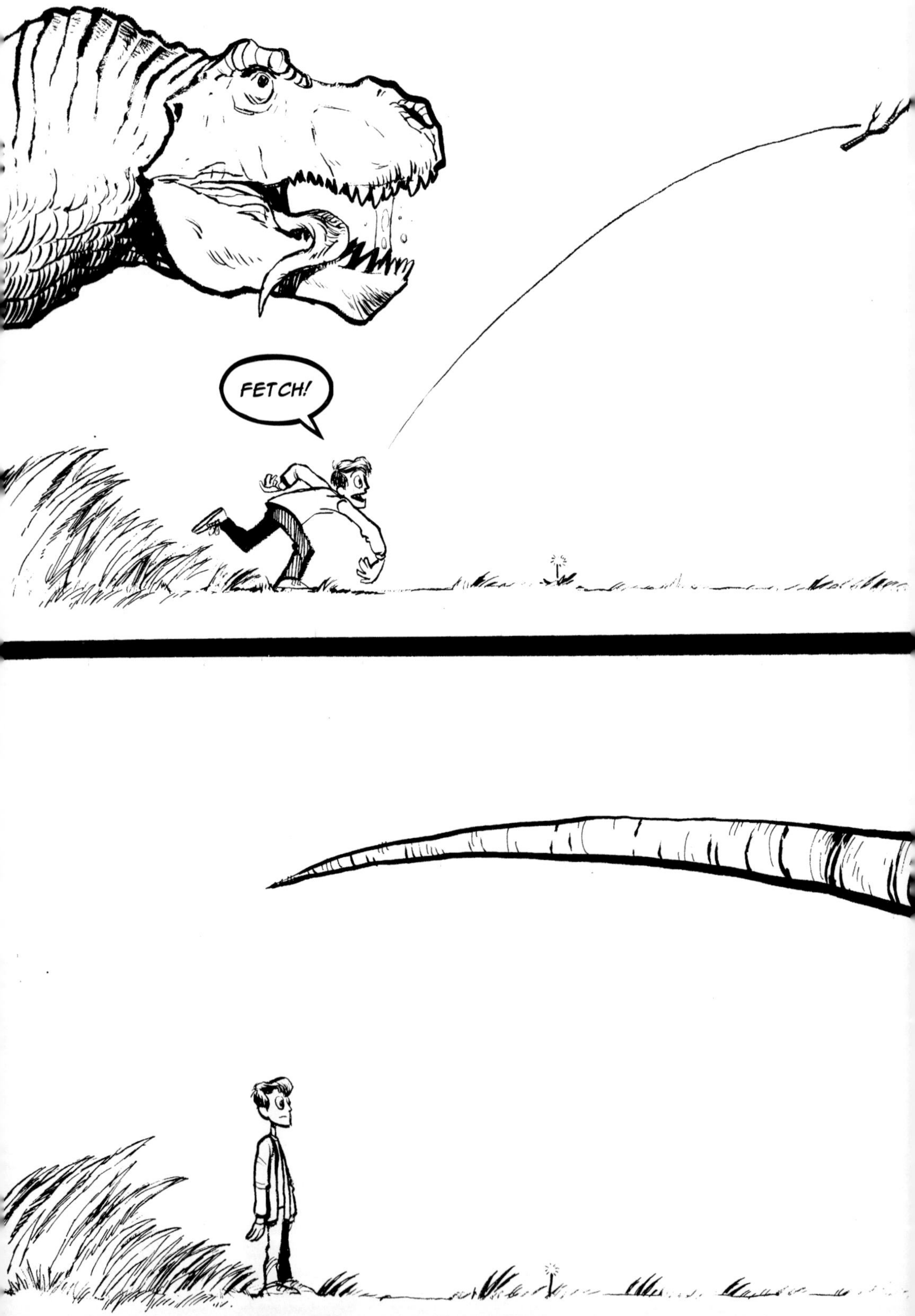
FETCH!

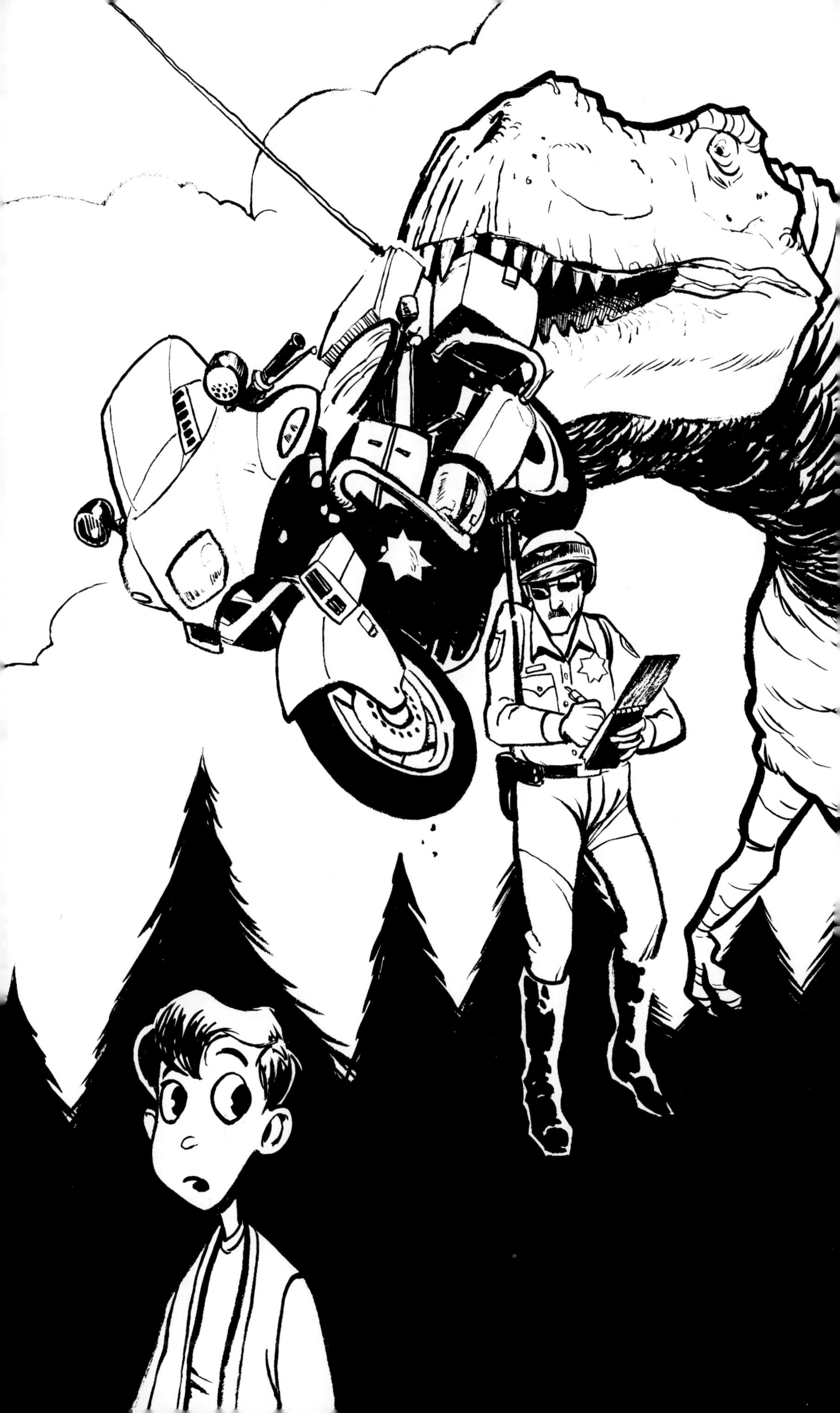

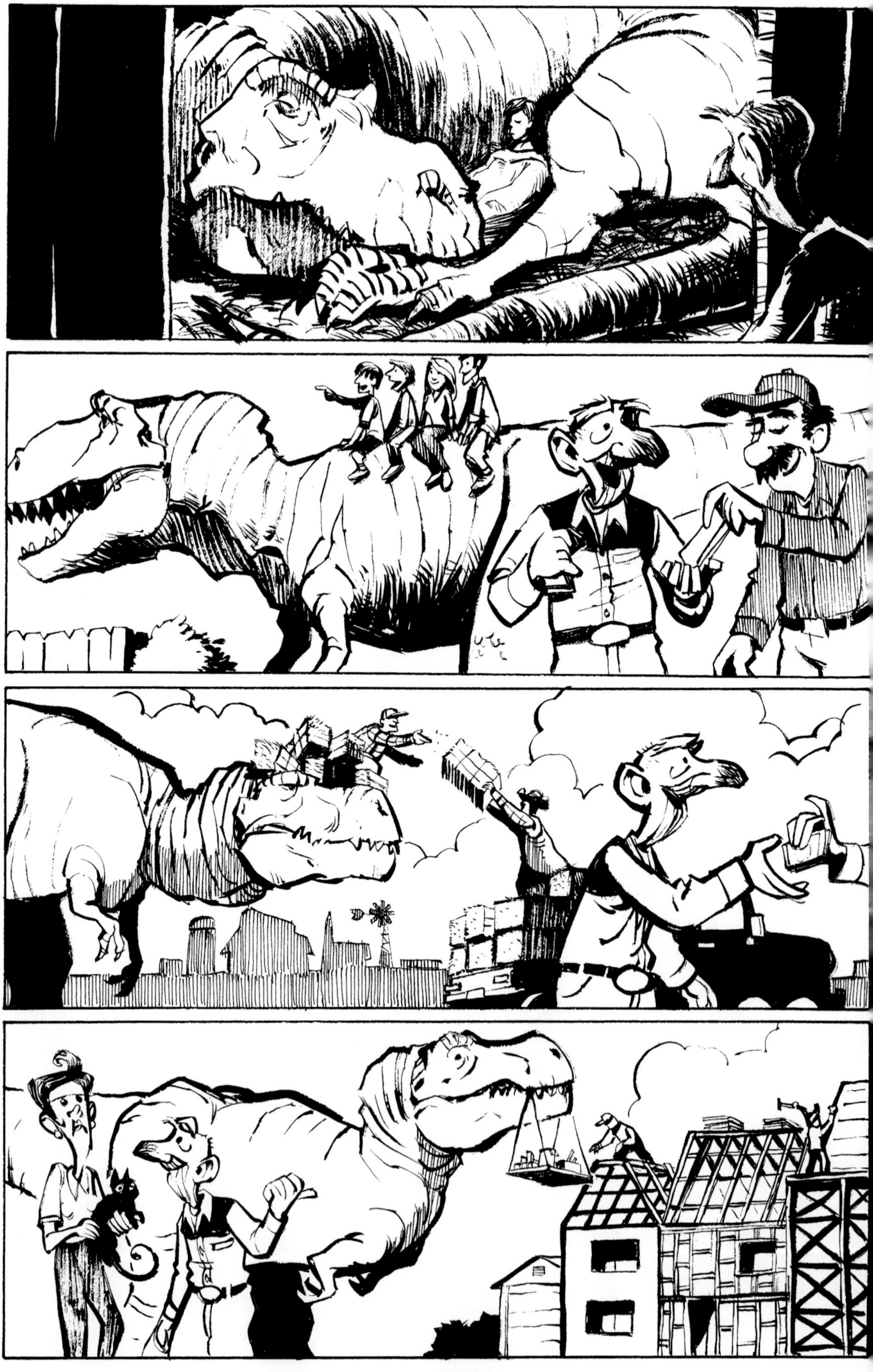

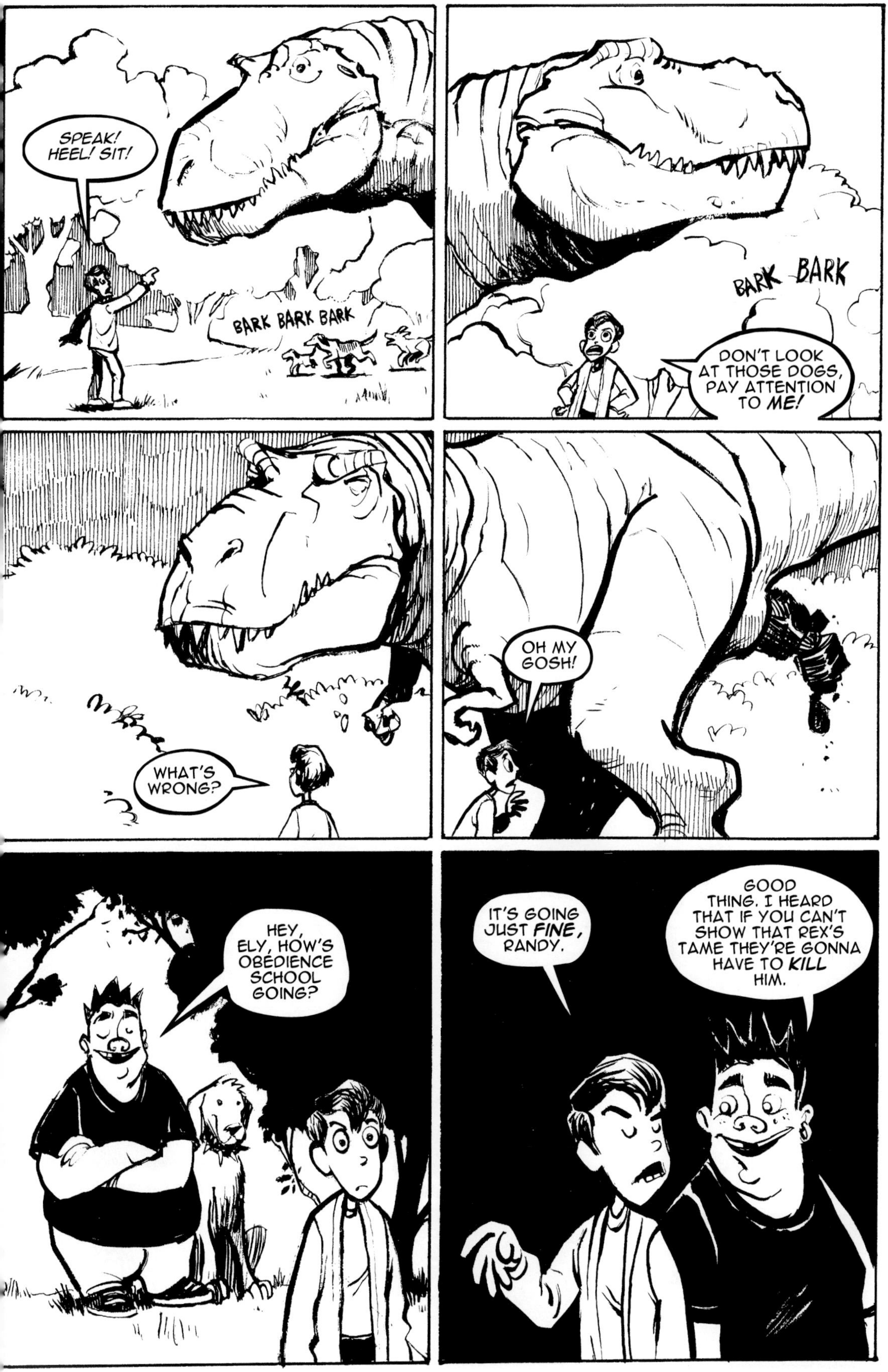
SPEAK! HEEL! SIT!
BARK BARK BARK
BARK BARK
DON'T LOOK AT THOSE DOGS, PAY ATTENTION TO *ME!*
WHAT'S WRONG?
OH MY GOSH!
HEY, ELY, HOW'S OBEDIENCE SCHOOL GOING?
IT'S GOING JUST *FINE*, RANDY.
GOOD THING. I HEARD THAT IF YOU CAN'T SHOW THAT REX'S TAME THEY'RE GONNA HAVE TO *KILL* HIM.

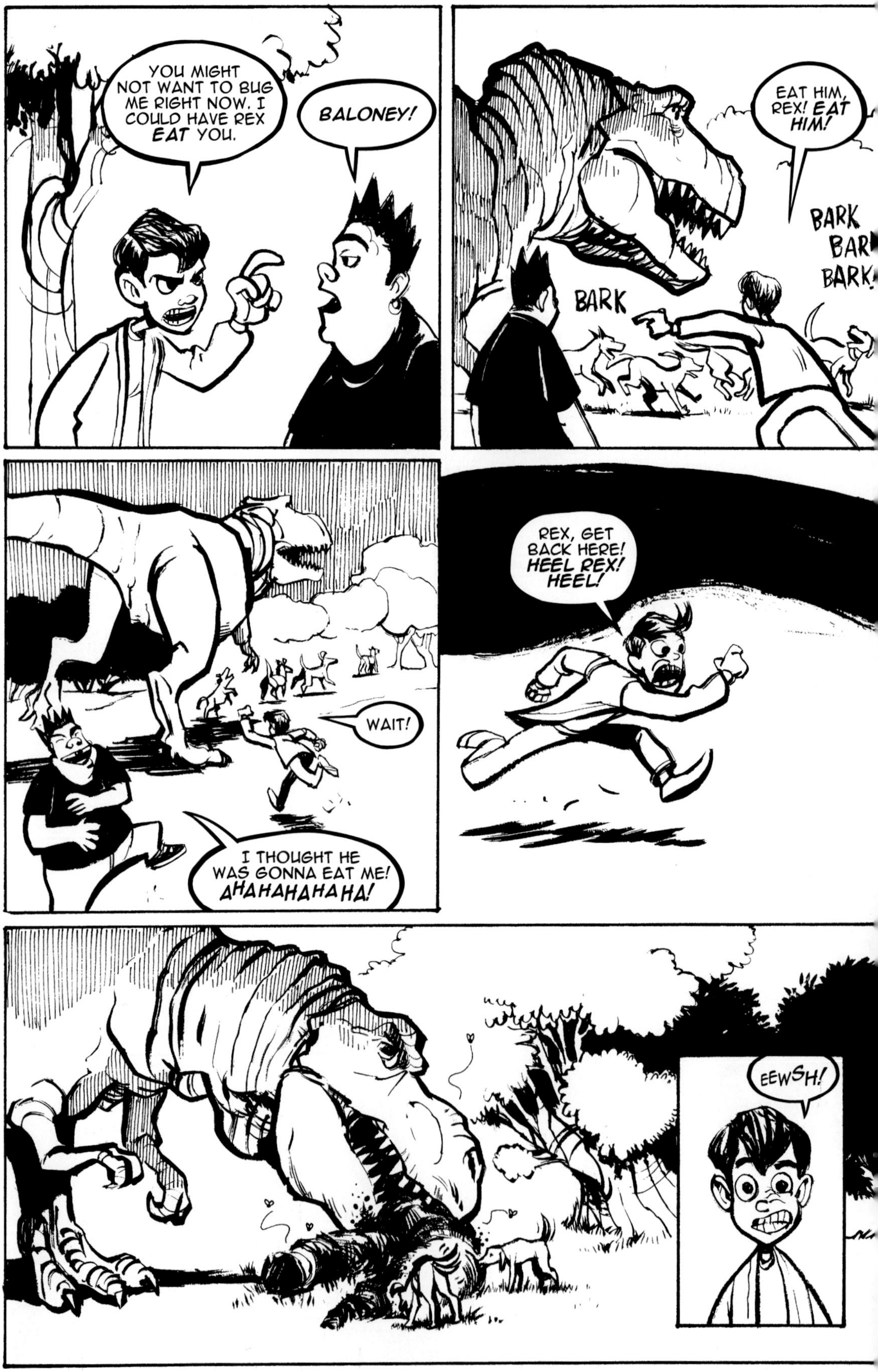
YOU MIGHT NOT WANT TO BUG ME RIGHT NOW. I COULD HAVE REX EAT YOU.
BALONEY!
EAT HIM, REX! EAT HIM!
BARK BARK BARK
BARK
WAIT!
I THOUGHT HE WAS GONNA EAT ME! AHAHAHAHAHA!
REX, GET BACK HERE! HEEL REX! HEEL!
EEWSH!

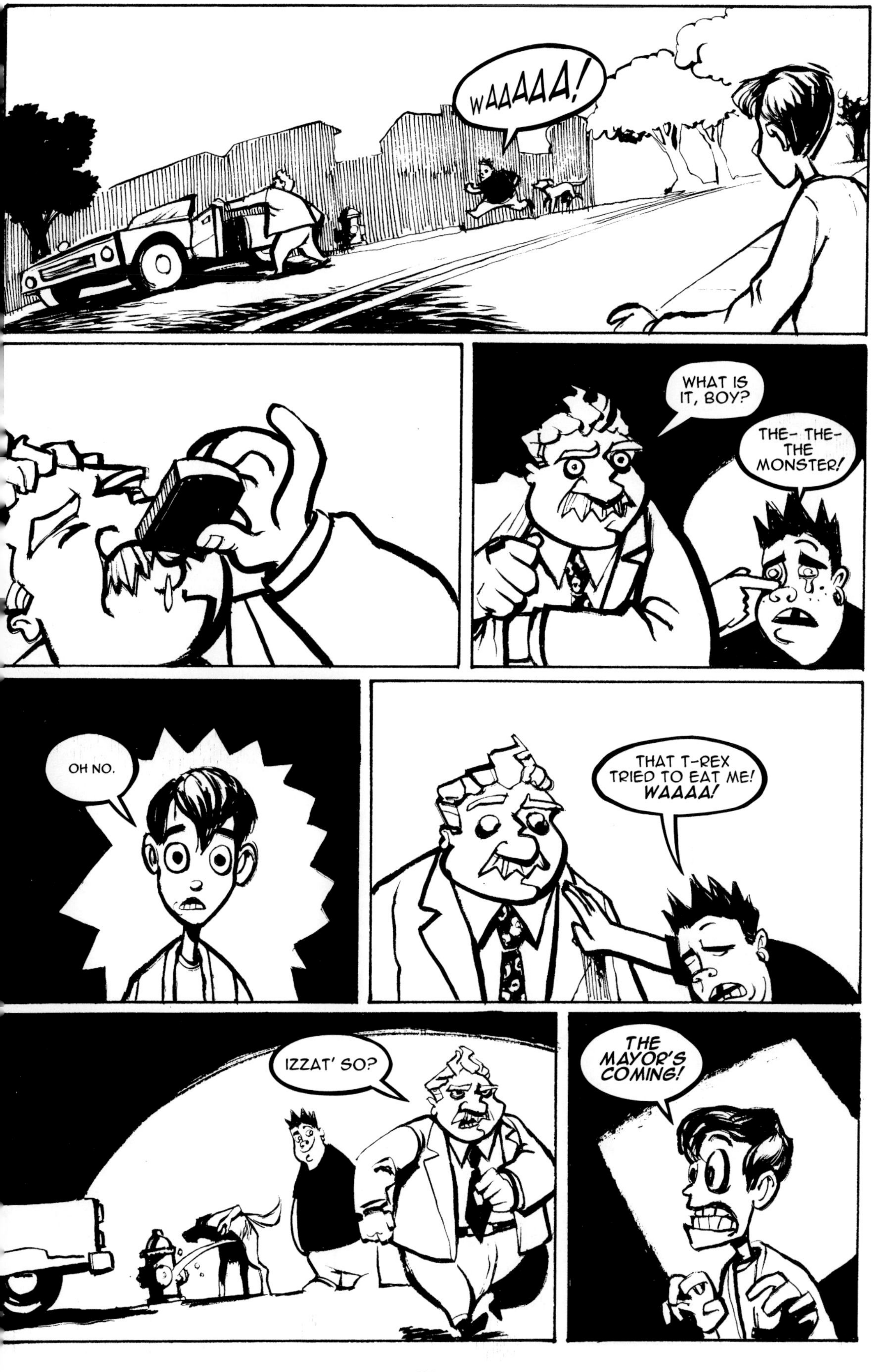
WAAAAA!
WHAT IS IT, BOY?
THE- THE- THE MONSTER!
OH NO.
THAT T-REX TRIED TO EAT ME! WAAAA!
IZZAT' SO?
THE MAYOR'S COMING!

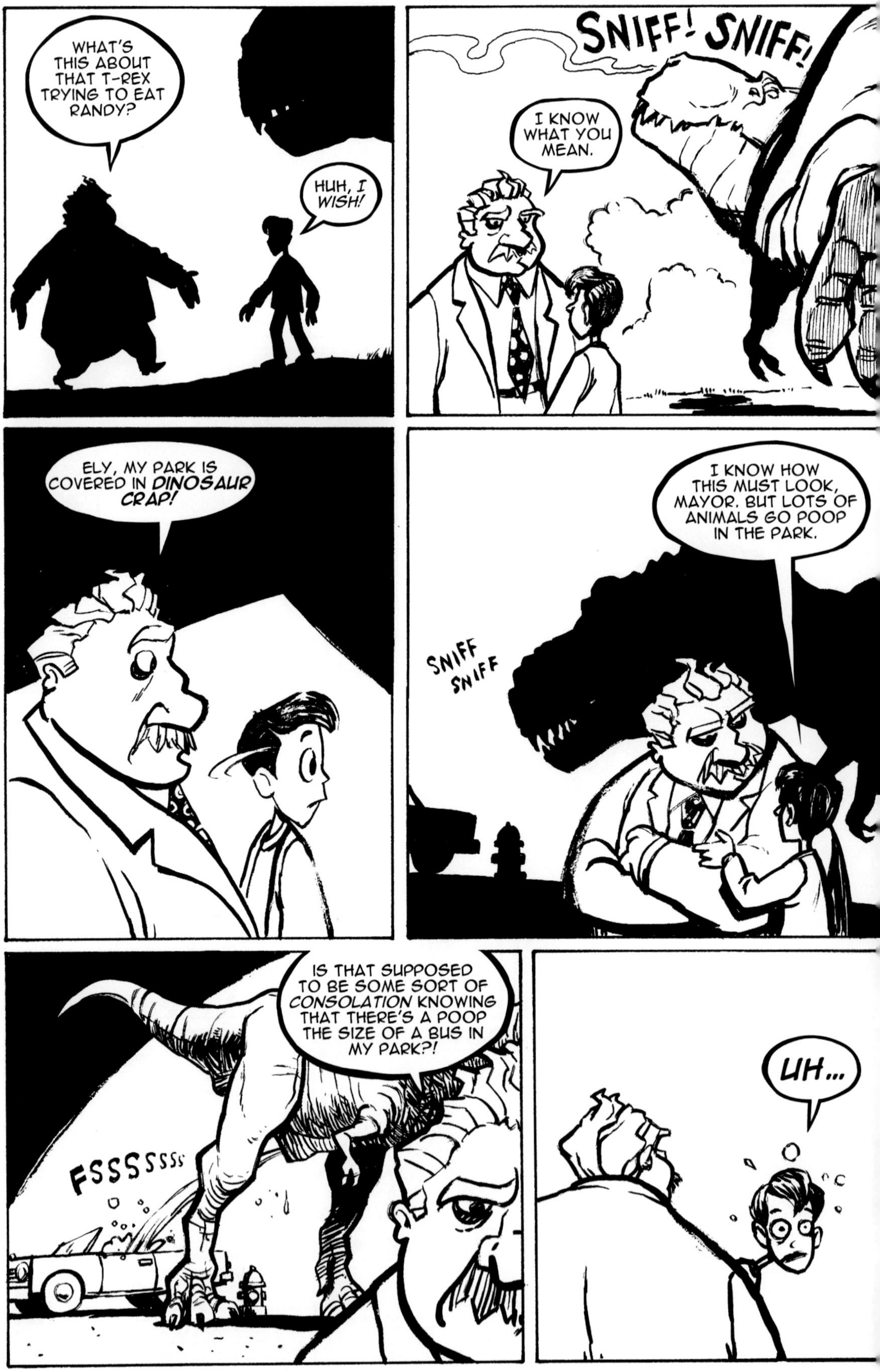
WHAT'S THIS ABOUT THAT T-REX TRYING TO EAT RANDY?
HUH, I WISH!
SNIFF! SNIFF!
I KNOW WHAT YOU MEAN.
ELY, MY PARK IS COVERED IN DINOSAUR CRAP!
I KNOW HOW THIS MUST LOOK, MAYOR. BUT LOTS OF ANIMALS GO POOP IN THE PARK.
SNIFF SNIFF
IS THAT SUPPOSED TO BE SOME SORT OF CONSOLATION KNOWING THAT THERE'S A POOP THE SIZE OF A BUS IN MY PARK?!
FSSSSSSS
UH...

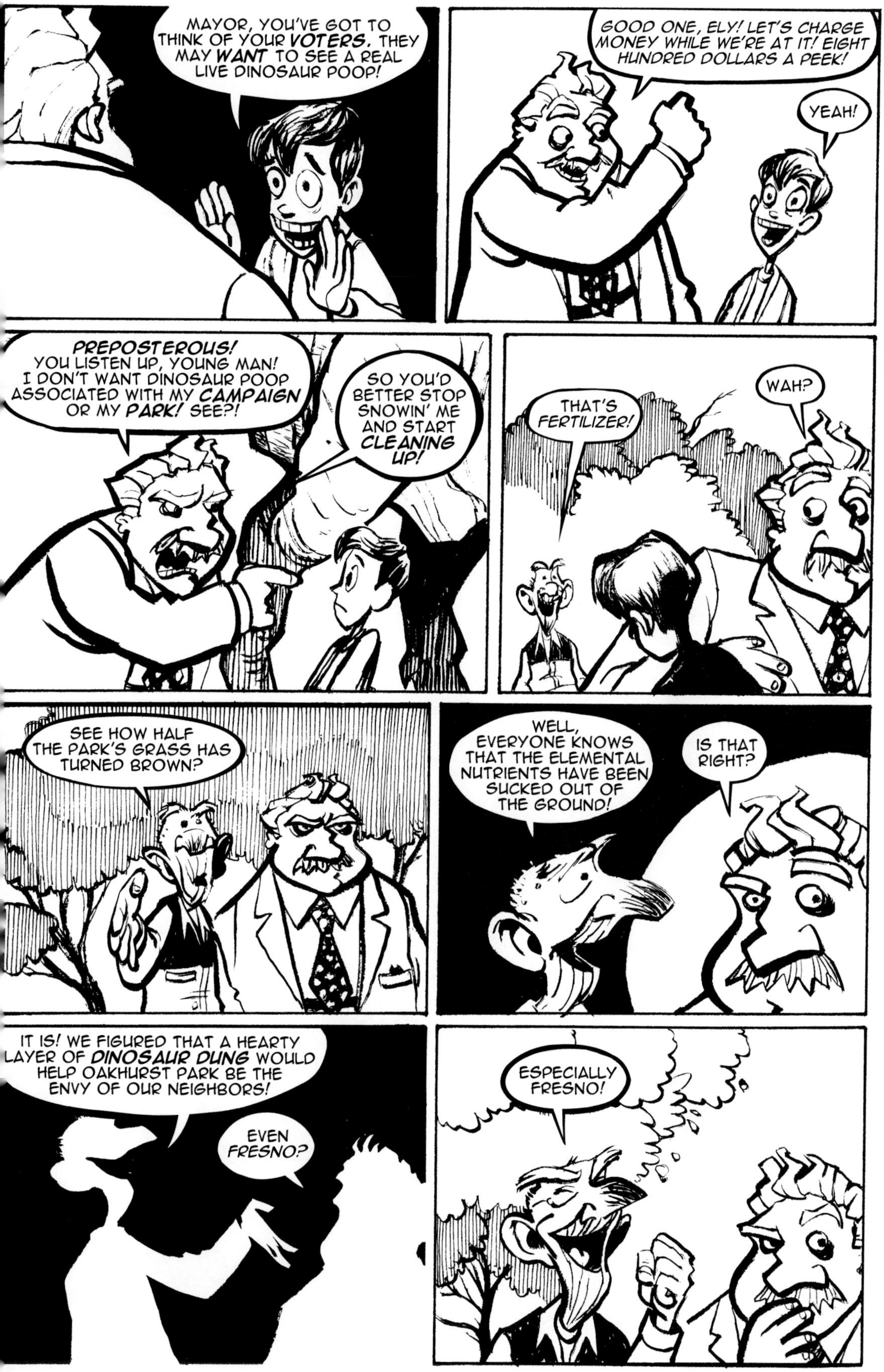
MAYOR, YOU'VE GOT TO THINK OF YOUR VOTERS. THEY MAY WANT TO SEE A REAL LIVE DINOSAUR POOP!
GOOD ONE, ELY! LET'S CHARGE MONEY WHILE WE'RE AT IT! EIGHT HUNDRED DOLLARS A PEEK!
YEAH!
PREPOSTEROUS! YOU LISTEN UP, YOUNG MAN! I DON'T WANT DINOSAUR POOP ASSOCIATED WITH MY CAMPAIGN OR MY PARK! SEE?!
SO YOU'D BETTER STOP SNOWIN' ME AND START CLEANING UP!
THAT'S FERTILIZER!
WAH?
SEE HOW HALF THE PARK'S GRASS HAS TURNED BROWN?
WELL, EVERYONE KNOWS THAT THE ELEMENTAL NUTRIENTS HAVE BEEN SUCKED OUT OF THE GROUND!
IS THAT RIGHT?
IT IS! WE FIGURED THAT A HEARTY LAYER OF DINOSAUR DUNG WOULD HELP OAKHURST PARK BE THE ENVY OF OUR NEIGHBORS!
EVEN FRESNO?
ESPECIALLY FRESNO!

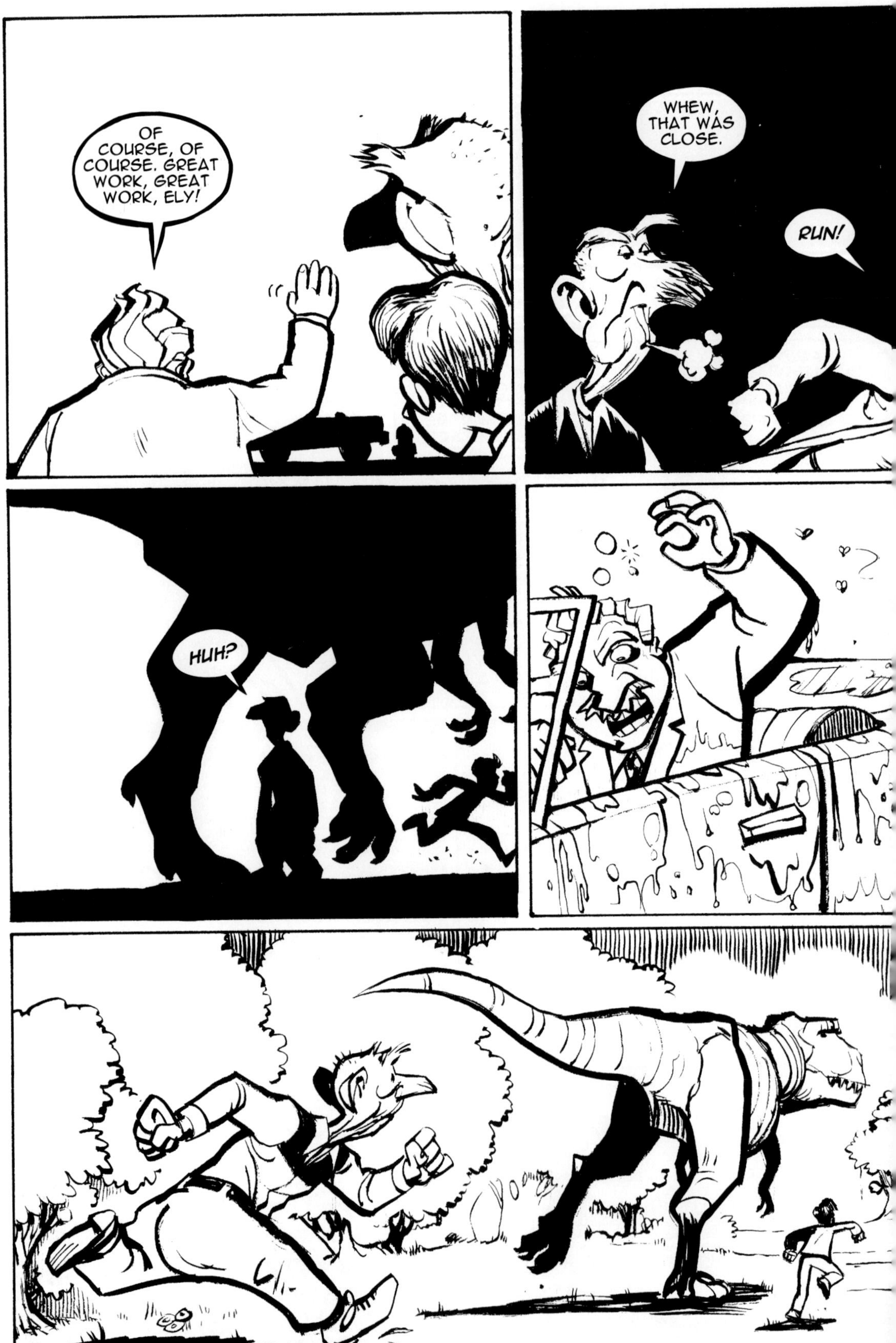
OF COURSE, OF COURSE. GREAT WORK, GREAT WORK, ELY!
WHEW, THAT WAS CLOSE.
RUN!
HUH?

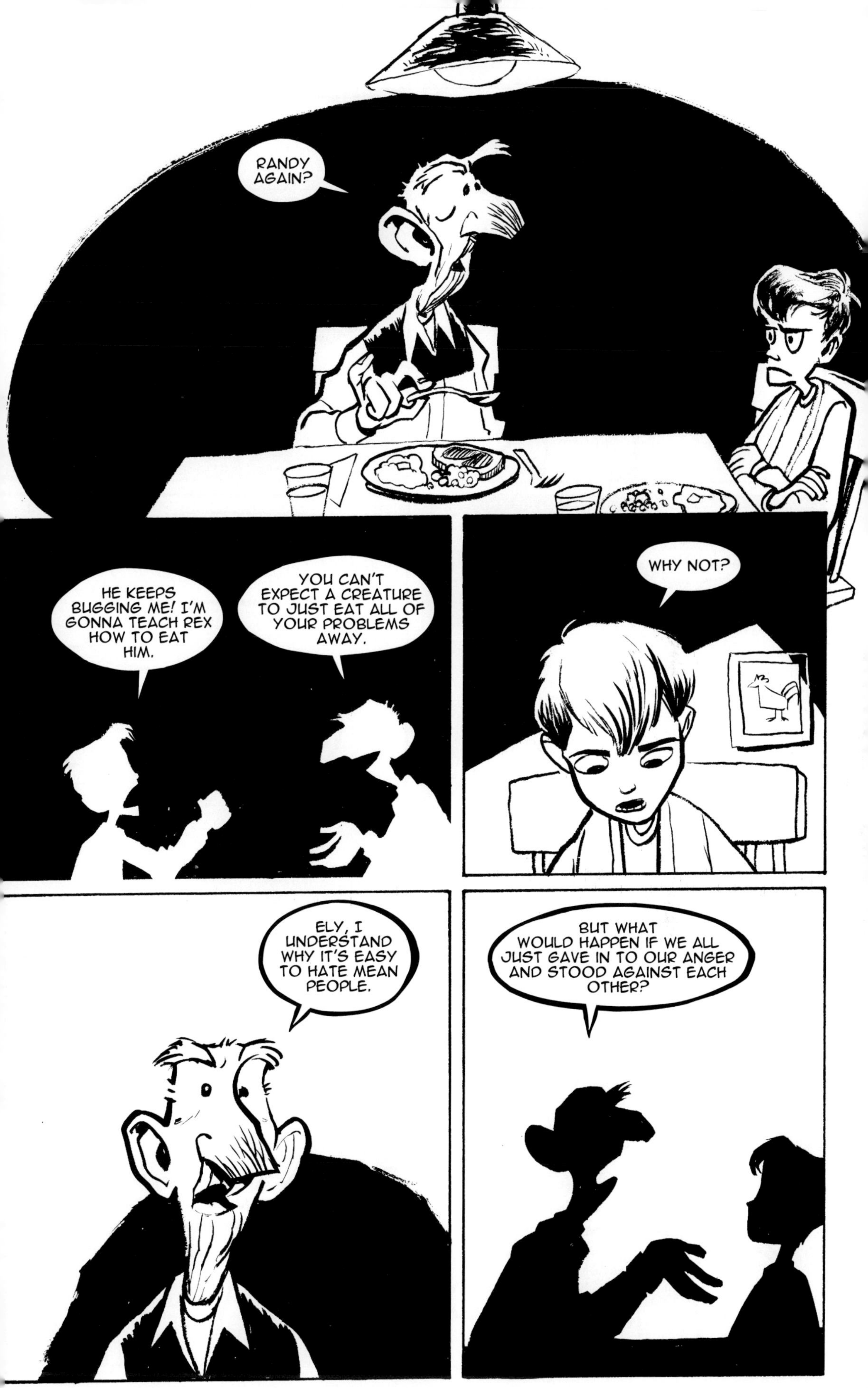
RANDY AGAIN?
HE KEEPS BUGGING ME! I'M GONNA TEACH REX HOW TO EAT HIM.
YOU CAN'T EXPECT A CREATURE TO JUST EAT ALL OF YOUR PROBLEMS AWAY.
WHY NOT?
ELY, I UNDERSTAND WHY IT'S EASY TO HATE MEAN PEOPLE.
BUT WHAT WOULD HAPPEN IF WE ALL JUST GAVE IN TO OUR ANGER AND STOOD AGAINST EACH OTHER?

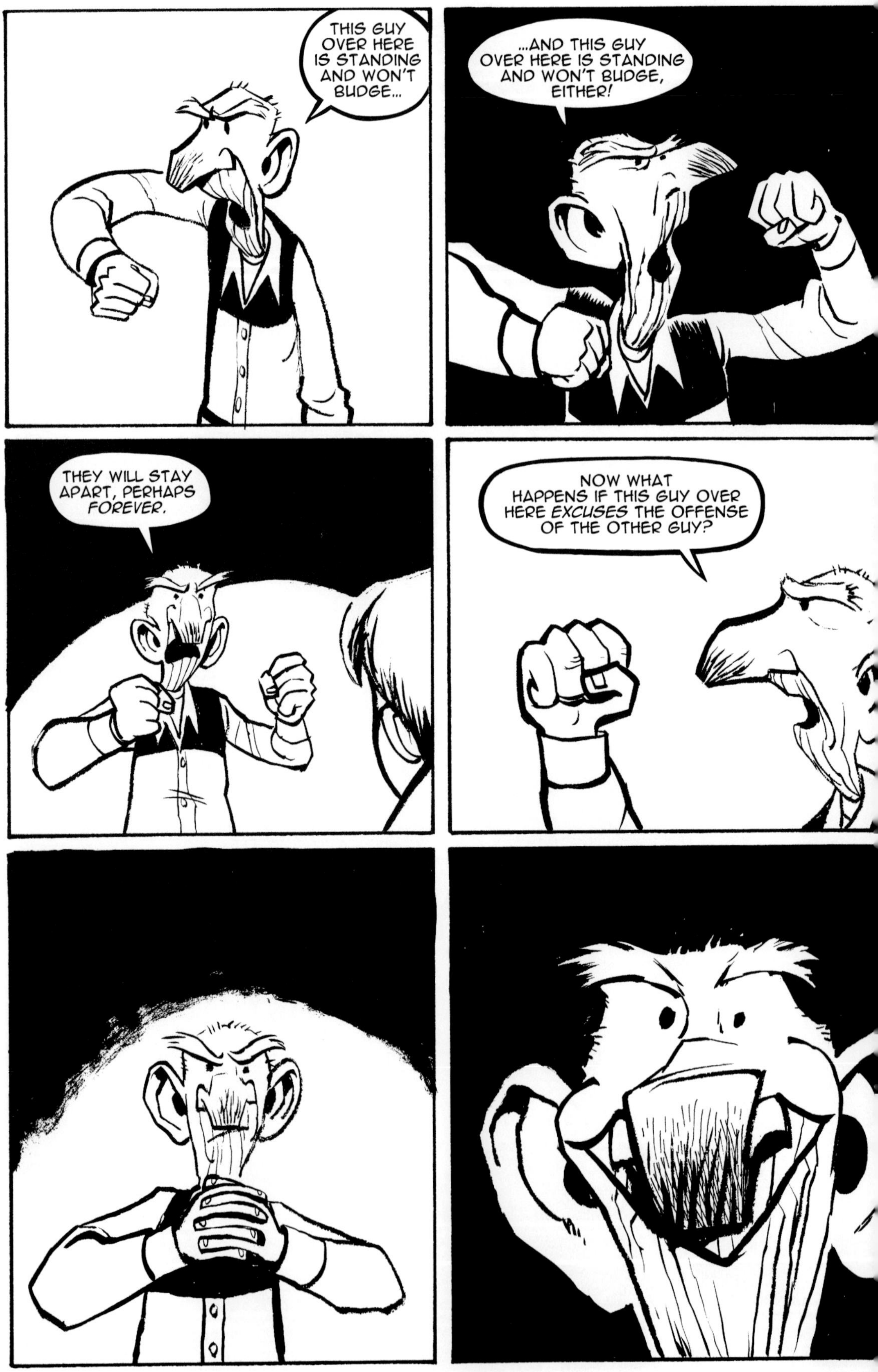
THIS GUY OVER HERE IS STANDING AND WON'T BUDGE...
...AND THIS GUY OVER HERE IS STANDING AND WON'T BUDGE, EITHER!
THEY WILL STAY APART, PERHAPS *FOREVER*.
NOW WHAT HAPPENS IF THIS GUY OVER HERE *EXCUSES* THE OFFENSE OF THE OTHER GUY?

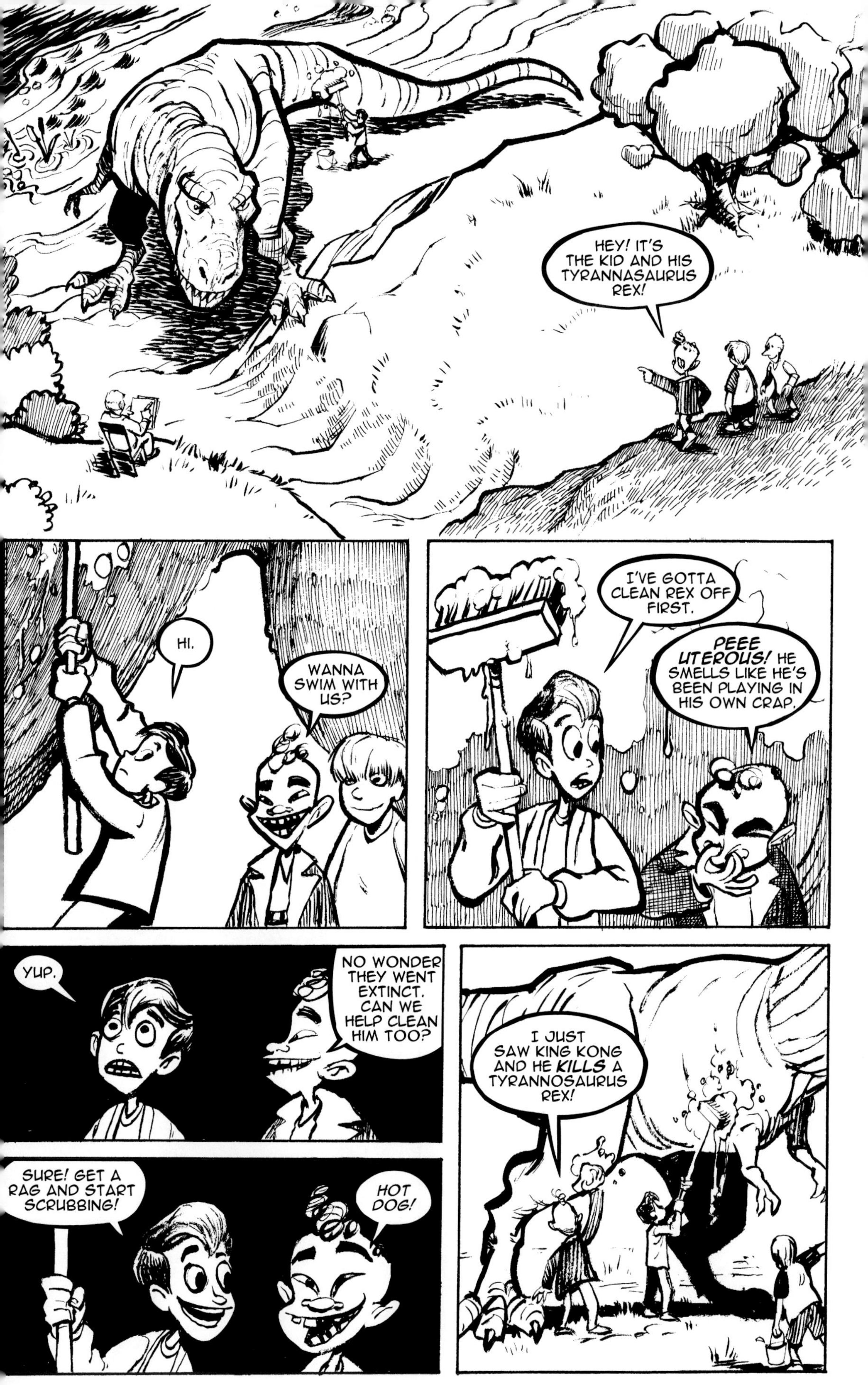
HEY! IT'S THE KID AND HIS TYRANNASAURUS REX!
HI.
WANNA SWIM WITH US?
I'VE GOTTA CLEAN REX OFF FIRST.
PEEE UTEROUS! HE SMELLS LIKE HE'S BEEN PLAYING IN HIS OWN CRAP.
YUP.
NO WONDER THEY WENT EXTINCT. CAN WE HELP CLEAN HIM TOO?
SURE! GET A RAG AND START SCRUBBING!
HOT DOG!
I JUST SAW KING KONG AND HE KILLS A TYRANNOSAURUS REX!

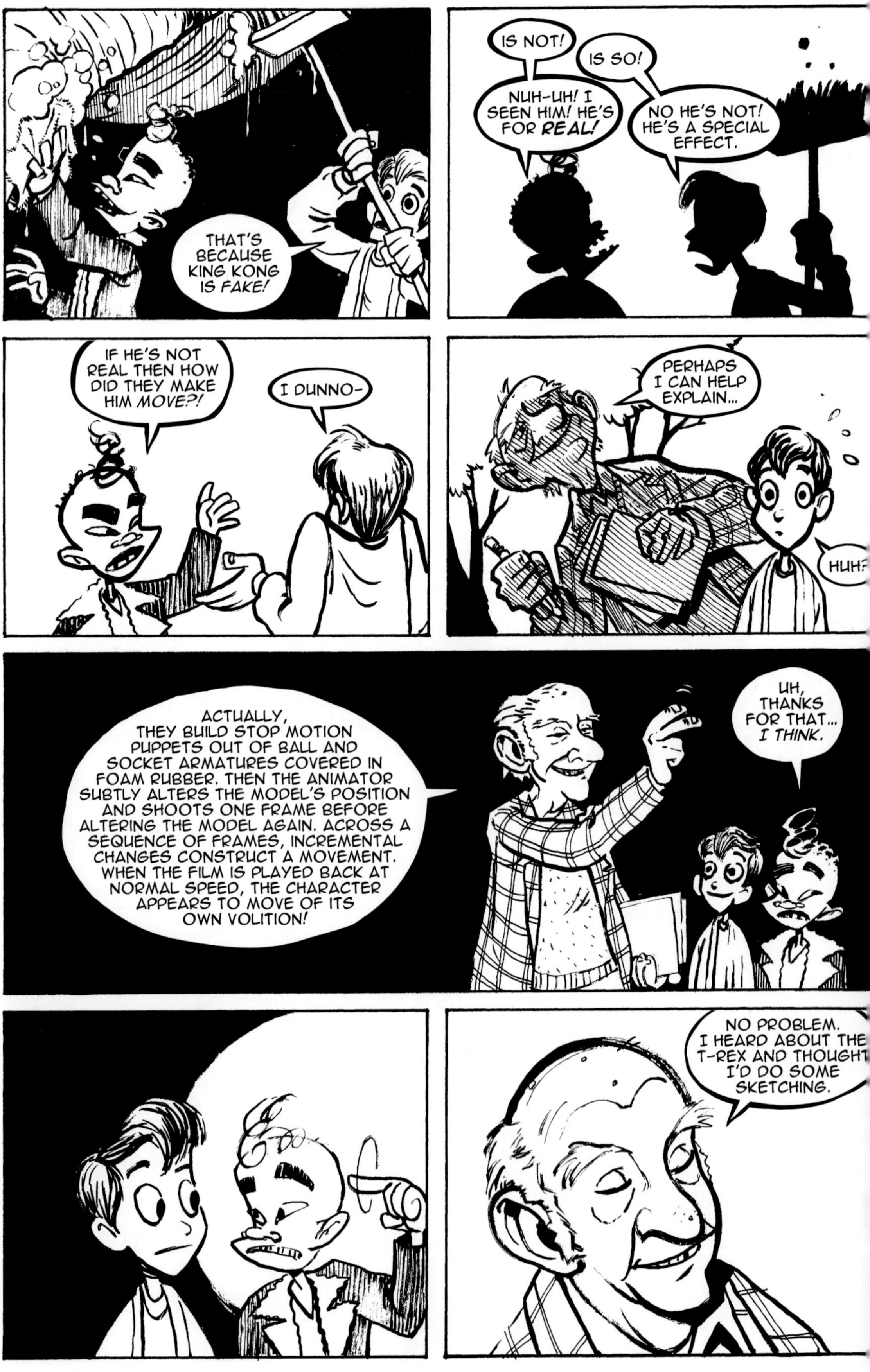
THAT'S BECAUSE KING KONG IS *FAKE!*
IS NOT!
NUH-UH! I SEEN HIM! HE'S FOR ***REAL!***
IS SO!
NO HE'S NOT! HE'S A SPECIAL EFFECT.
IF HE'S NOT REAL THEN HOW DID THEY MAKE HIM *MOVE?!*
I DUNNO-
PERHAPS I CAN HELP EXPLAIN...
HUH?
ACTUALLY, THEY BUILD STOP MOTION PUPPETS OUT OF BALL AND SOCKET ARMATURES COVERED IN FOAM RUBBER. THEN THE ANIMATOR SUBTLY ALTERS THE MODEL'S POSITION AND SHOOTS ONE FRAME BEFORE ALTERING THE MODEL AGAIN. ACROSS A SEQUENCE OF FRAMES, INCREMENTAL CHANGES CONSTRUCT A MOVEMENT. WHEN THE FILM IS PLAYED BACK AT NORMAL SPEED, THE CHARACTER APPEARS TO MOVE OF ITS OWN VOLITION!
UH, THANKS FOR THAT... *I THINK.*
NO PROBLEM. I HEARD ABOUT THE T-REX AND THOUGHT I'D DO SOME SKETCHING.

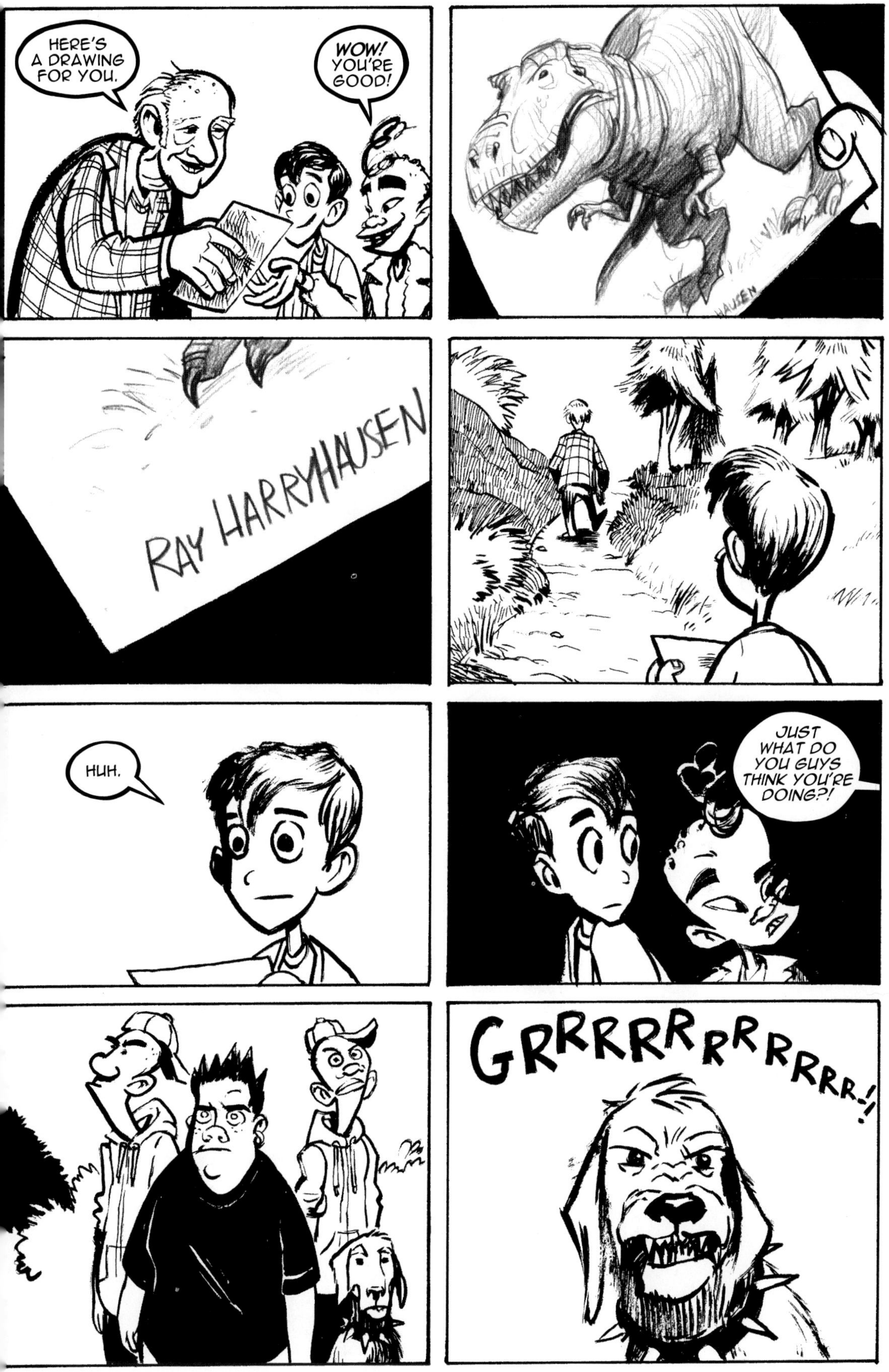
HERE'S A DRAWING FOR YOU.
WOW! YOU'RE GOOD!
HAUSEN
RAY HARRYHAUSEN
HUH.
JUST WHAT DO YOU GUYS THINK YOU'RE DOING?!
GRRRRRRRRRRRR-!

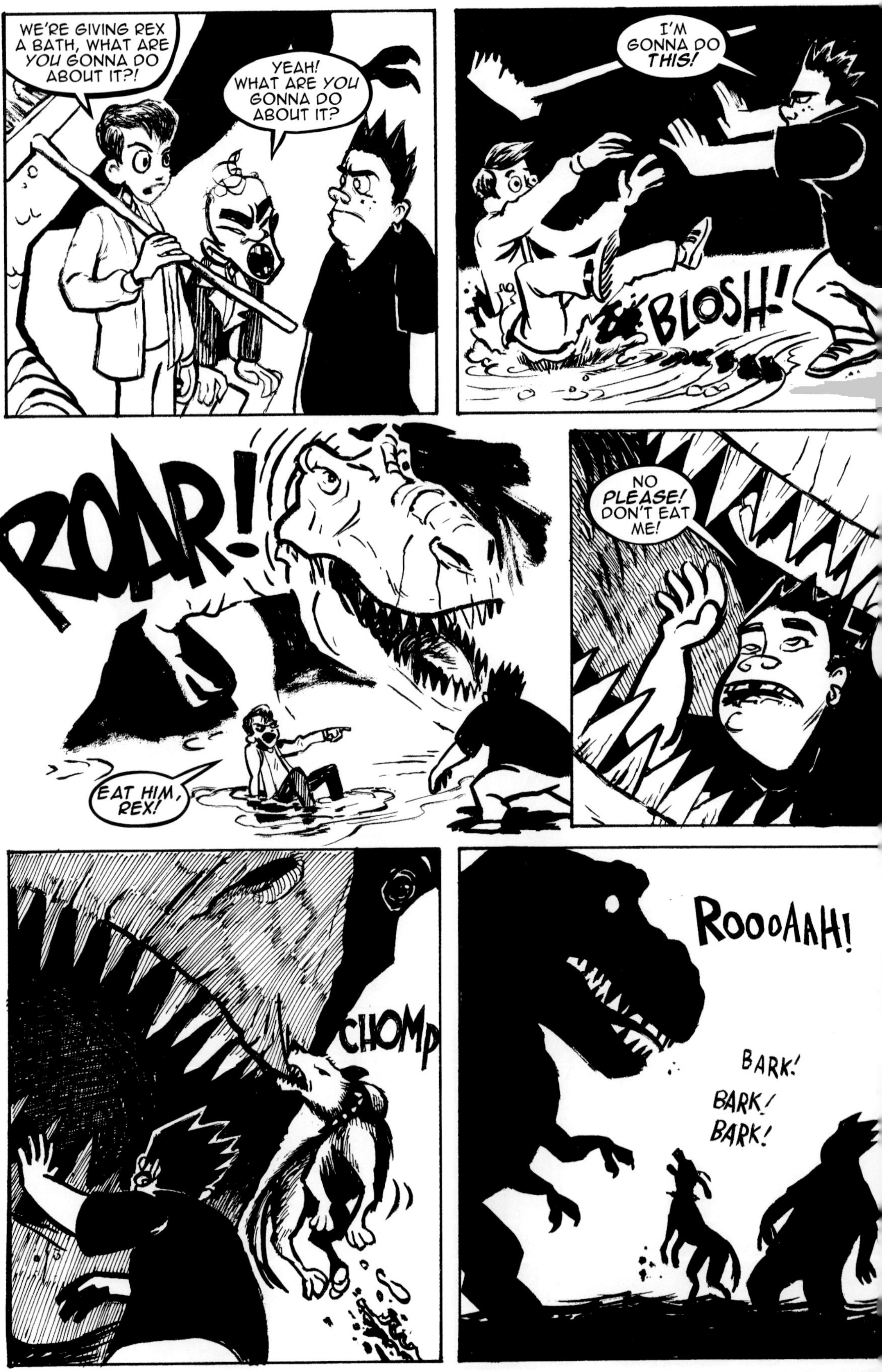
WE'RE GIVING REX A BATH, WHAT ARE *YOU* GONNA DO ABOUT IT?!
YEAH! WHAT ARE *YOU* GONNA DO ABOUT IT?
I'M GONNA DO **THIS!**
BLOSH!
ROAR!
EAT HIM, REX!
NO *PLEASE!* DON'T EAT ME!
CHOMP
ROOOAAH!
BARK!
BARK!
BARK!

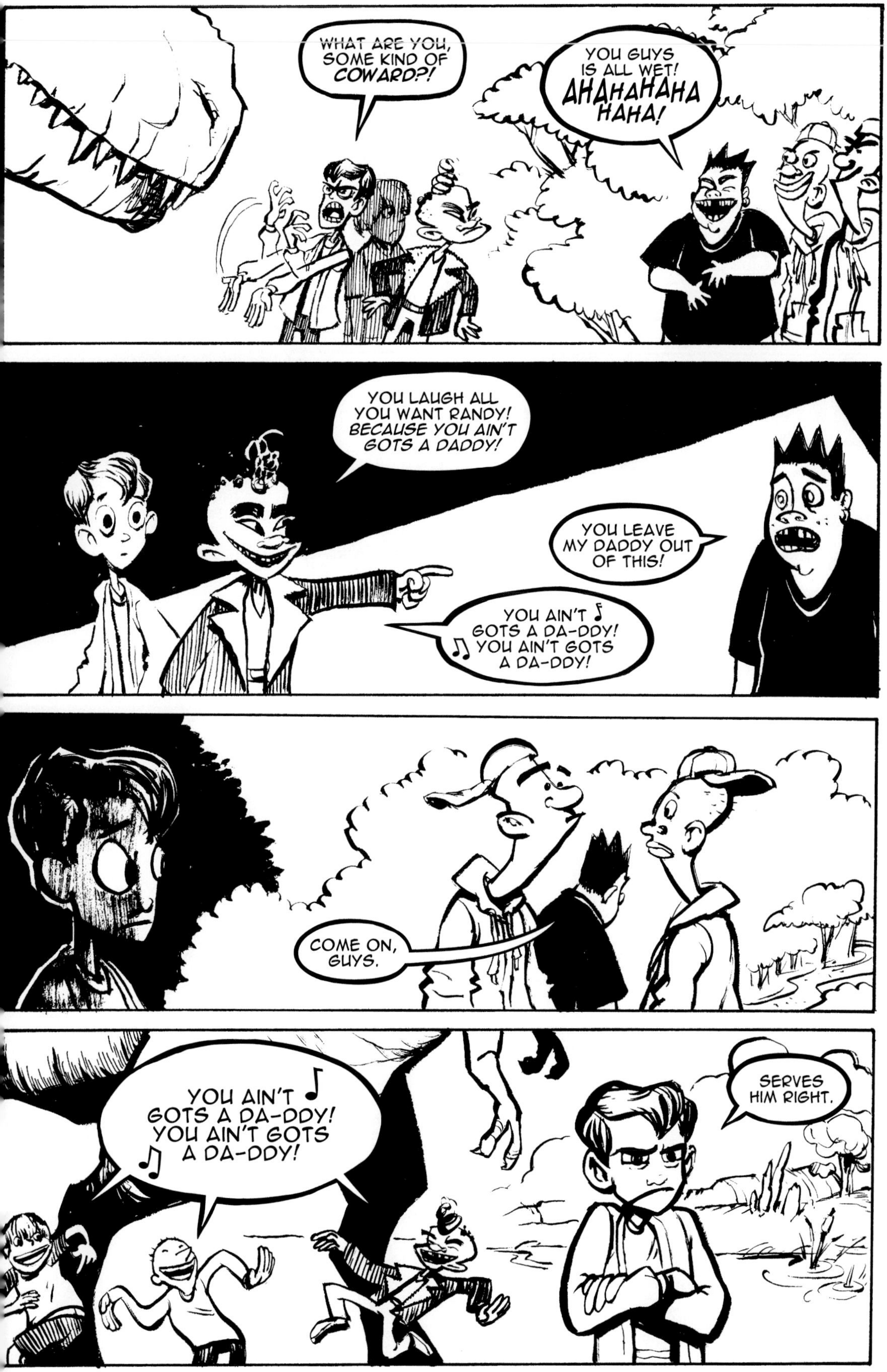
WHAT ARE YOU, SOME KIND OF COWARD?!
YOU GUYS IS ALL WET! AHAHAHAHA HAHA!
YOU LAUGH ALL YOU WANT RANDY! BECAUSE YOU AIN'T GOTS A DADDY!
YOU LEAVE MY DADDY OUT OF THIS!
YOU AIN'T GOTS A DA-DDY! YOU AIN'T GOTS A DA-DDY!
COME ON, GUYS.
YOU AIN'T GOTS A DA-DDY! YOU AIN'T GOTS A DA-DDY!
SERVES HIM RIGHT.

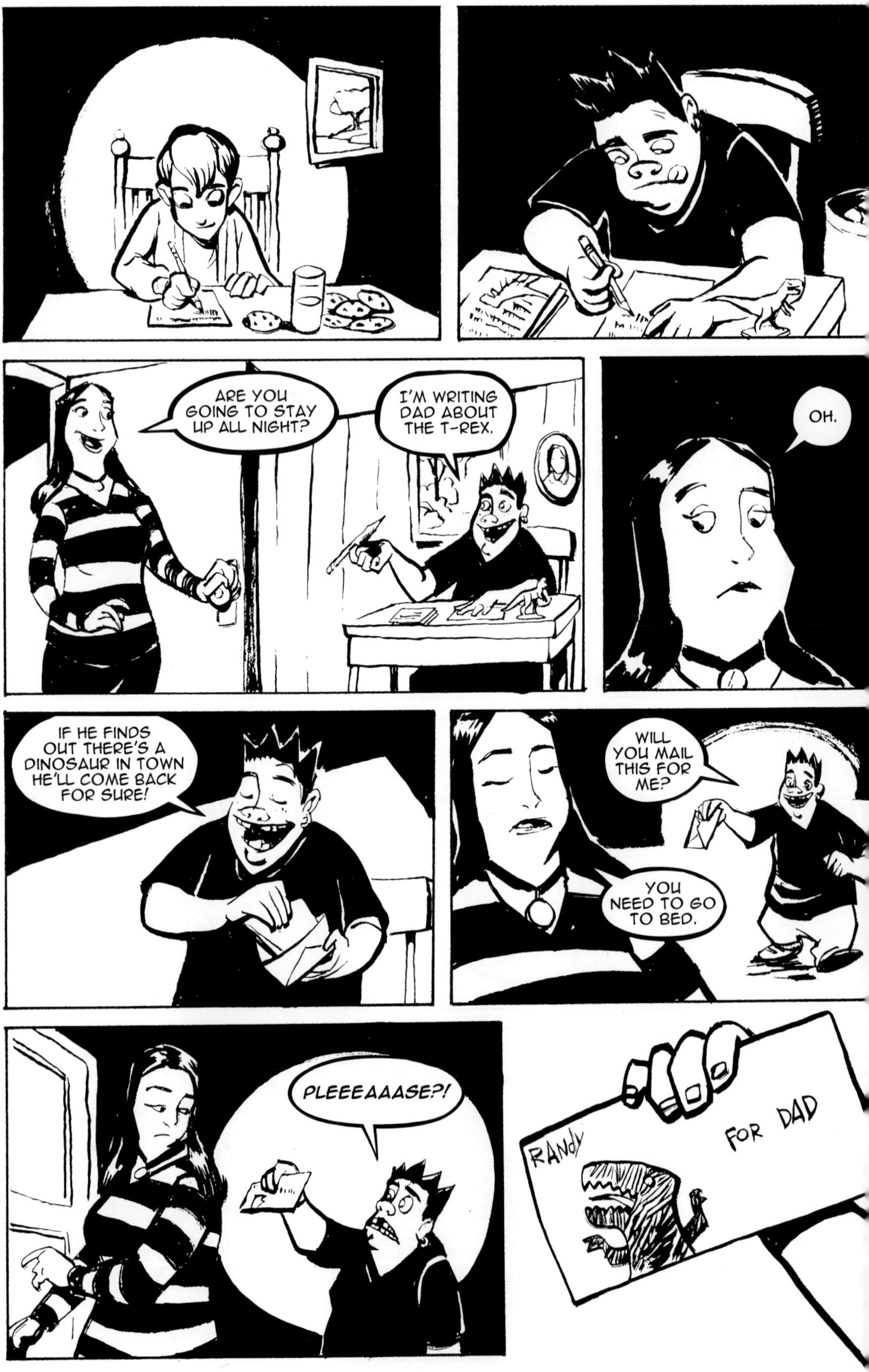
ARE YOU GOING TO STAY UP ALL NIGHT?
I'M WRITING DAD ABOUT THE T-REX.
OH.
IF HE FINDS OUT THERE'S A DINOSAUR IN TOWN HE'LL COME BACK FOR SURE!
WILL YOU MAIL THIS FOR ME?
YOU NEED TO GO TO BED.
PLEEEAAAASE?!
RANdy
FOR DAD

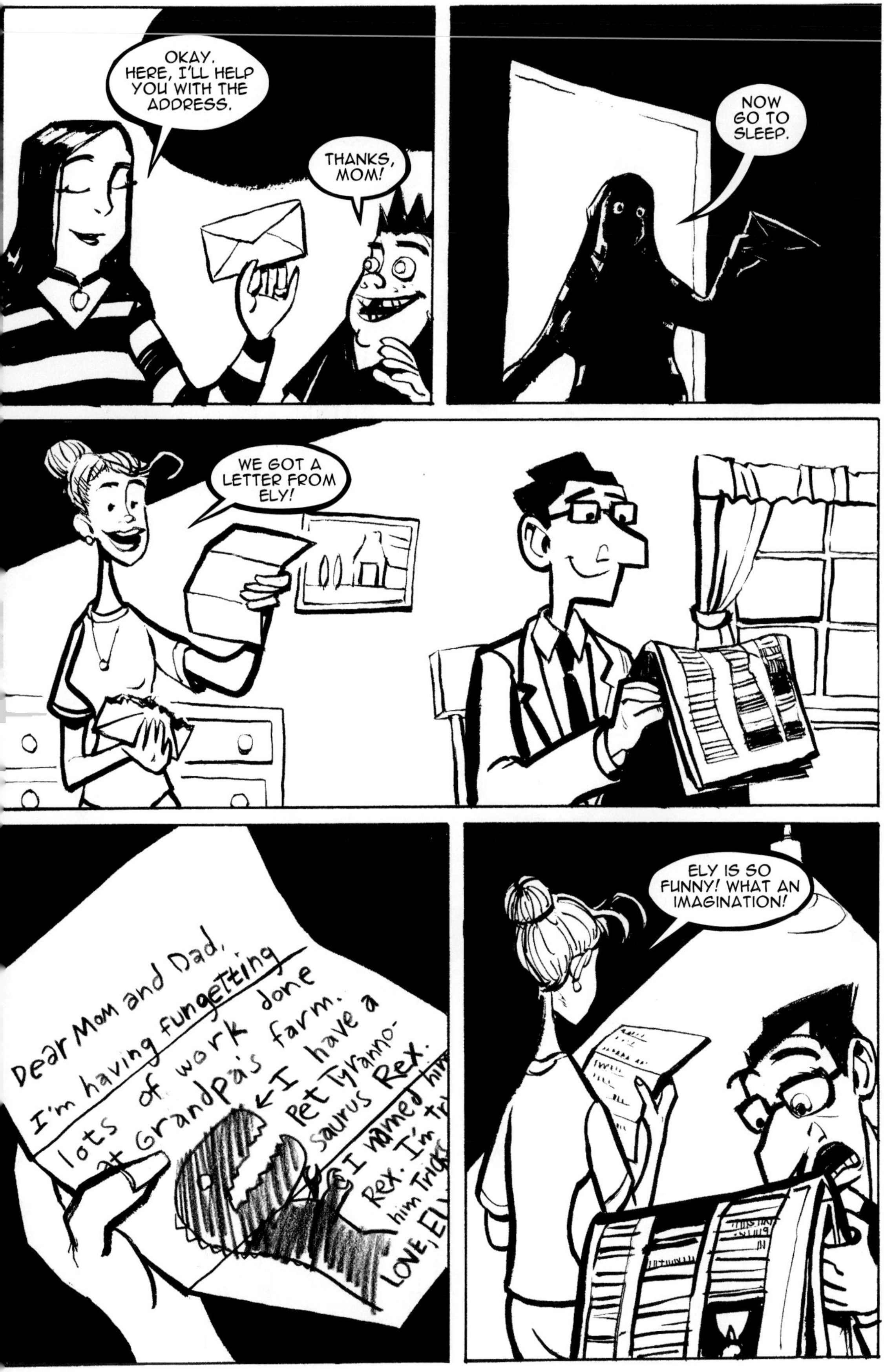

OKAY. HERE, I'LL HELP YOU WITH THE ADDRESS.
THANKS, MOM!
NOW GO TO SLEEP.
WE GOT A LETTER FROM ELY!
Dear Mom and Dad,
I'm having fungetting
lots of work done
at Grandpa's farm.
I have a pet Tyranno-saurus Rex.
ELY IS SO FUNNY! WHAT AN IMAGINATION!

HONEY?

t program
ere students
etail facilities
s learned in the
situations.
y give students the
learned skills, but
nts close to
work and
el. are

Ely and his pet Tyrannosaurus Rex... scientists are baffled... would befriend what he... prey... Tevision says, "We were... organized and at... participating... turnout...

THIS IS THE HEROIC STORY OF TEN-YEAR OLD ELY AND HIS TYRANNOSAURUS REX.

BBBNEWS

BEHOLD THEIR ATTEMPT TO DEFY ALL ODDS TO SAVE A CAT DROWNING IN A TWENTY FOOT ABANDONED WELLSHAFT!

BB

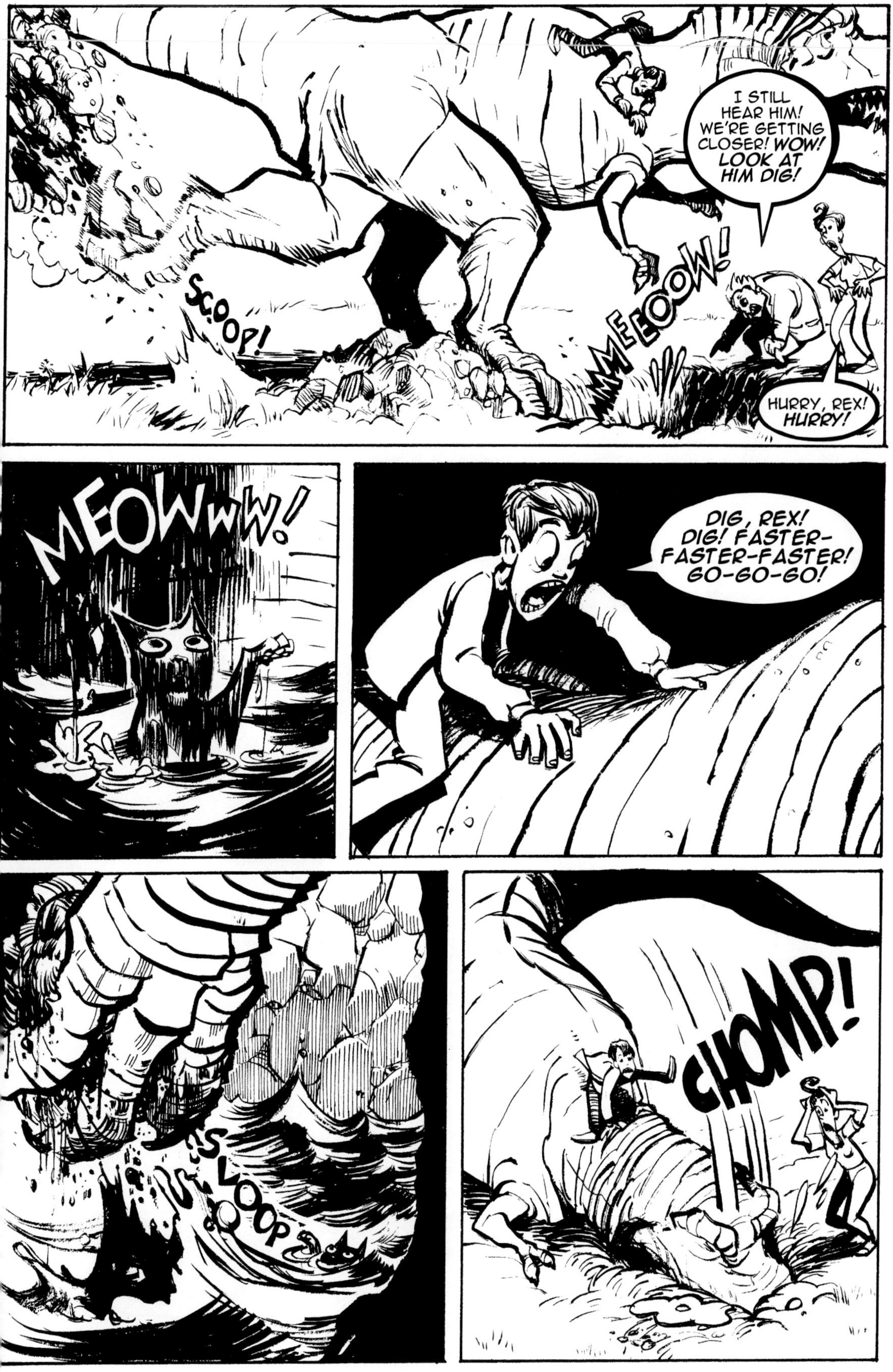
I STILL HEAR HIM! WE'RE GETTING CLOSER! WOW! LOOK AT HIM DIG!
SCOOP!
MMEOOW!
HURRY, REX! HURRY!
MEOWWW!
DIG, REX! DIG! FASTER-FASTER-FASTER! GO-GO-GO!
SSLOOP
CHOMP!

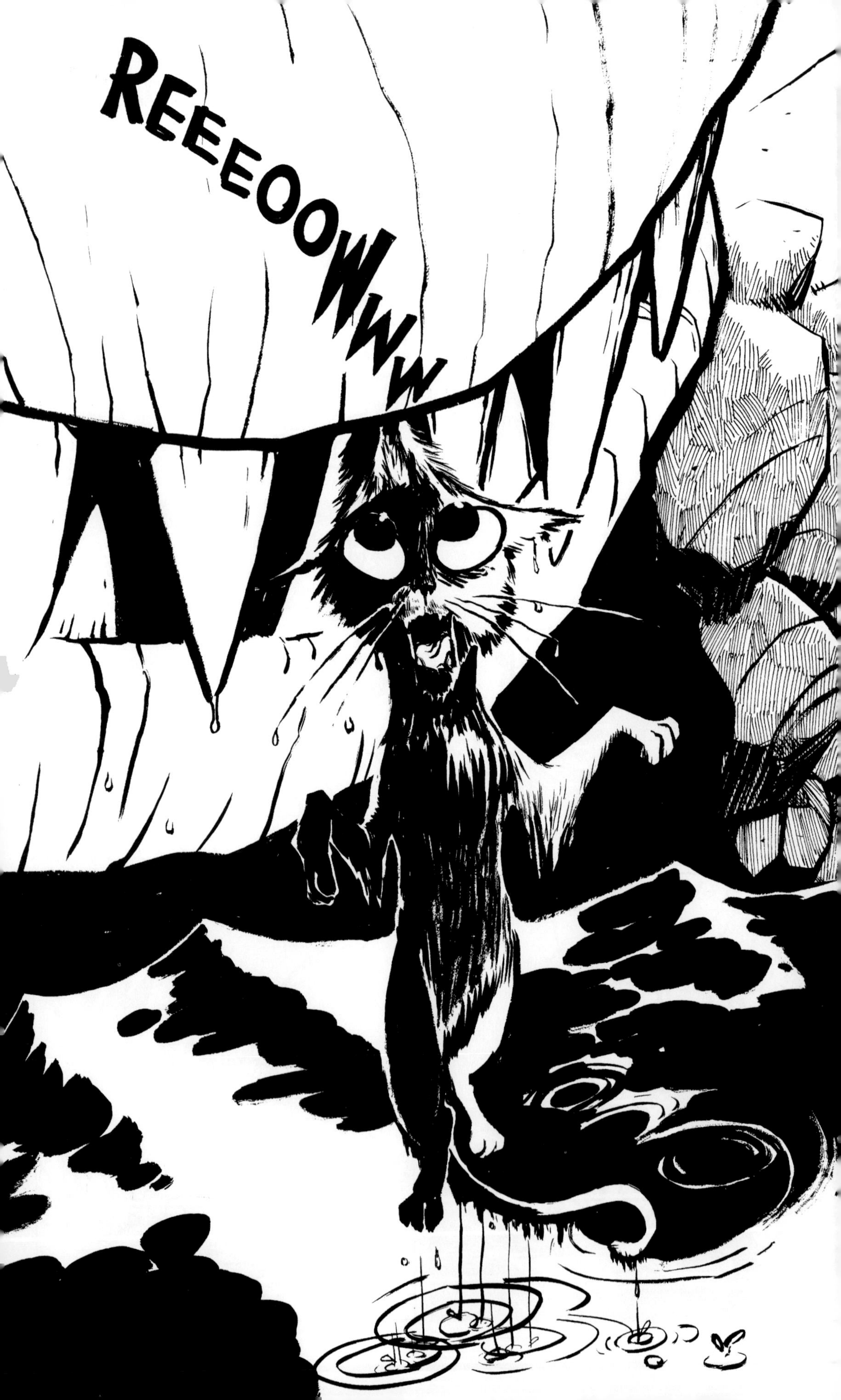
REEEOOOWWW

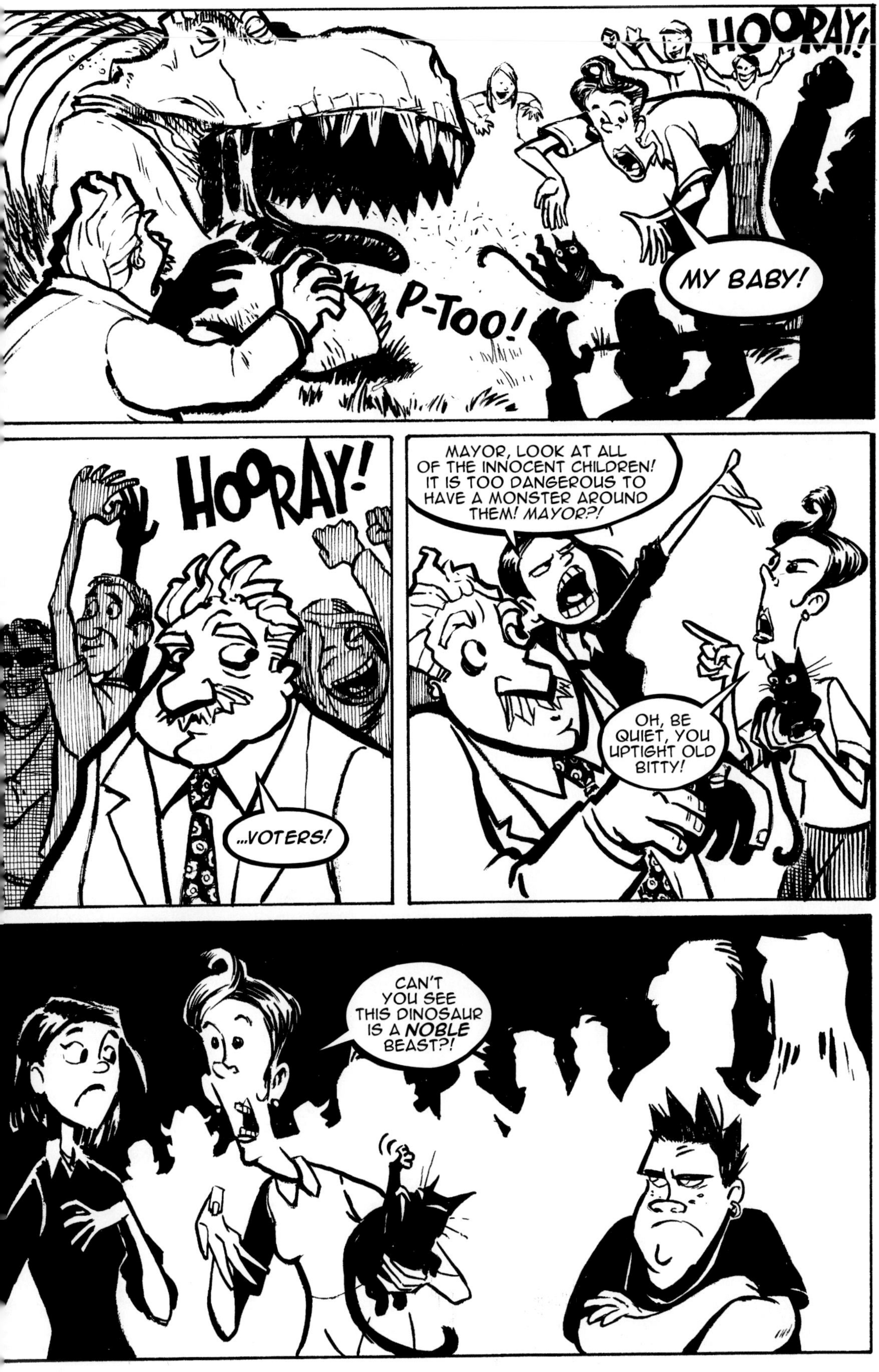
HOORAY!
P-TOO!
MY BABY!
HOORAY!
...VOTERS!
MAYOR, LOOK AT ALL OF THE INNOCENT CHILDREN! IT IS TOO DANGEROUS TO HAVE A MONSTER AROUND THEM! MAYOR?!
OH, BE QUIET, YOU UPTIGHT OLD BITTY!
CAN'T YOU SEE THIS DINOSAUR IS A NOBLE BEAST?!

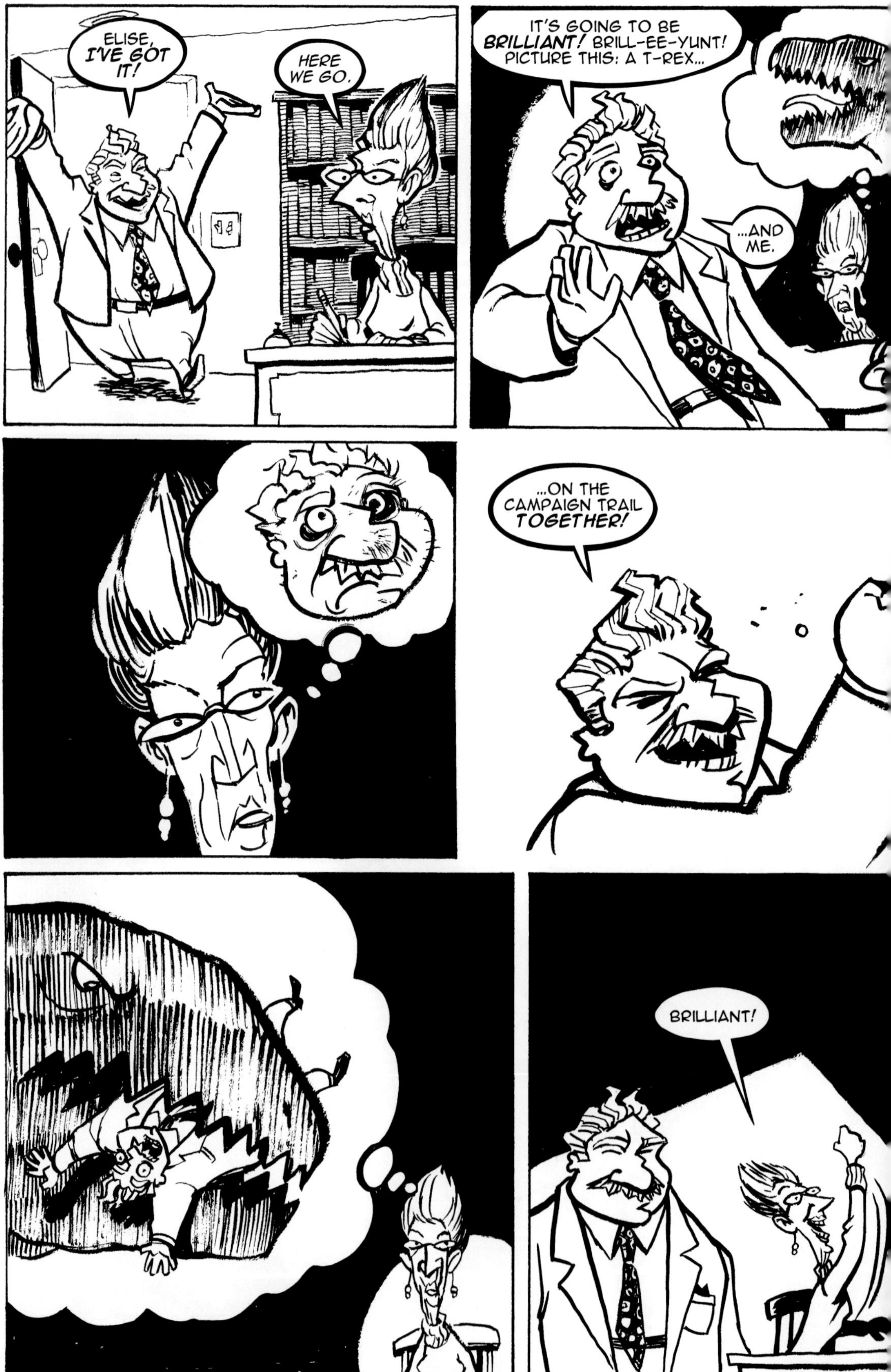

ELISE, I'VE GOT IT!
HERE WE GO.
IT'S GOING TO BE BRILLIANT! BRILL-EE-YUNT! PICTURE THIS: A T-REX...
...AND ME.
...ON THE CAMPAIGN TRAIL TOGETHER!
BRILLIANT!

SIT I SAY! SIT DOWN!

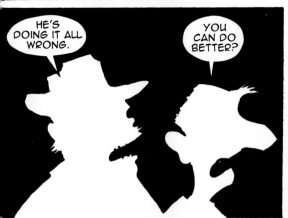

HE'S DOING IT ALL WRONG.

YOU CAN DO BETTER?

COMPARED TO TEACHING A LLAMA TO SIT? TEACHING A DINOSAUR WOULD BE A PIECE O' FLAN.

STEP ASIDE. YOU HAVE TO SHOW HIM WHO IS THE BOSS.

HOW DO I DO THAT?

YOU HAVE TO GET HIS ATTENTION.

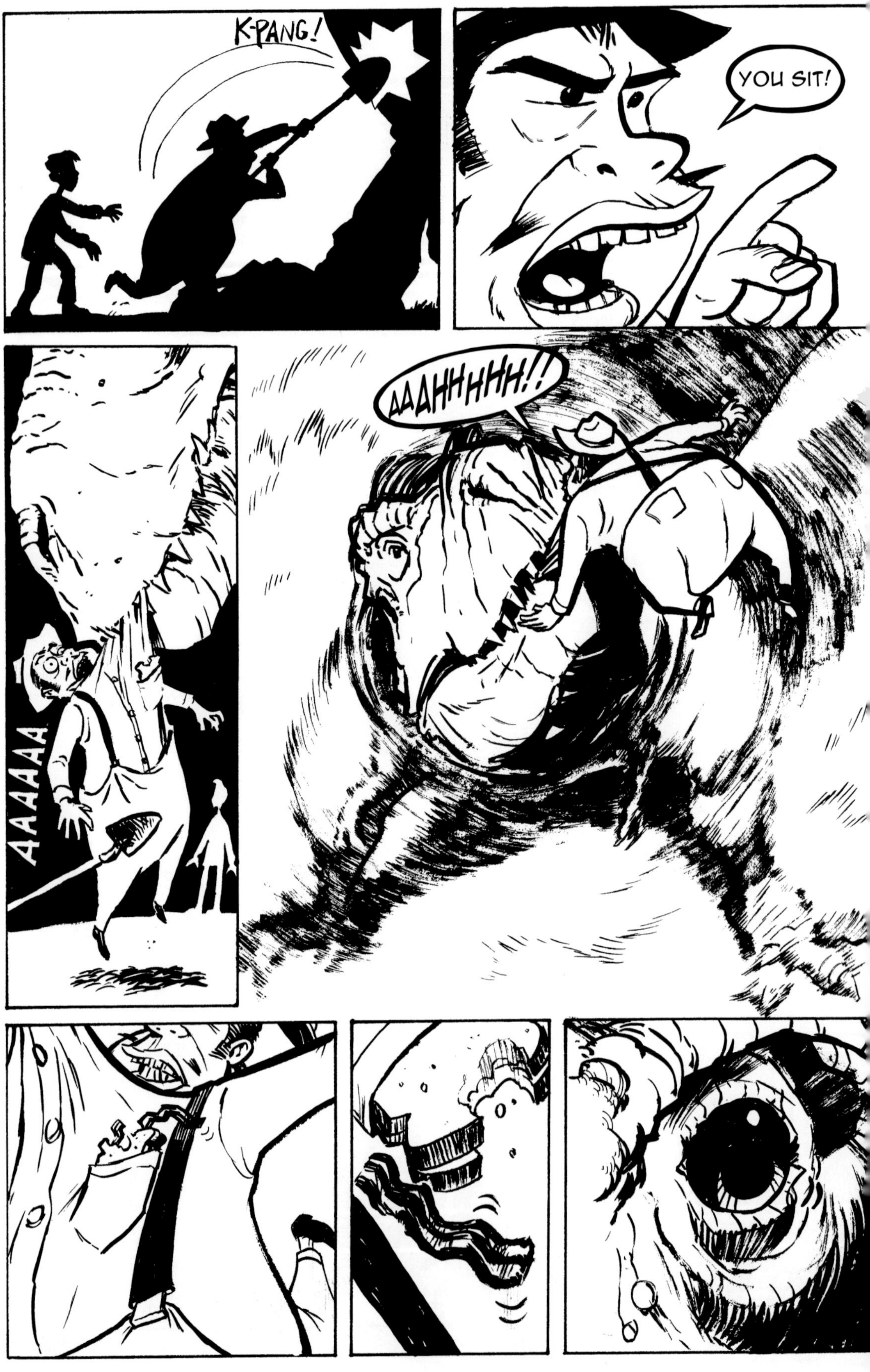
K-PANG!
YOU SIT!
AAAAAA
AAAHHHHH!!

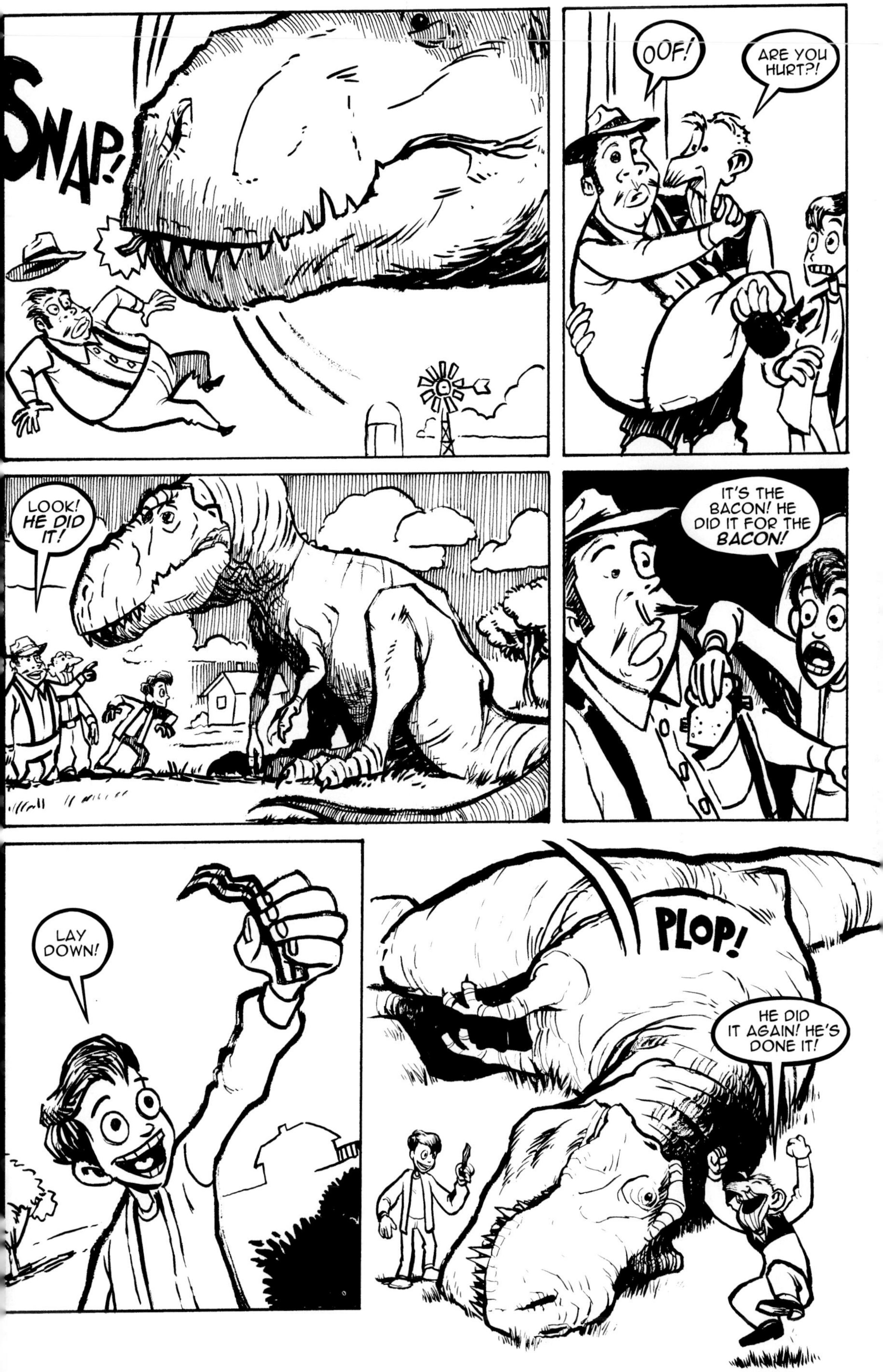
SNAP!
OOF!
ARE YOU HURT?!
LOOK! HE DID IT!
IT'S THE BACON! HE DID IT FOR THE BACON!
LAY DOWN!
PLOP!
HE DID IT AGAIN! HE'S DONE IT!

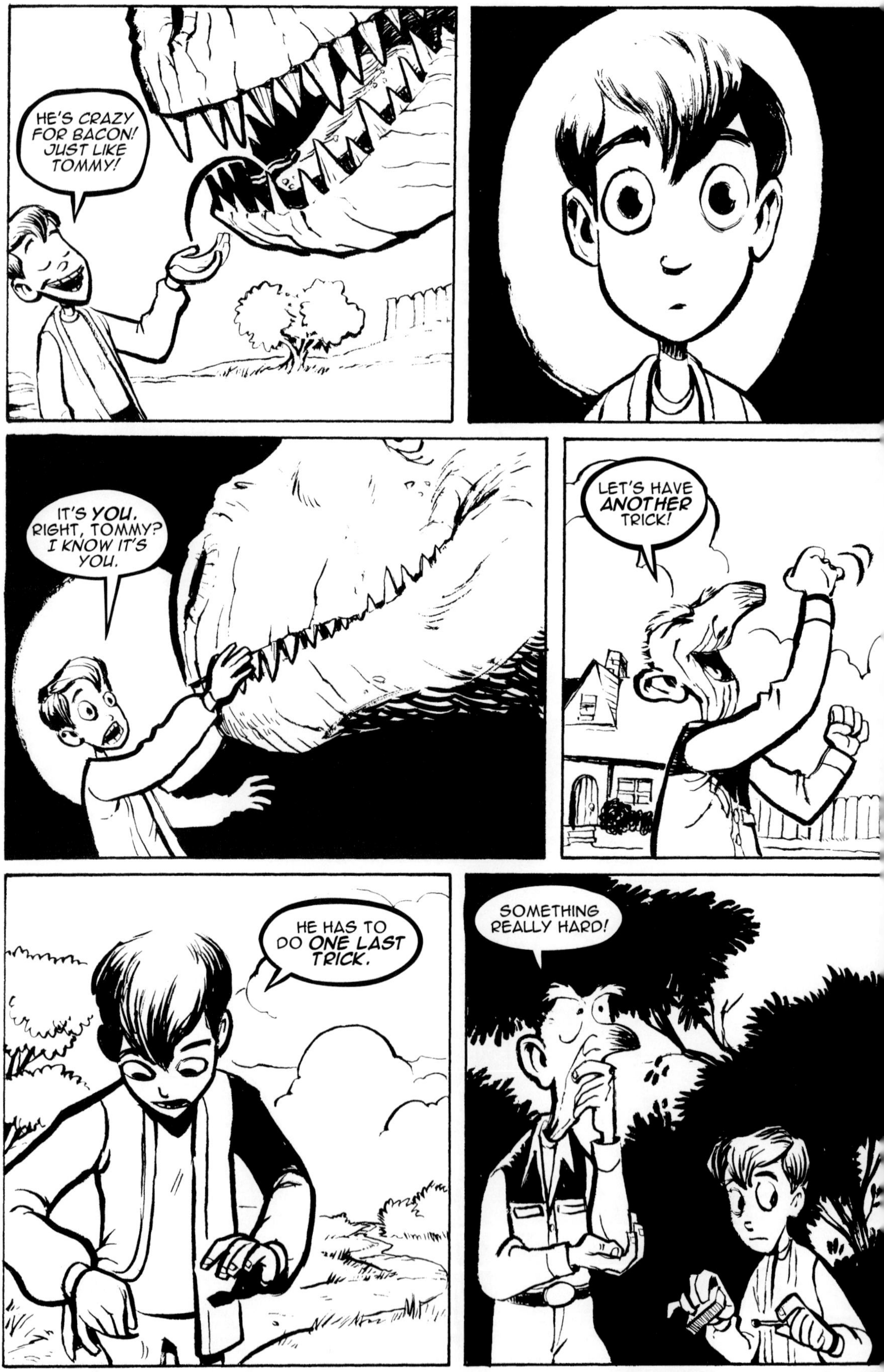
HE'S CRAZY FOR BACON! JUST LIKE TOMMY!
IT'S YOU. RIGHT, TOMMY? I KNOW IT'S YOU.
LET'S HAVE ANOTHER TRICK!
HE HAS TO DO ONE LAST TRICK.
SOMETHING REALLY HARD!

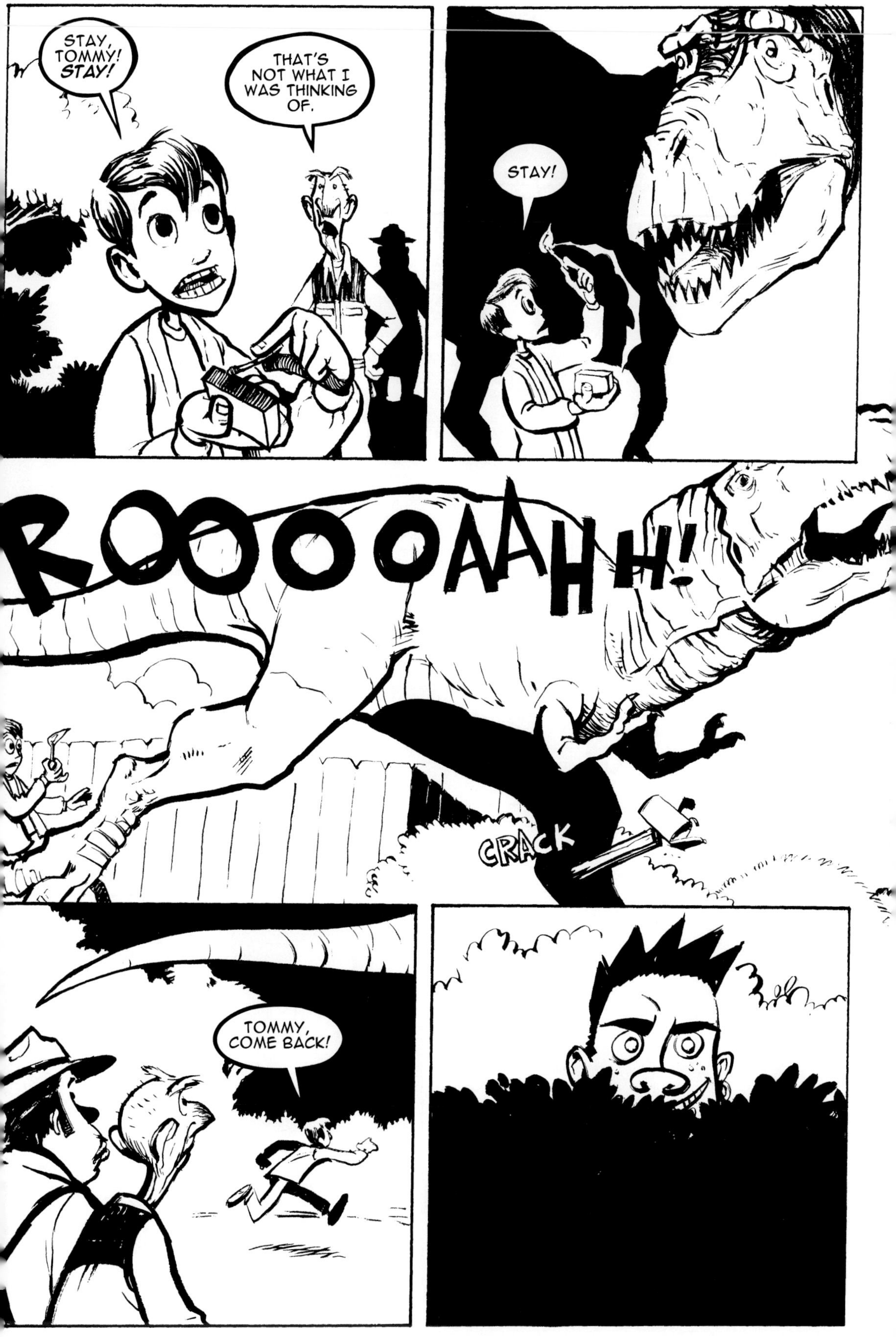
STAY, TOMMY! STAY!
THAT'S NOT WHAT I WAS THINKING OF.
STAY!
ROOOOAAHH!
CRACK
TOMMY, COME BACK!

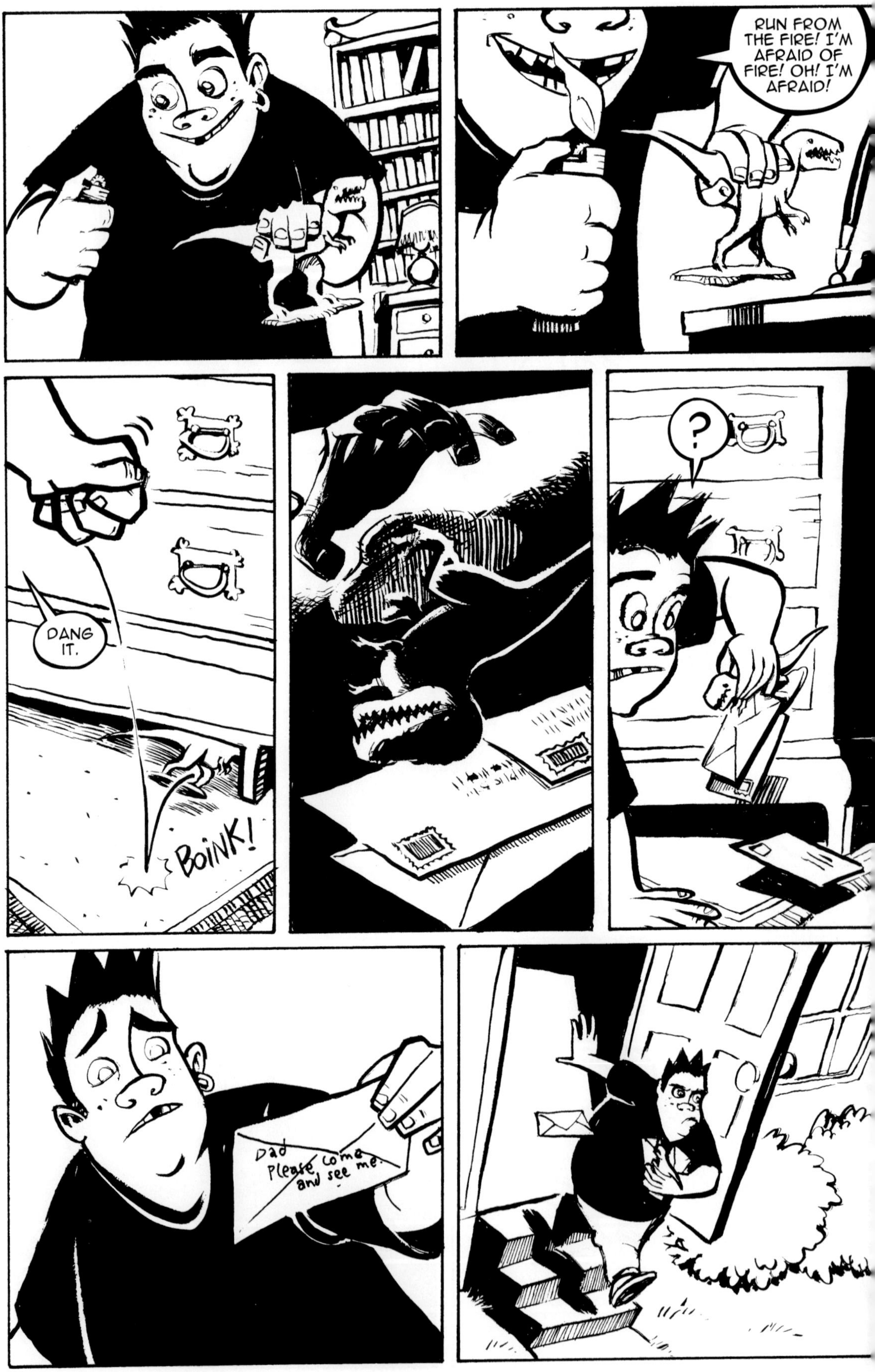
RUN FROM THE FIRE! I'M AFRAID OF FIRE! OH! I'M AFRAID!
DANG IT.
BOINK!
?
Dad Please come and see me.

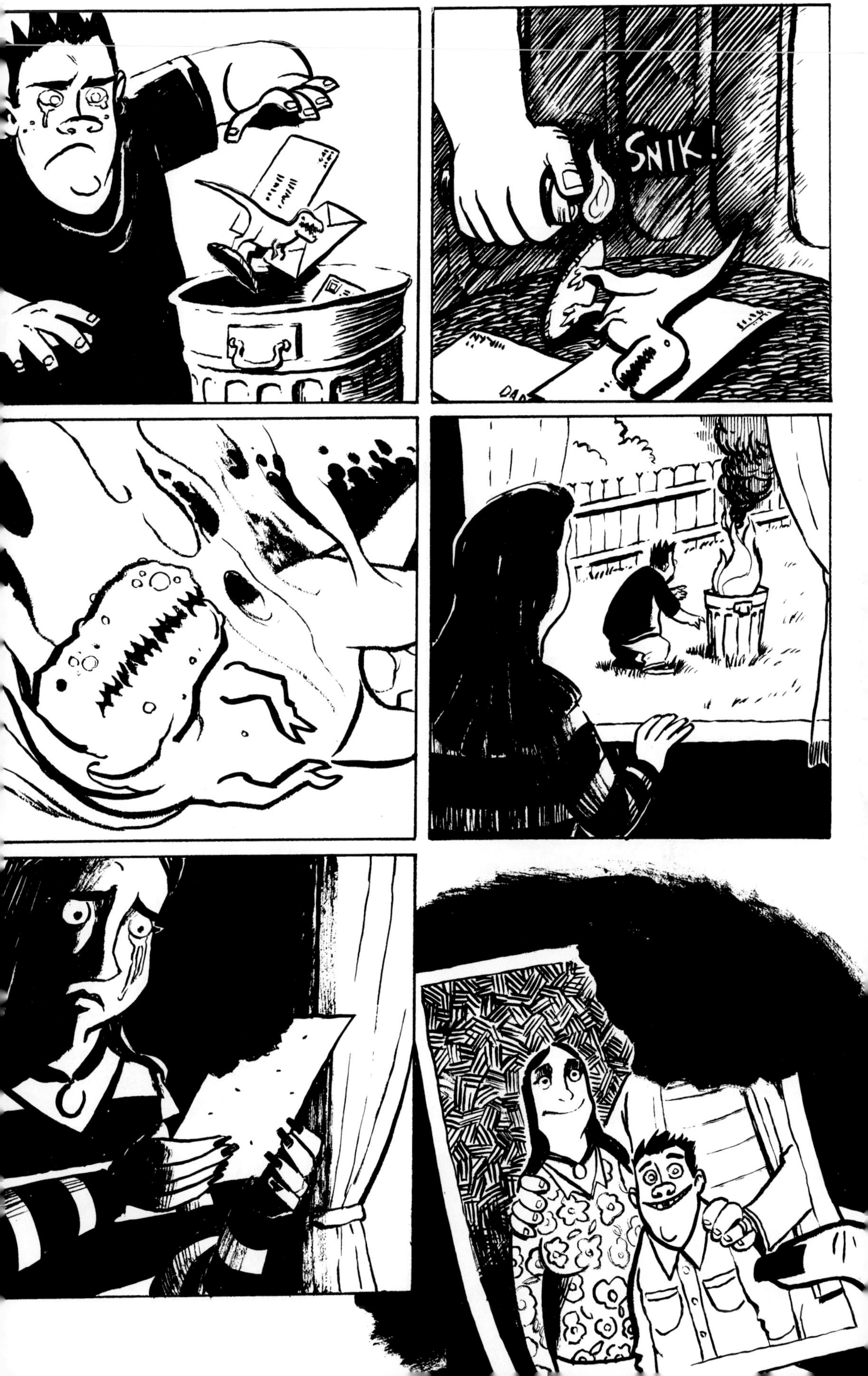
SNIK!
DAD

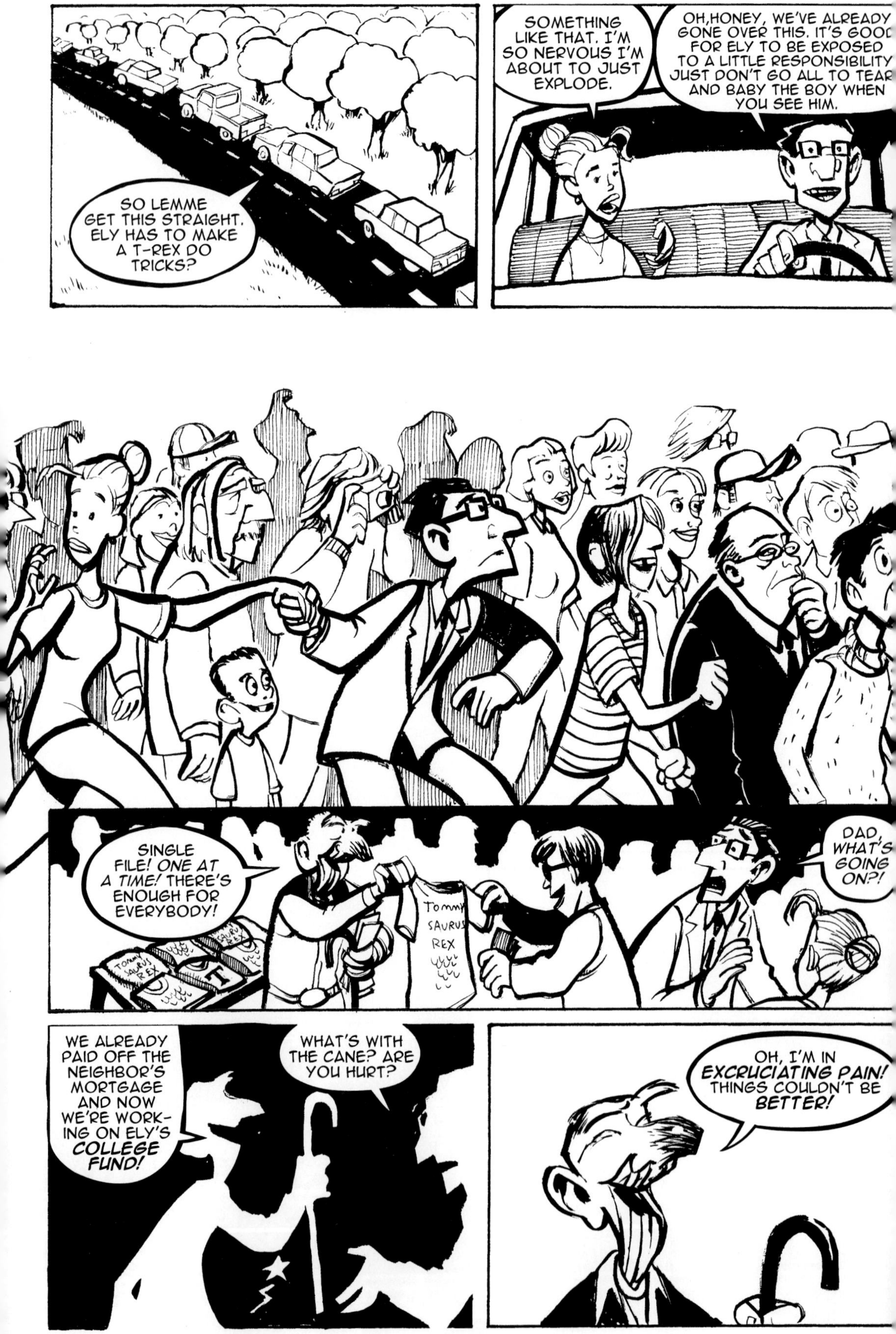

SO LEMME GET THIS STRAIGHT. ELY HAS TO MAKE A T-REX DO TRICKS?
SOMETHING LIKE THAT. I'M SO NERVOUS I'M ABOUT TO JUST EXPLODE.
OH,HONEY, WE'VE ALREADY GONE OVER THIS. IT'S GOOD FOR ELY TO BE EXPOSED TO A LITTLE RESPONSIBILITY. JUST DON'T GO ALL TO TEAR AND BABY THE BOY WHEN YOU SEE HIM.
SINGLE FILE! *ONE AT A TIME!* THERE'S ENOUGH FOR EVERYBODY!
TOMMY SAURUS REX
DAD, WHAT'S GOING ON?!
WE ALREADY PAID OFF THE NEIGHBOR'S MORTGAGE AND NOW WE'RE WORKING ON ELY'S ***COLLEGE FUND!***
WHAT'S WITH THE CANE? ARE YOU HURT?
OH, I'M IN ***EXCRUCIATING PAIN!*** THINGS COULDN'T BE ***BETTER!***

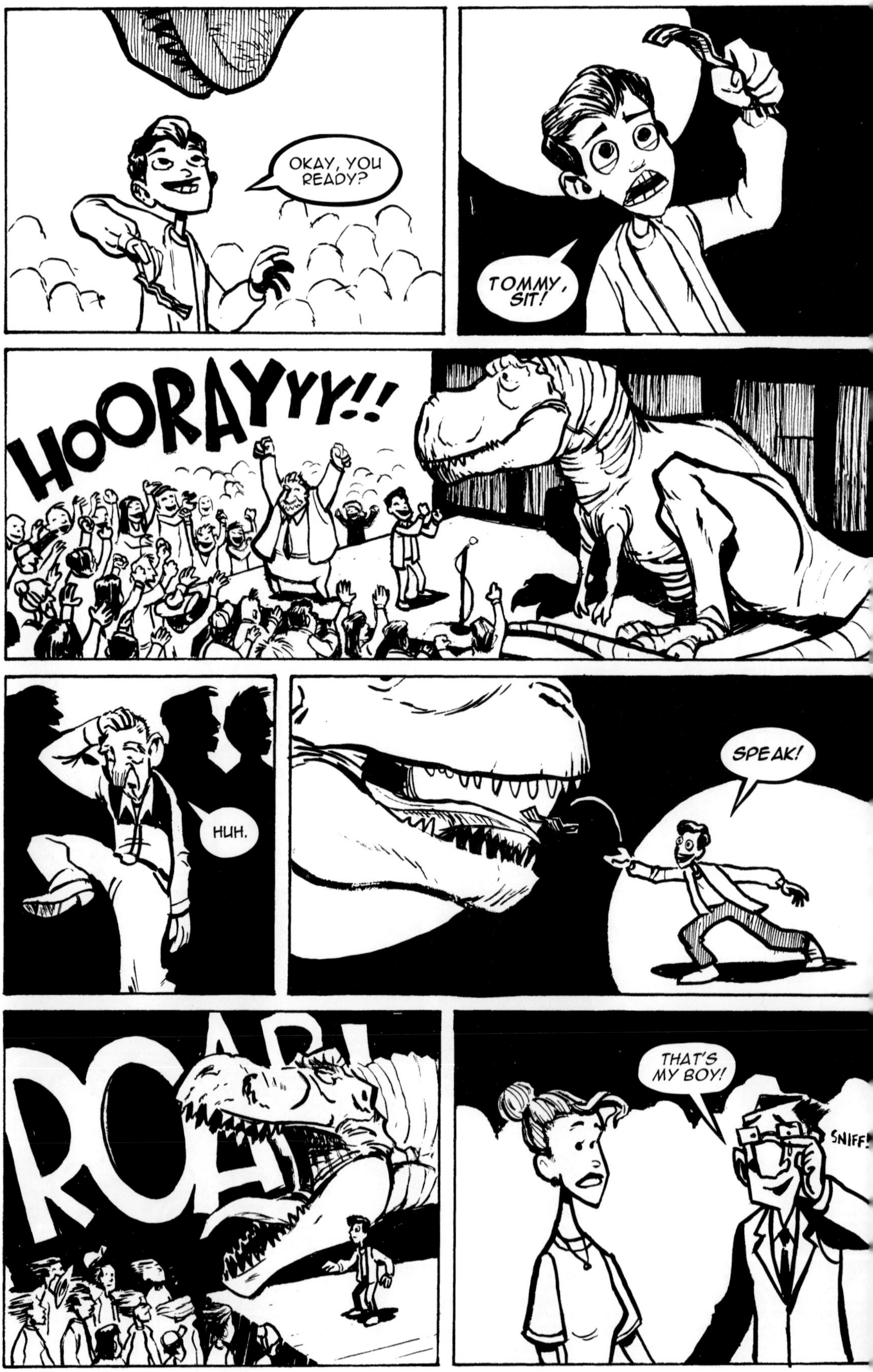
OKAY, YOU READY?
TOMMY, SIT!
HOORAYYY!!
HUH.
SPEAK!
ROAR!
THAT'S MY BOY!
SNIFF!

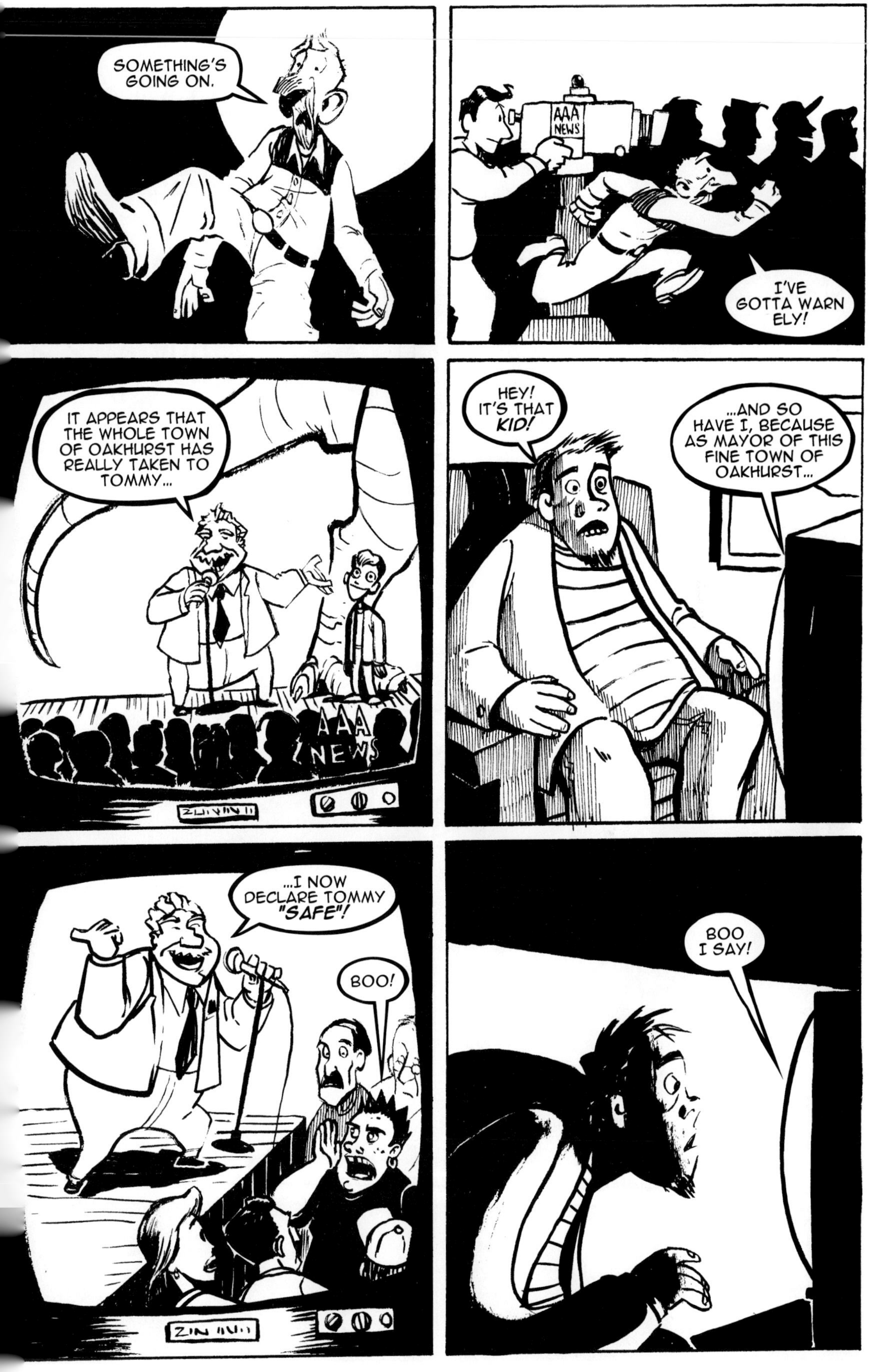
SOMETHING'S GOING ON.
AAA NEWS
I'VE GOTTA WARN ELY!
IT APPEARS THAT THE WHOLE TOWN OF OAKHURST HAS REALLY TAKEN TO TOMMY...
AAA NEWS
HEY! IT'S THAT KID!
...AND SO HAVE I, BECAUSE AS MAYOR OF THIS FINE TOWN OF OAKHURST...
...I NOW DECLARE TOMMY "SAFE"!
BOO!
BOO I SAY!

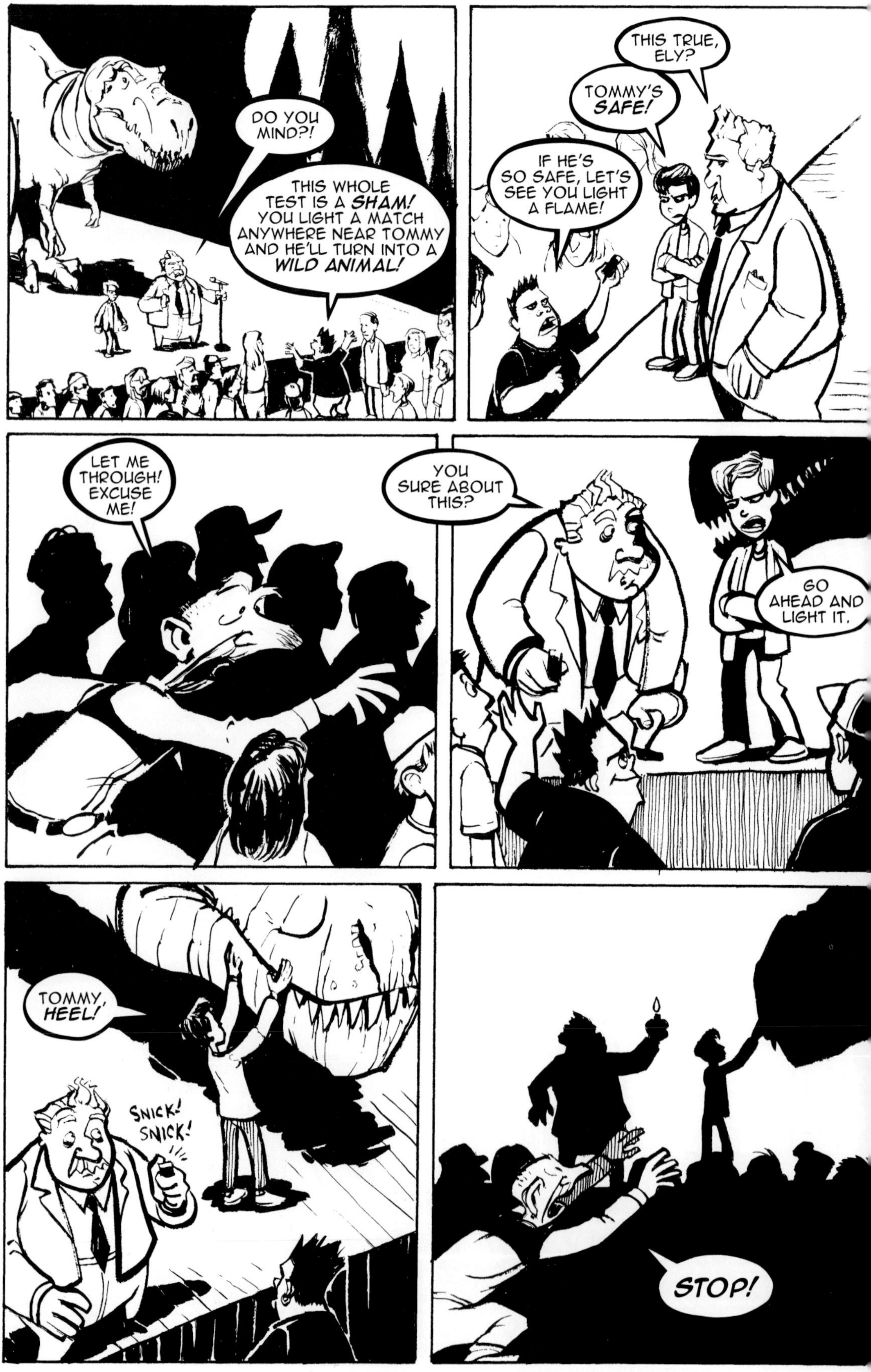
DO YOU MIND?!
THIS WHOLE TEST IS A SHAM! YOU LIGHT A MATCH ANYWHERE NEAR TOMMY AND HE'LL TURN INTO A WILD ANIMAL!
THIS TRUE, ELY?
TOMMY'S SAFE!
IF HE'S SO SAFE, LET'S SEE YOU LIGHT A FLAME!
LET ME THROUGH! EXCUSE ME!
YOU SURE ABOUT THIS?
GO AHEAD AND LIGHT IT.
TOMMY, HEEL!
SNICK! SNICK!
STOP!

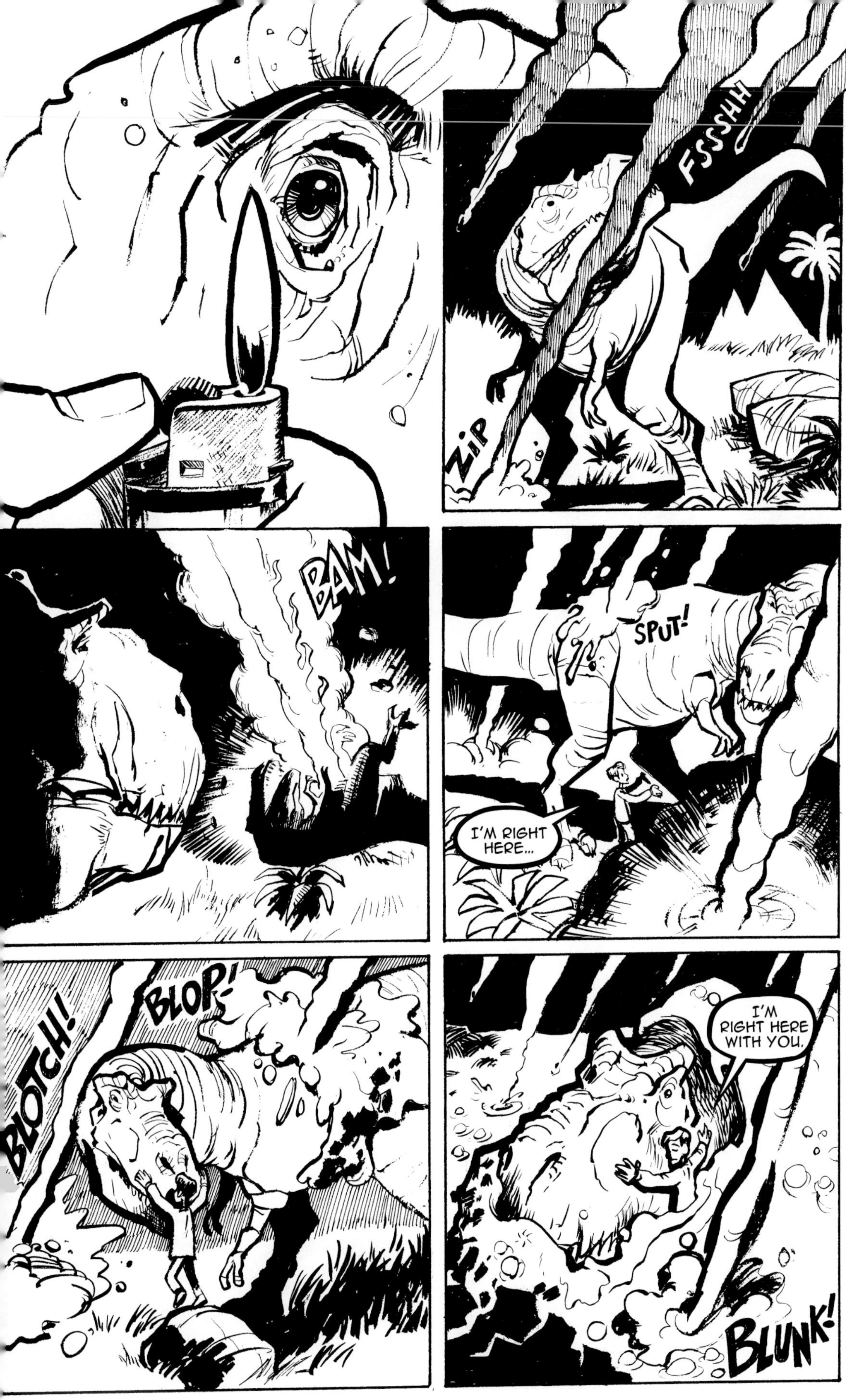
FSSSHH
ZIP
BAM!
SPUT!
I'M RIGHT HERE...
BLOTCH!
BLOP!
I'M RIGHT HERE WITH YOU.
BLUNK!

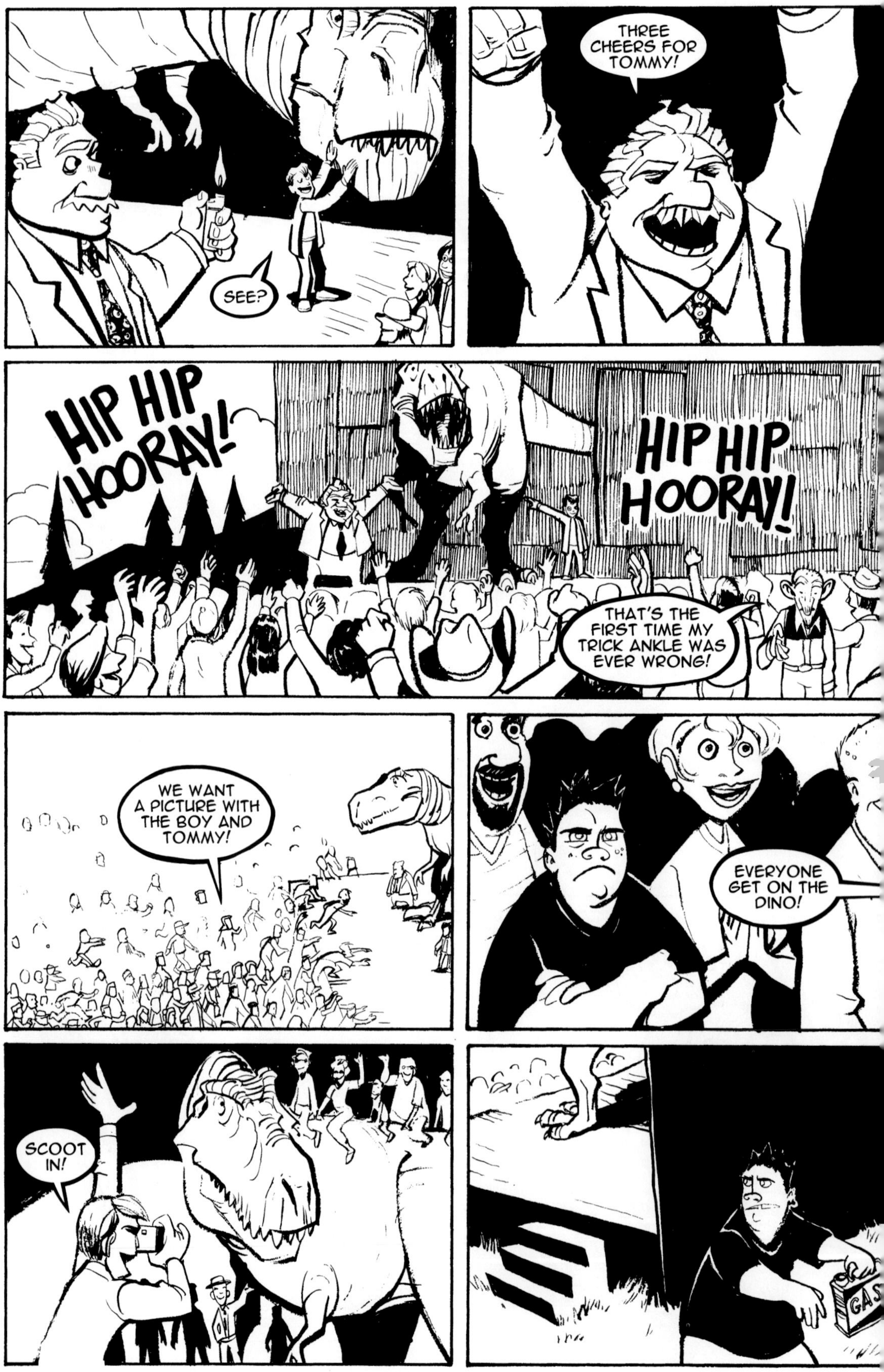
SEE?
THREE CHEERS FOR TOMMY!
HIP HIP HOORAY!
HIP HIP HOORAY!
THAT'S THE FIRST TIME MY TRICK ANKLE WAS EVER WRONG!
WE WANT A PICTURE WITH THE BOY AND TOMMY!
EVERYONE GET ON THE DINO!
SCOOT IN!
GAS

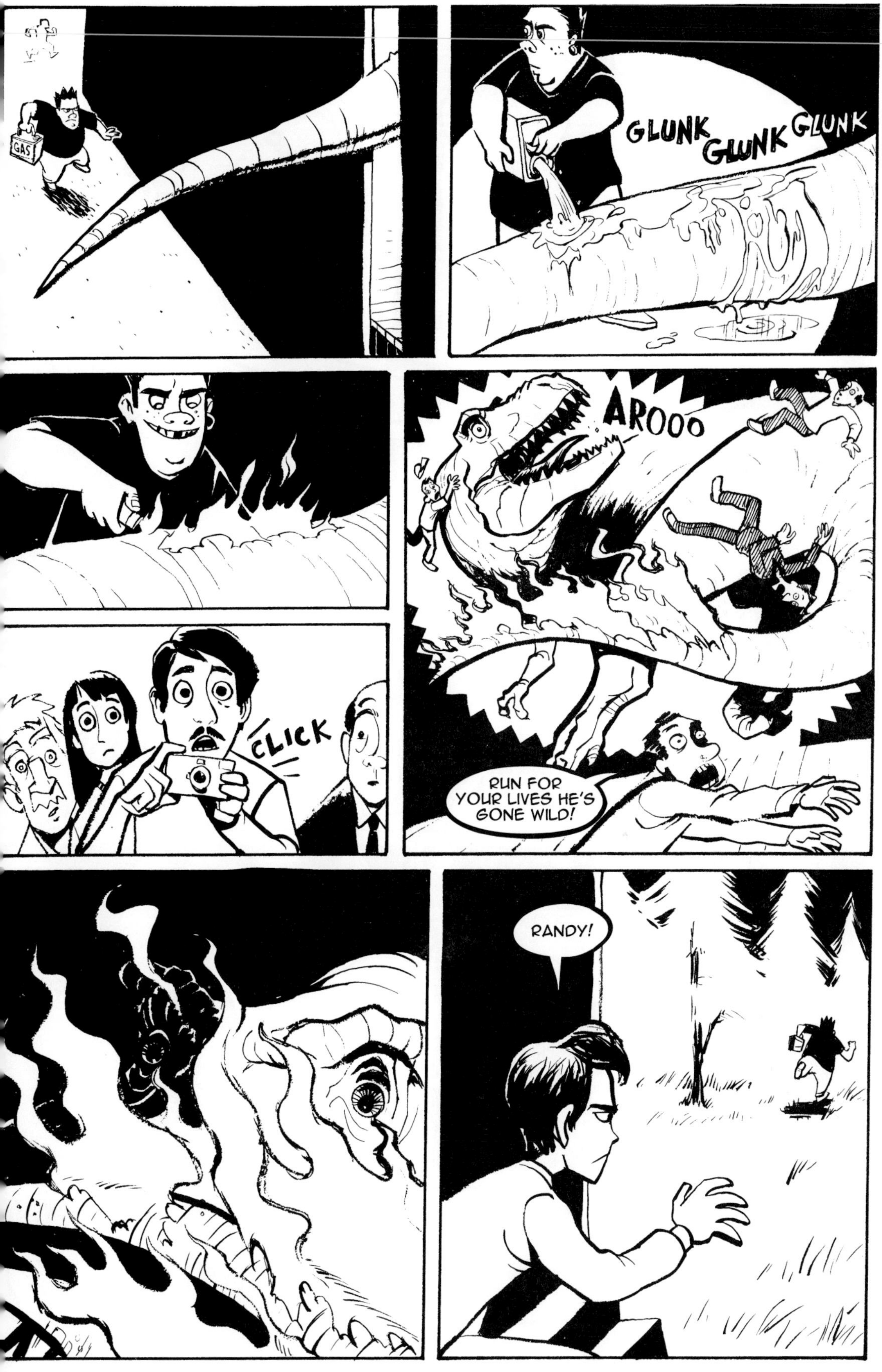
GAS
GLUNK GLUNK GLUNK
AROOO
CLICK
RUN FOR YOUR LIVES HE'S GONE WILD!
RANDY!

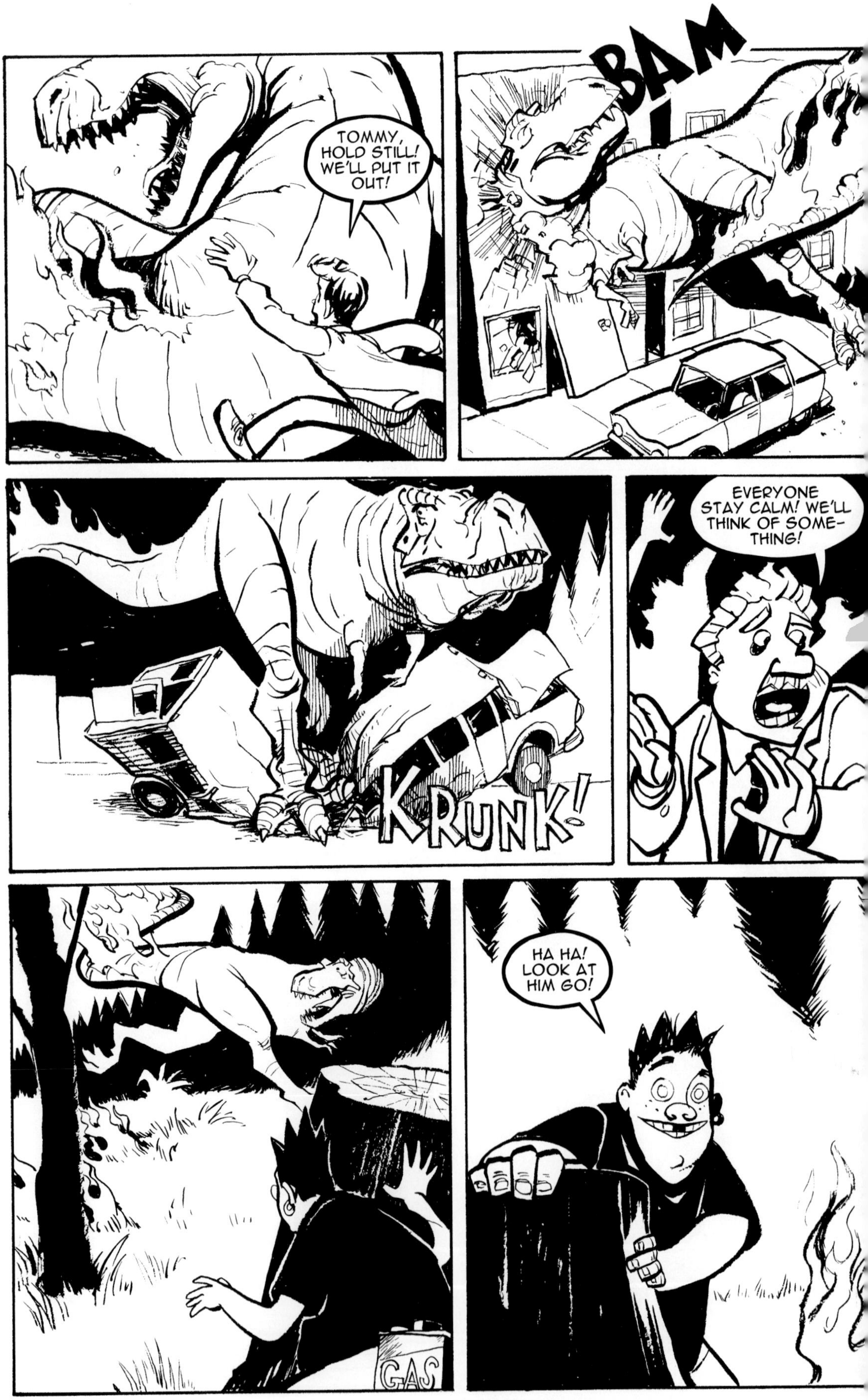
TOMMY, HOLD STILL! WE'LL PUT IT OUT!
BAM
KRUNK!
EVERYONE STAY CALM! WE'LL THINK OF SOME-THING!
GAS
HA HA! LOOK AT HIM GO!

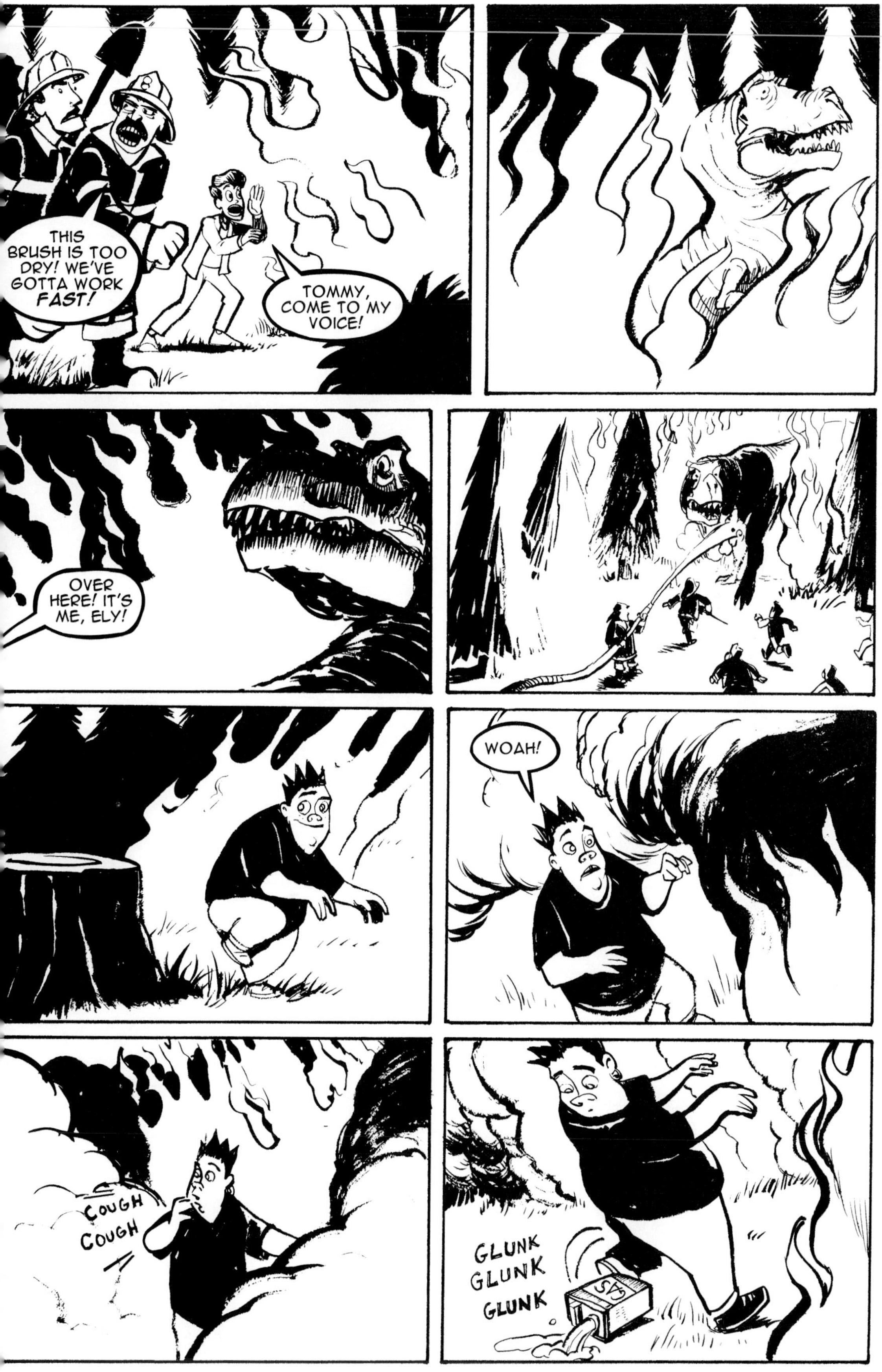
THIS BRUSH IS TOO DRY! WE'VE GOTTA WORK FAST!
TOMMY, COME TO MY VOICE!
OVER HERE! IT'S ME, ELY!
WOAH!
COUGH
COUGH
GLUNK
GLUNK
GLUNK

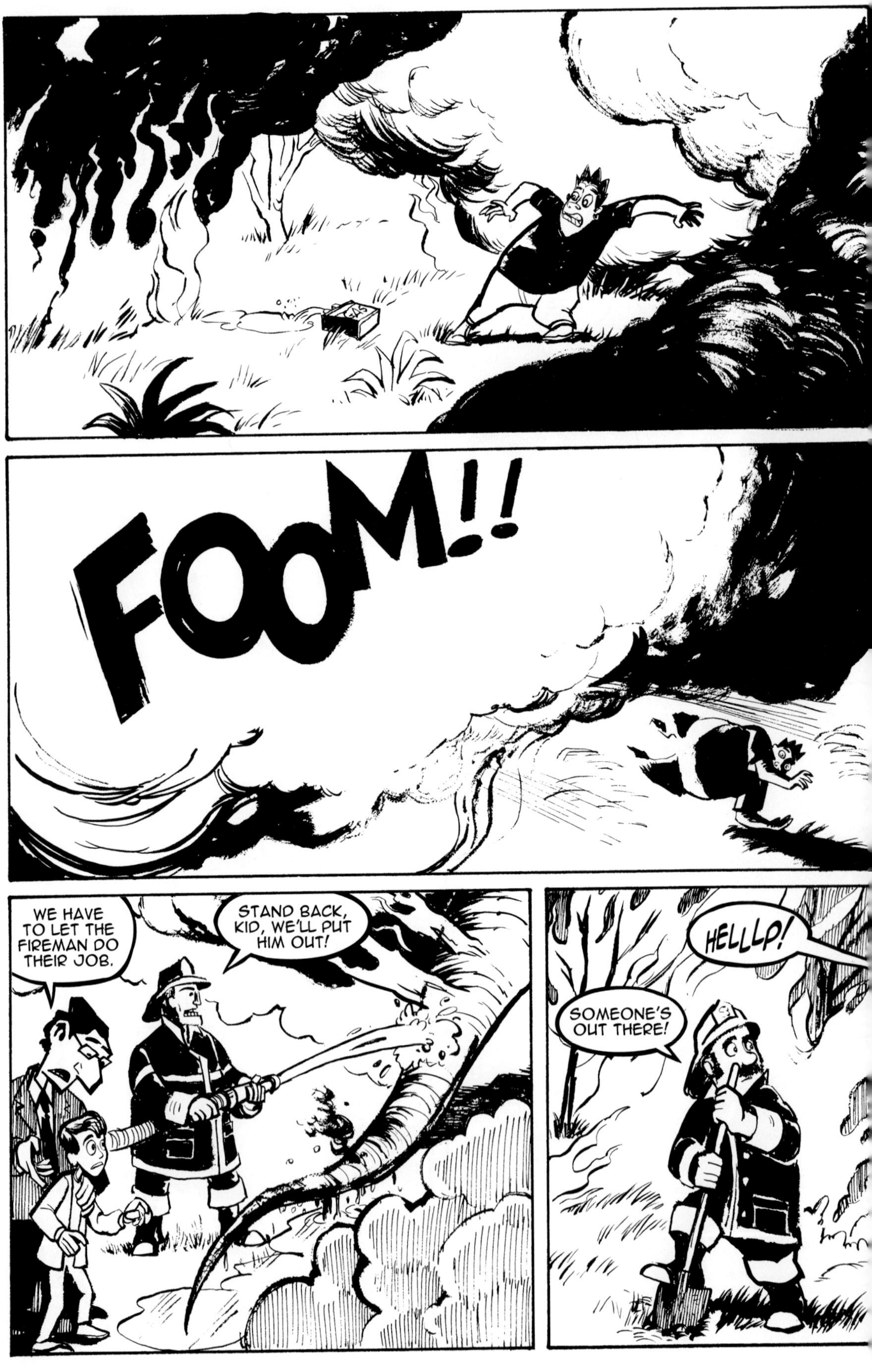
FOOM!!
WE HAVE TO LET THE FIREMAN DO THEIR JOB.
STAND BACK, KID, WE'LL PUT HIM OUT!
HELLLP!
SOMEONE'S OUT THERE!

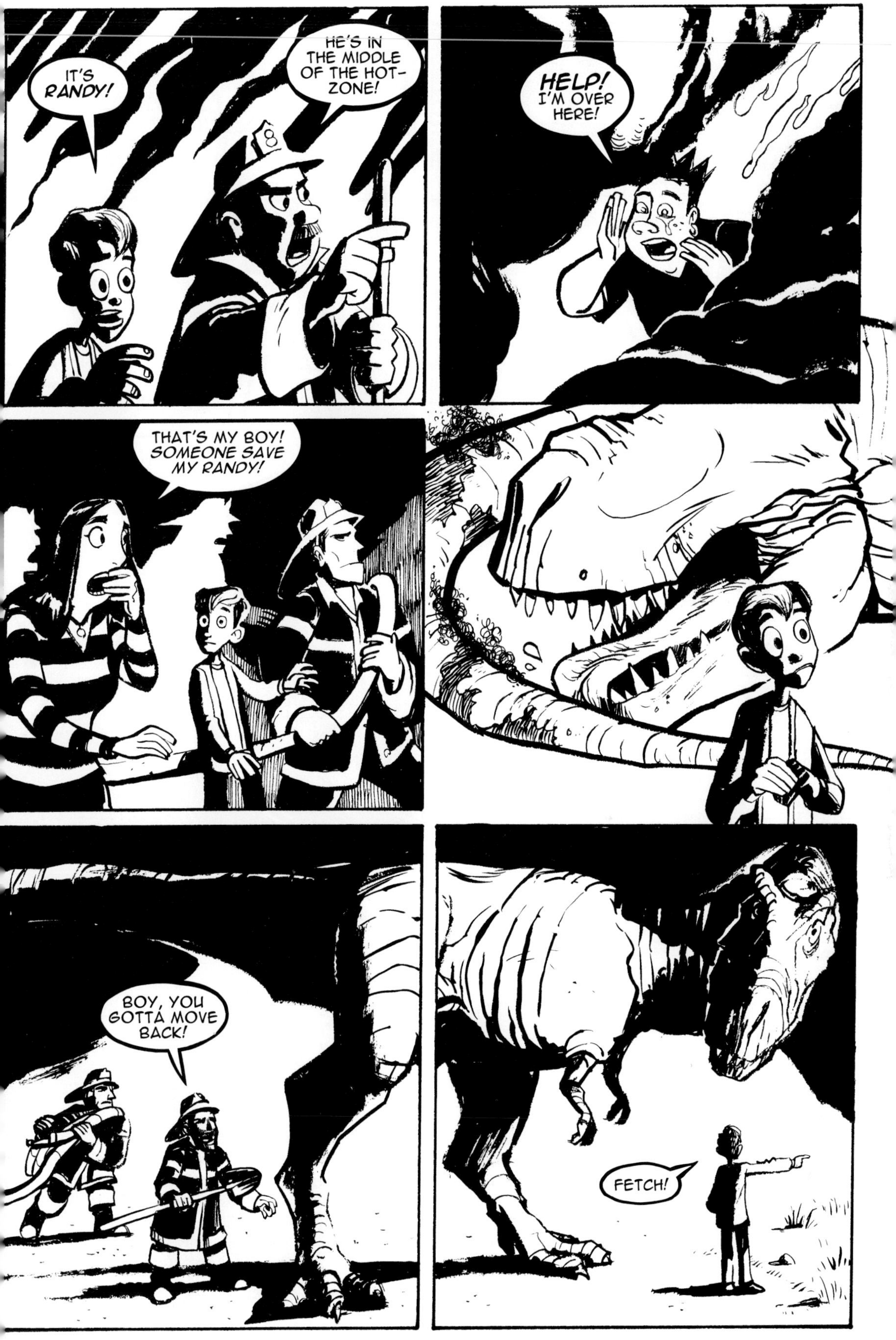
IT'S RANDY!
HE'S IN THE MIDDLE OF THE HOT-ZONE!
HELP! I'M OVER HERE!
THAT'S MY BOY! SOMEONE SAVE MY RANDY!
BOY, YOU GOTTA MOVE BACK!
FETCH!

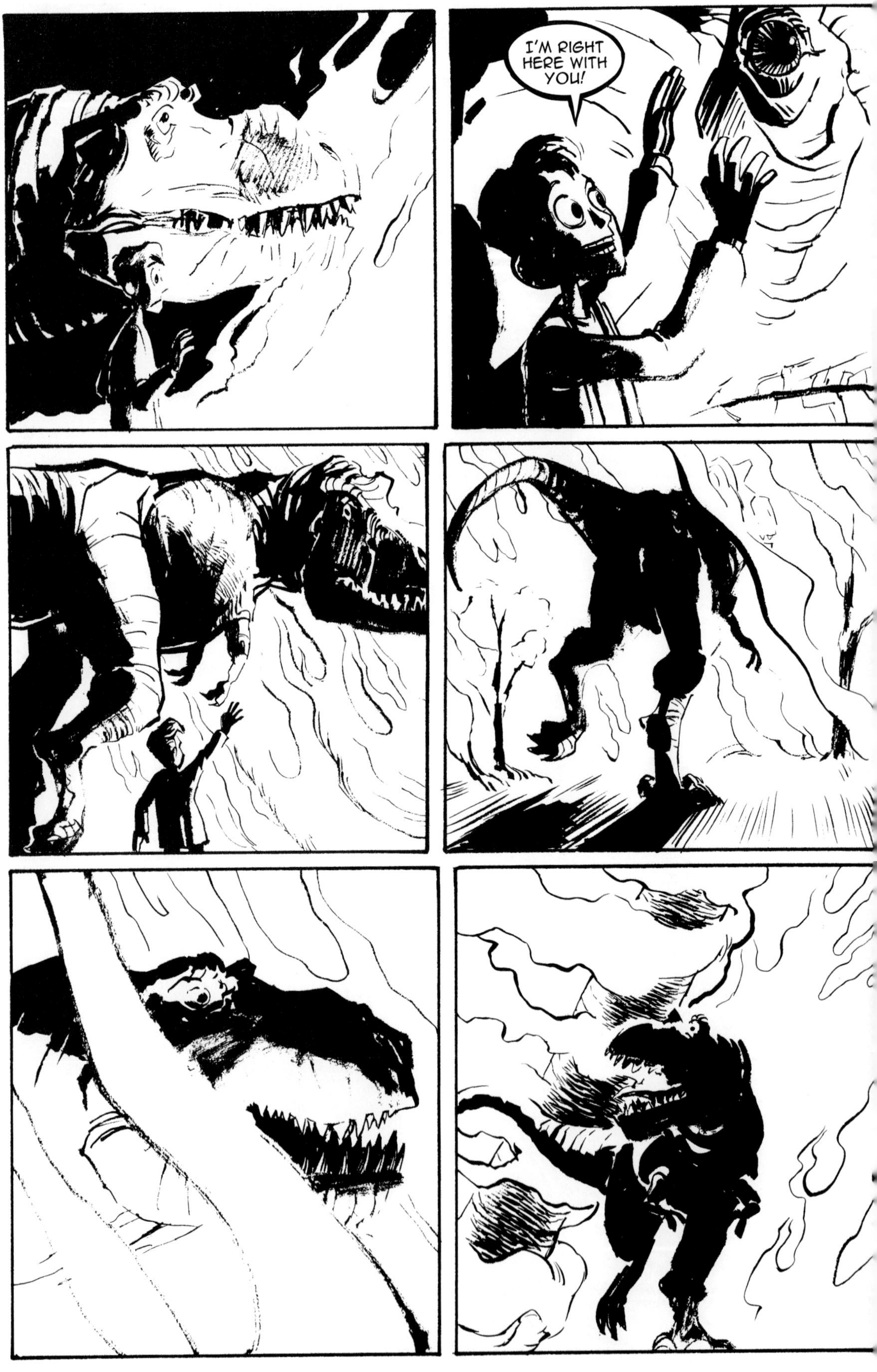
I'M RIGHT HERE WITH YOU!

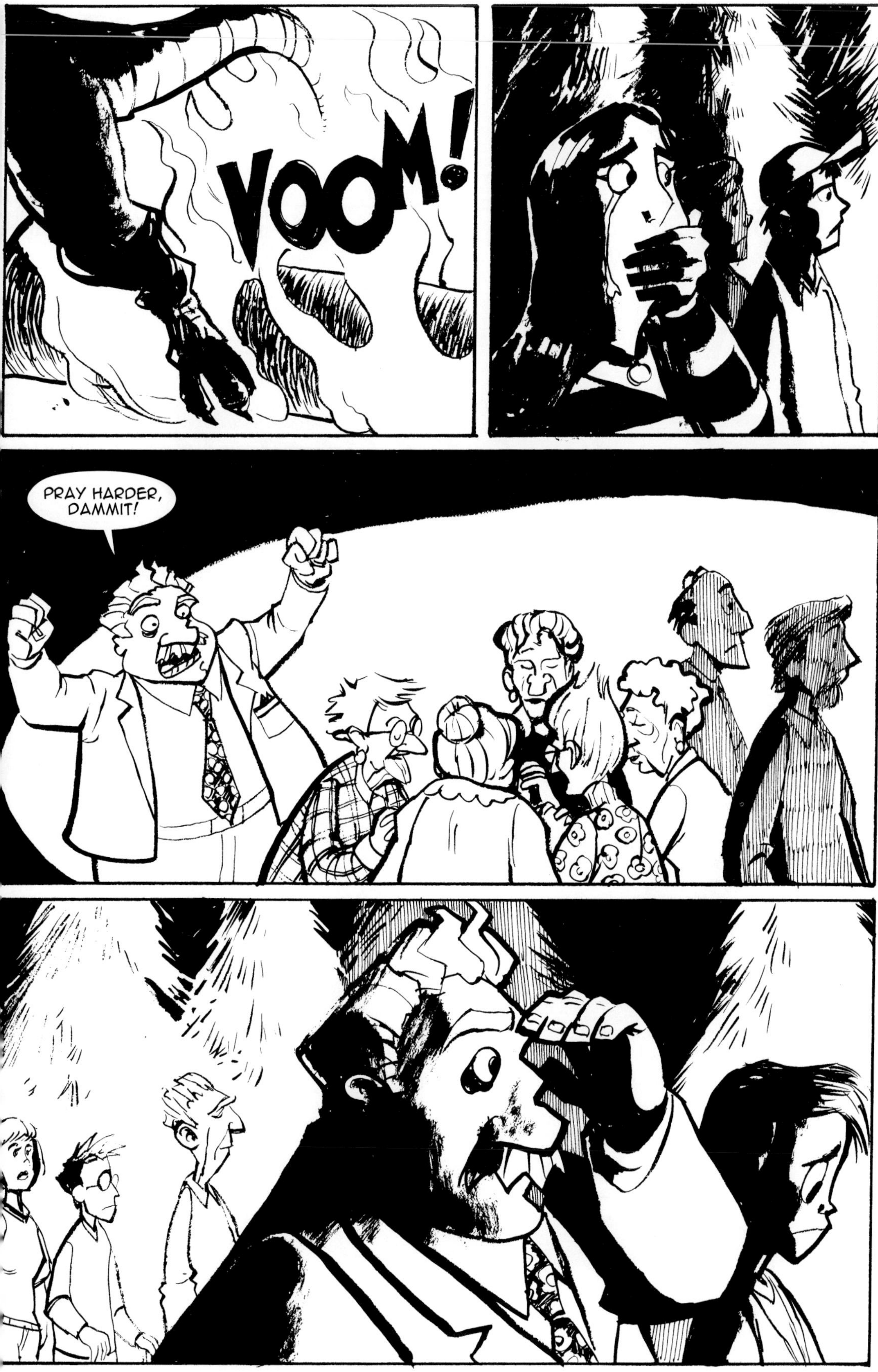
VOOM!
PRAY HARDER, DAMMIT!

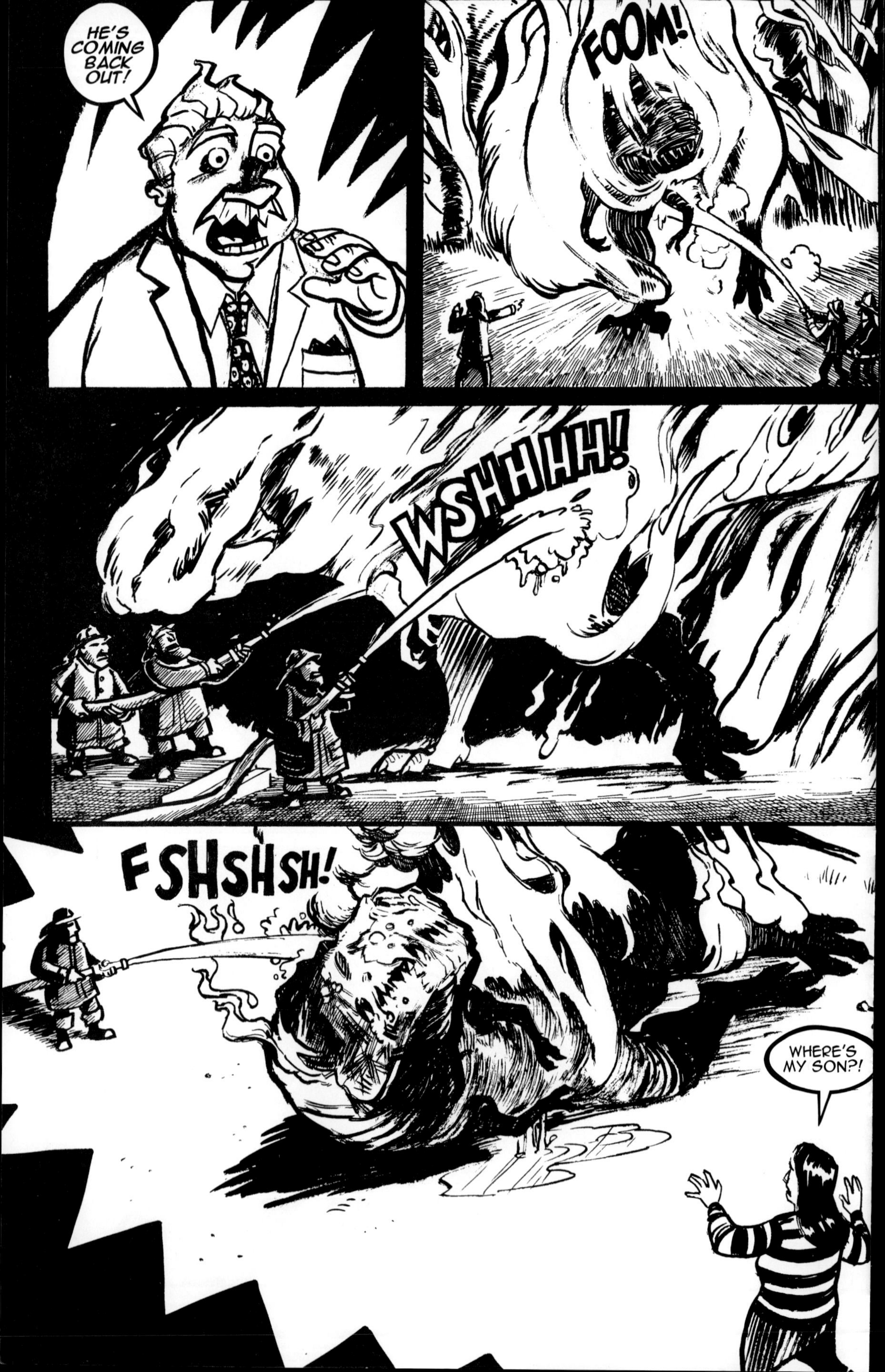
HE'S COMING BACK OUT!
FOOM!
WSHHHHH!
FSHSHSH!
WHERE'S MY SON?!

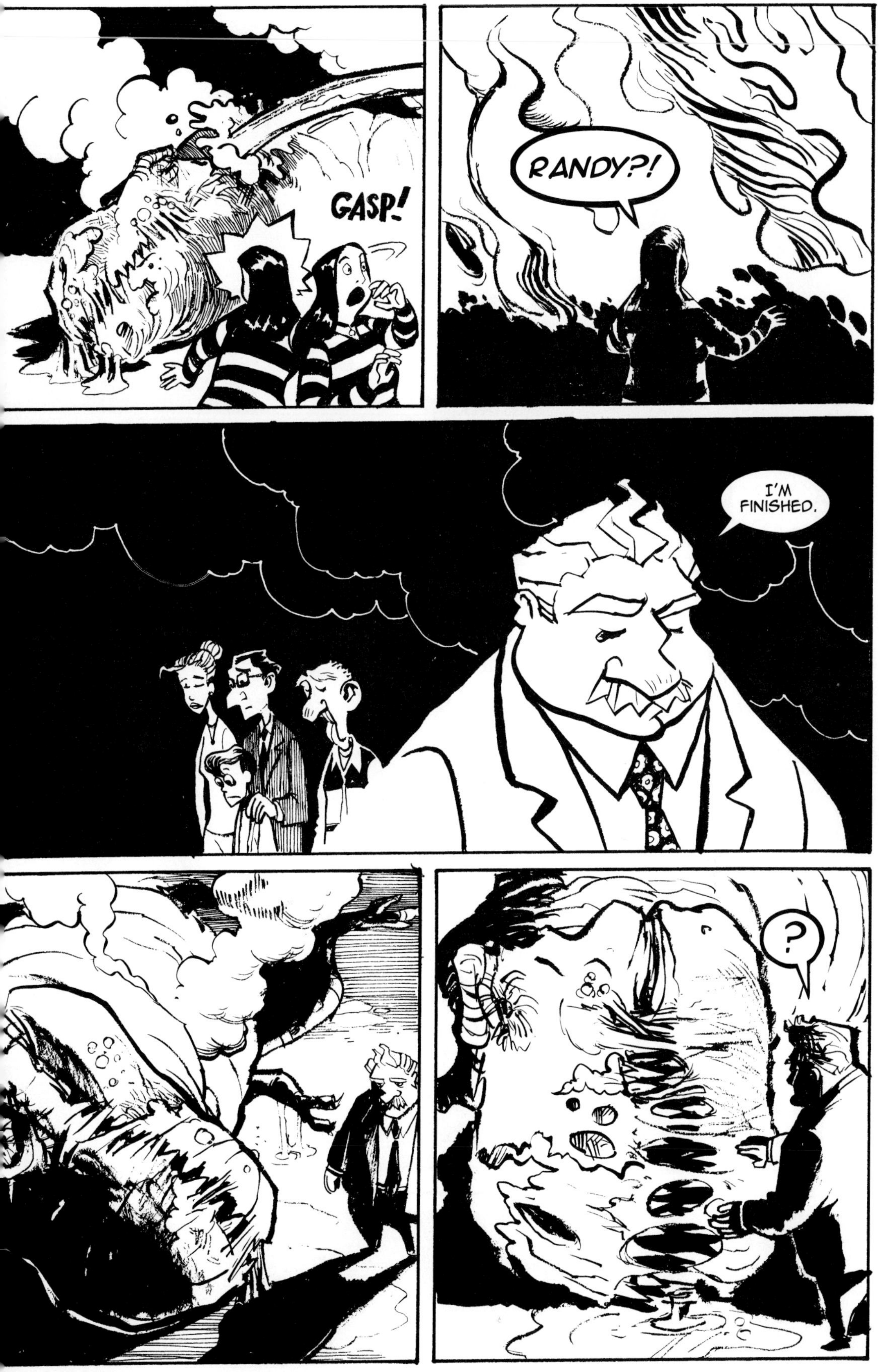
GASP!
RANDY?!
I'M FINISHED.
?

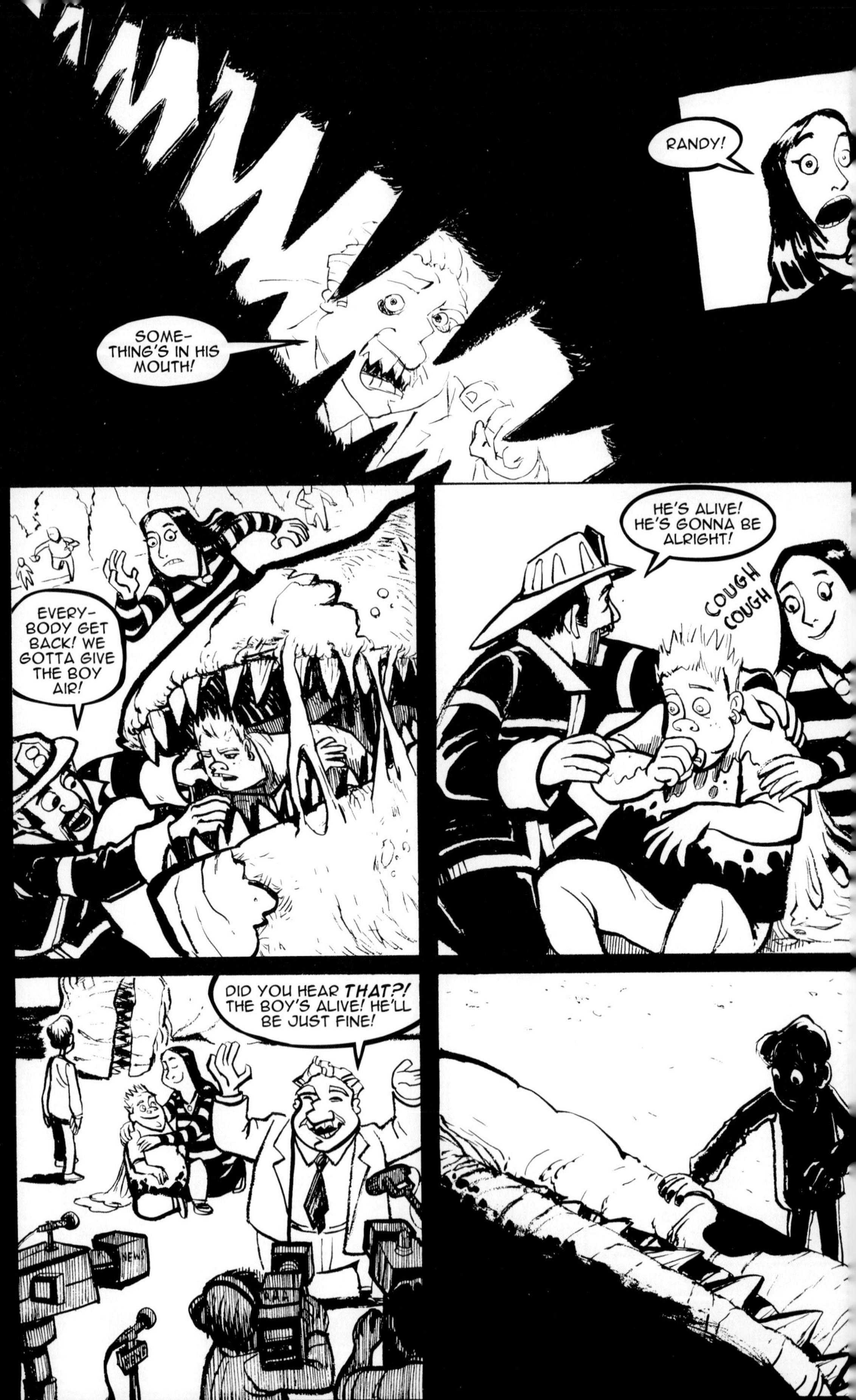
RANDY!
SOME-THING'S IN HIS MOUTH!
EVERY-BODY GET BACK! WE GOTTA GIVE THE BOY AIR!
HE'S ALIVE! HE'S GONNA BE ALRIGHT!
COUGH COUGH
DID YOU HEAR THAT?! THE BOY'S ALIVE! HE'LL BE JUST FINE!
NEWS

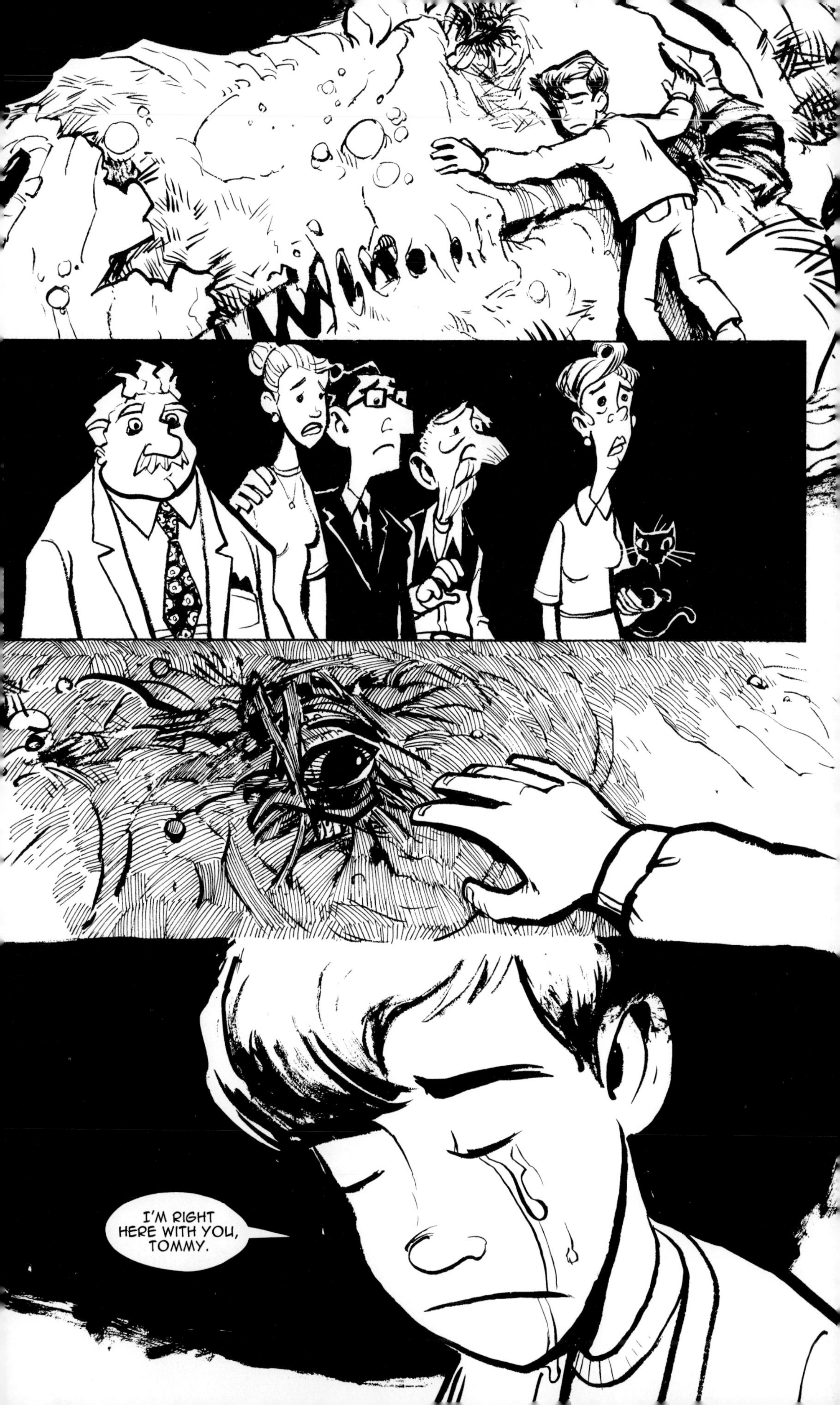
I'M RIGHT HERE WITH YOU, TOMMY.

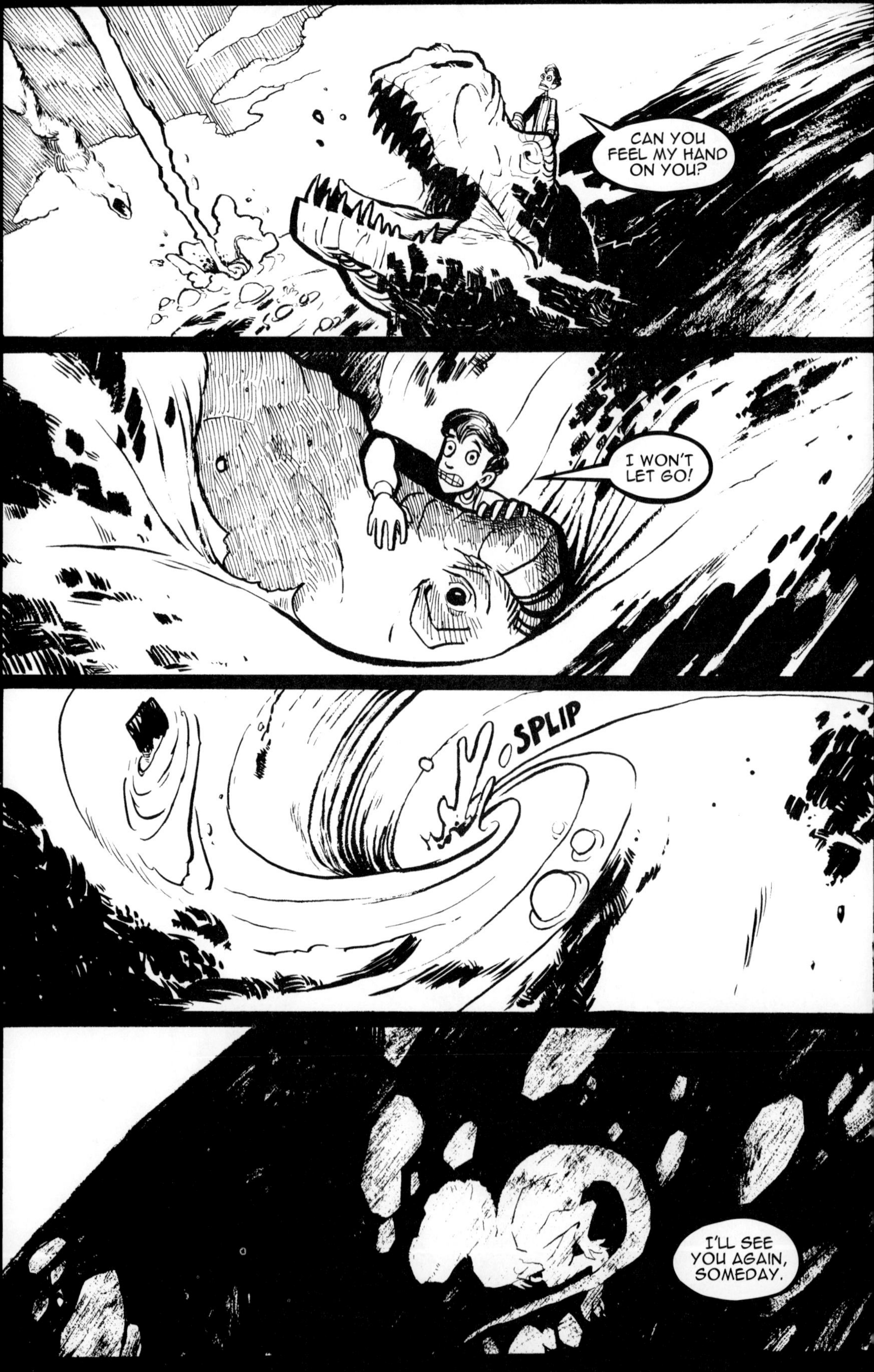
CAN YOU FEEL MY HAND ON YOU?
I WON'T LET GO!
SPLIP
I'LL SEE YOU AGAIN, SOMEDAY.

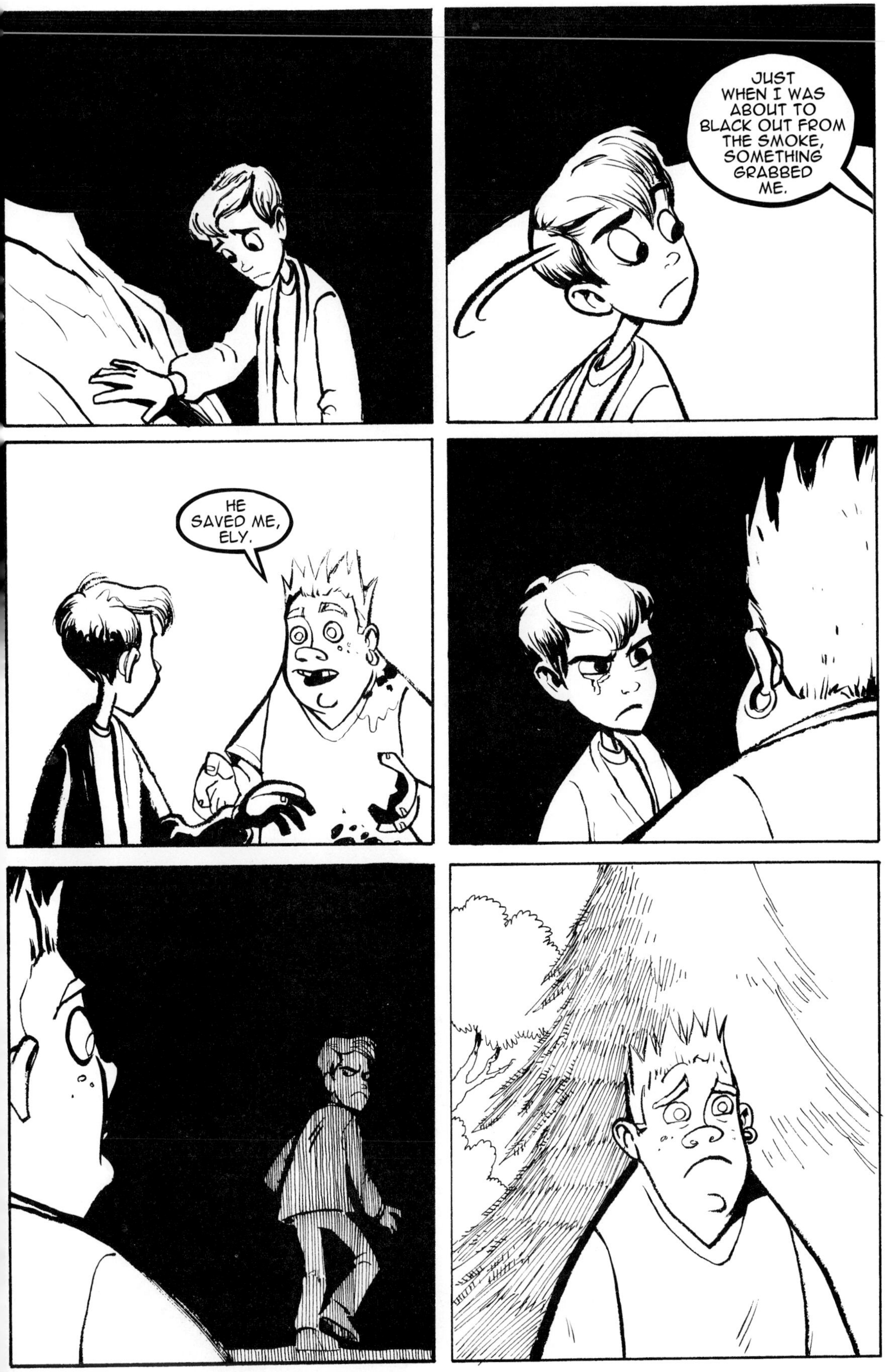
JUST WHEN I WAS ABOUT TO BLACK OUT FROM THE SMOKE, SOMETHING GRABBED ME.
HE SAVED ME, ELY.

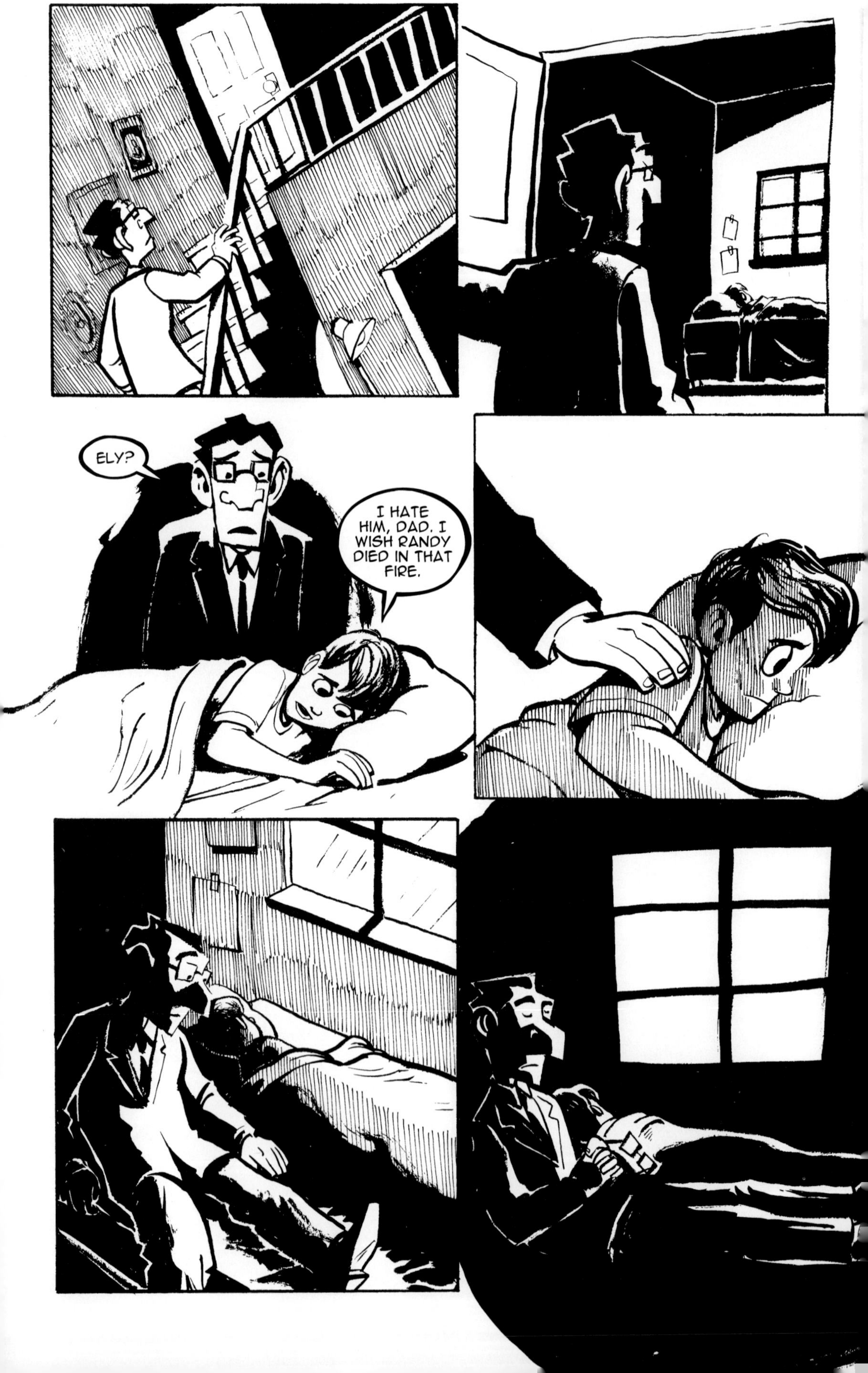
ELY?
I HATE HIM, DAD. I WISH RANDY DIED IN THAT FIRE.

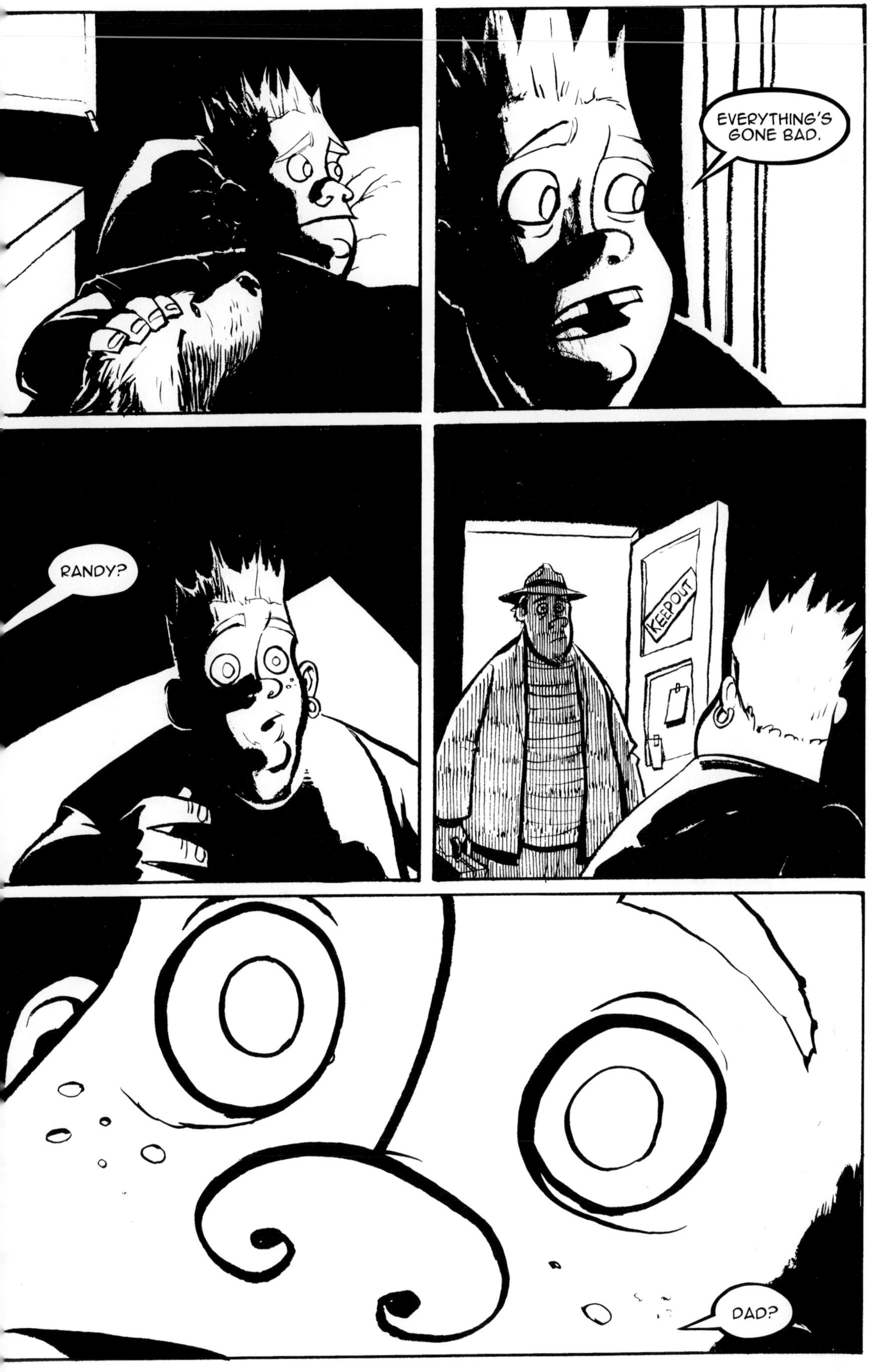
EVERYTHING'S GONE BAD.
RANDY?
KEEPOUT
DAD?

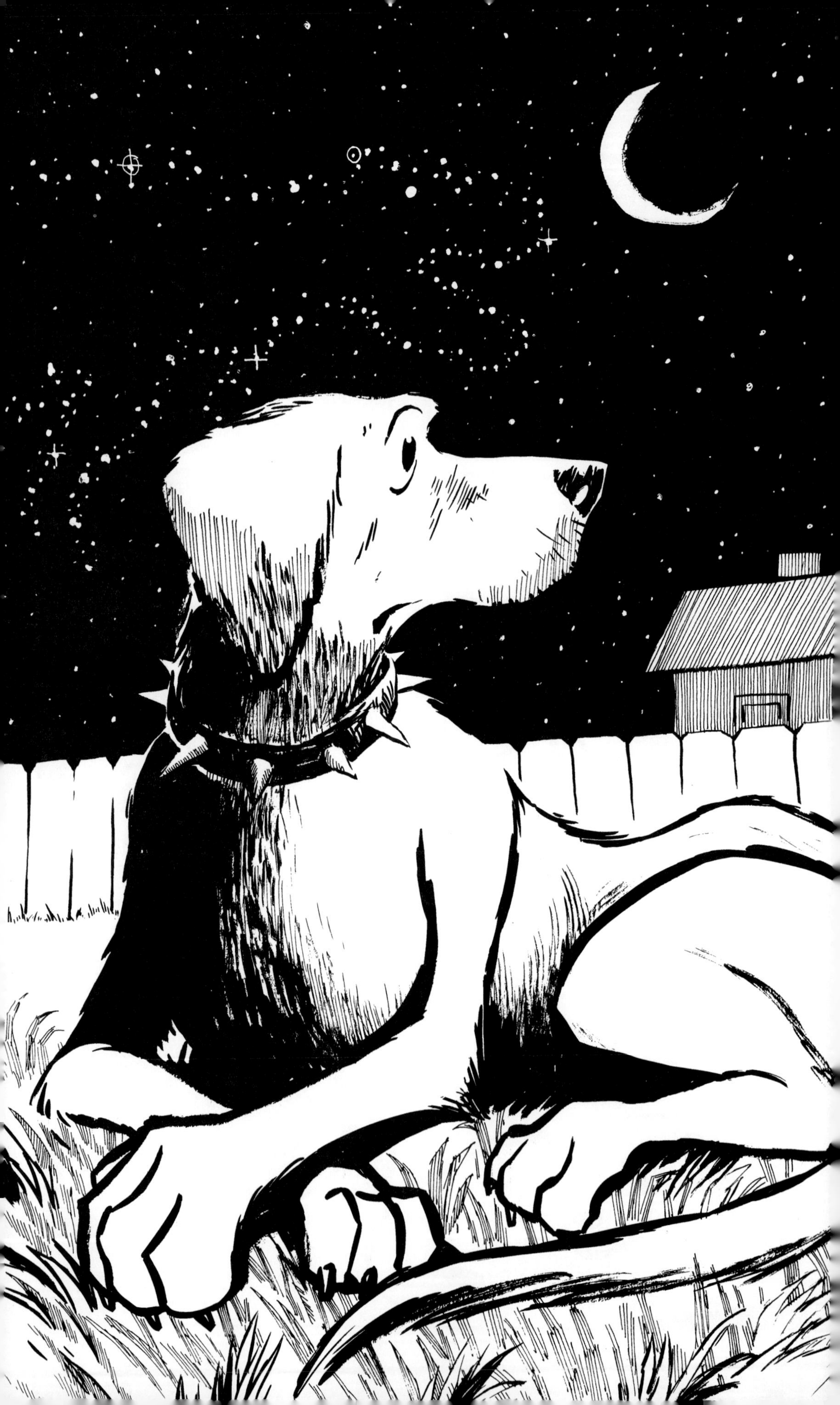

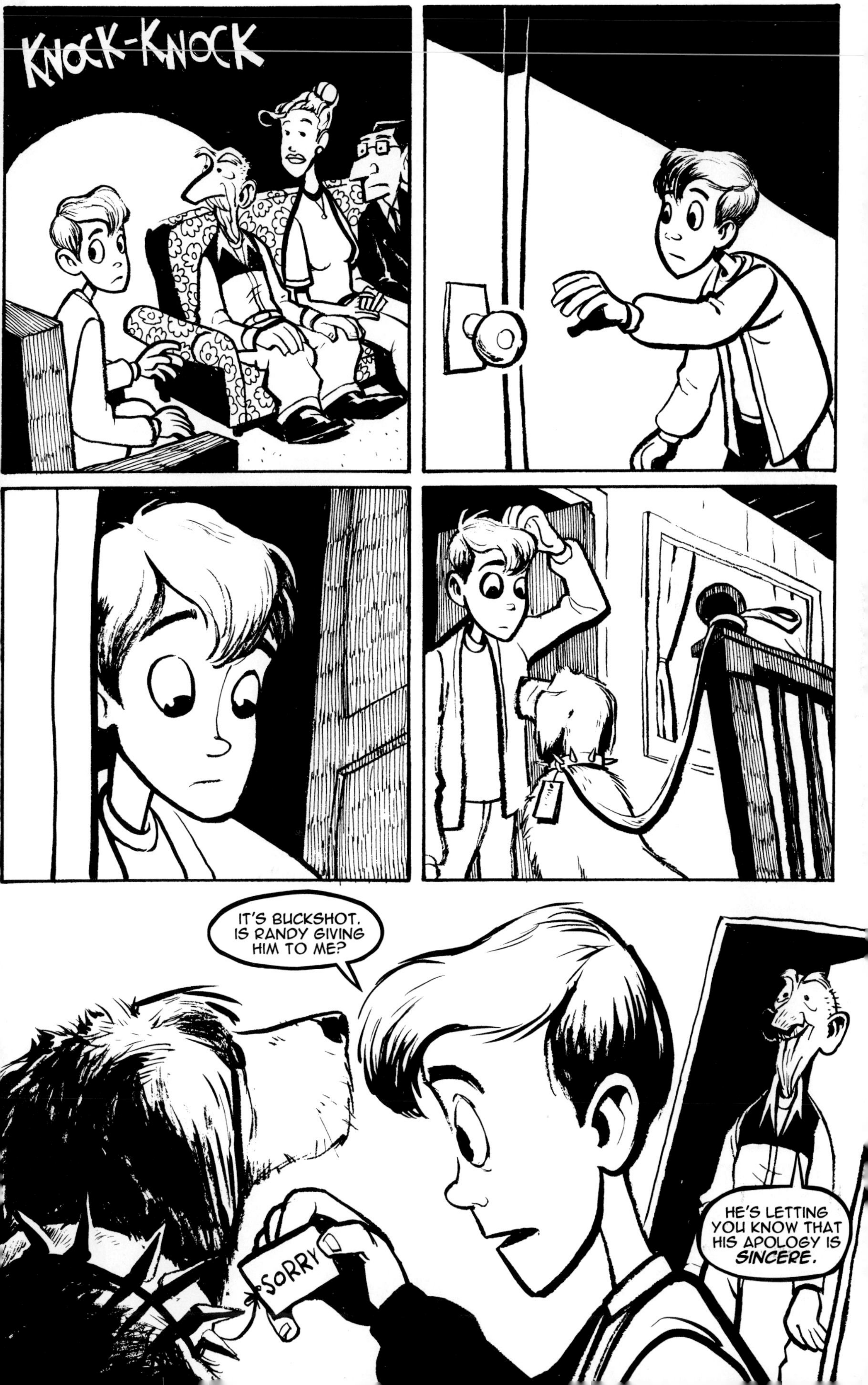
KNOCK-KNOCK
IT'S BUCKSHOT. IS RANDY GIVING HIM TO ME?
SORRY
HE'S LETTING YOU KNOW THAT HIS APOLOGY IS SINCERE.

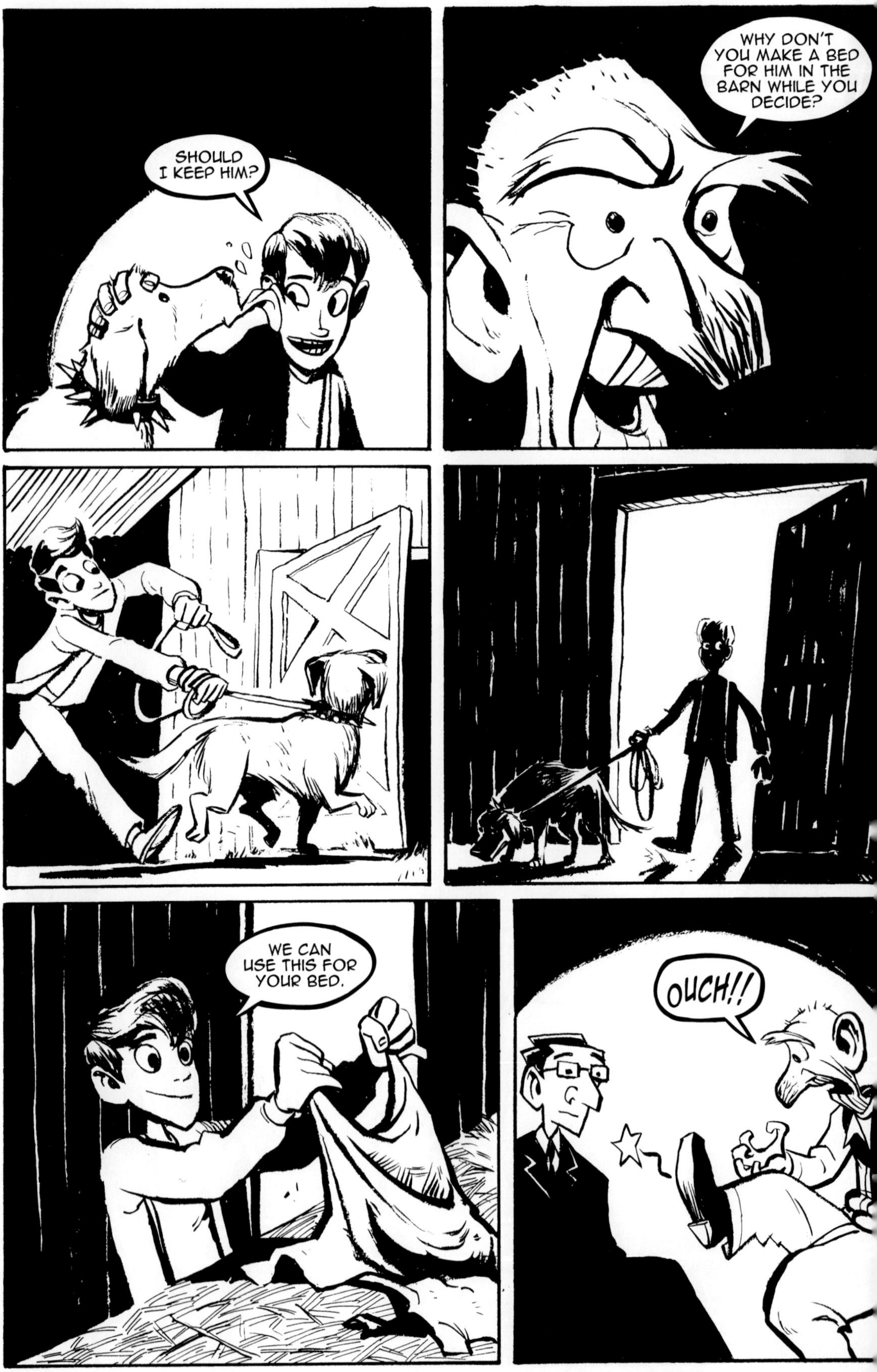
SHOULD I KEEP HIM?
WHY DON'T YOU MAKE A BED FOR HIM IN THE BARN WHILE YOU DECIDE?
WE CAN USE THIS FOR YOUR BED.
OUCH!!

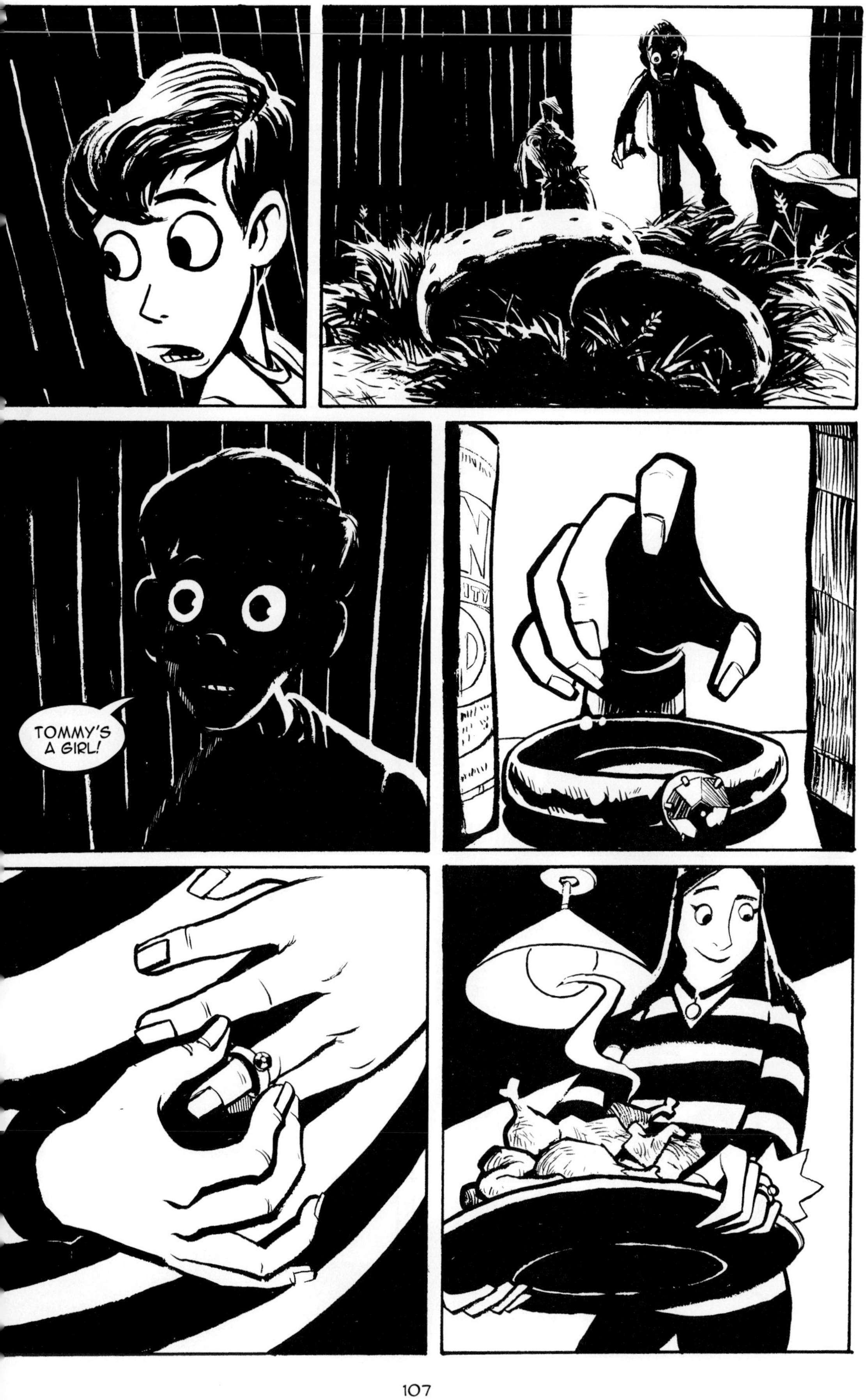
TOMMY'S A GIRL!

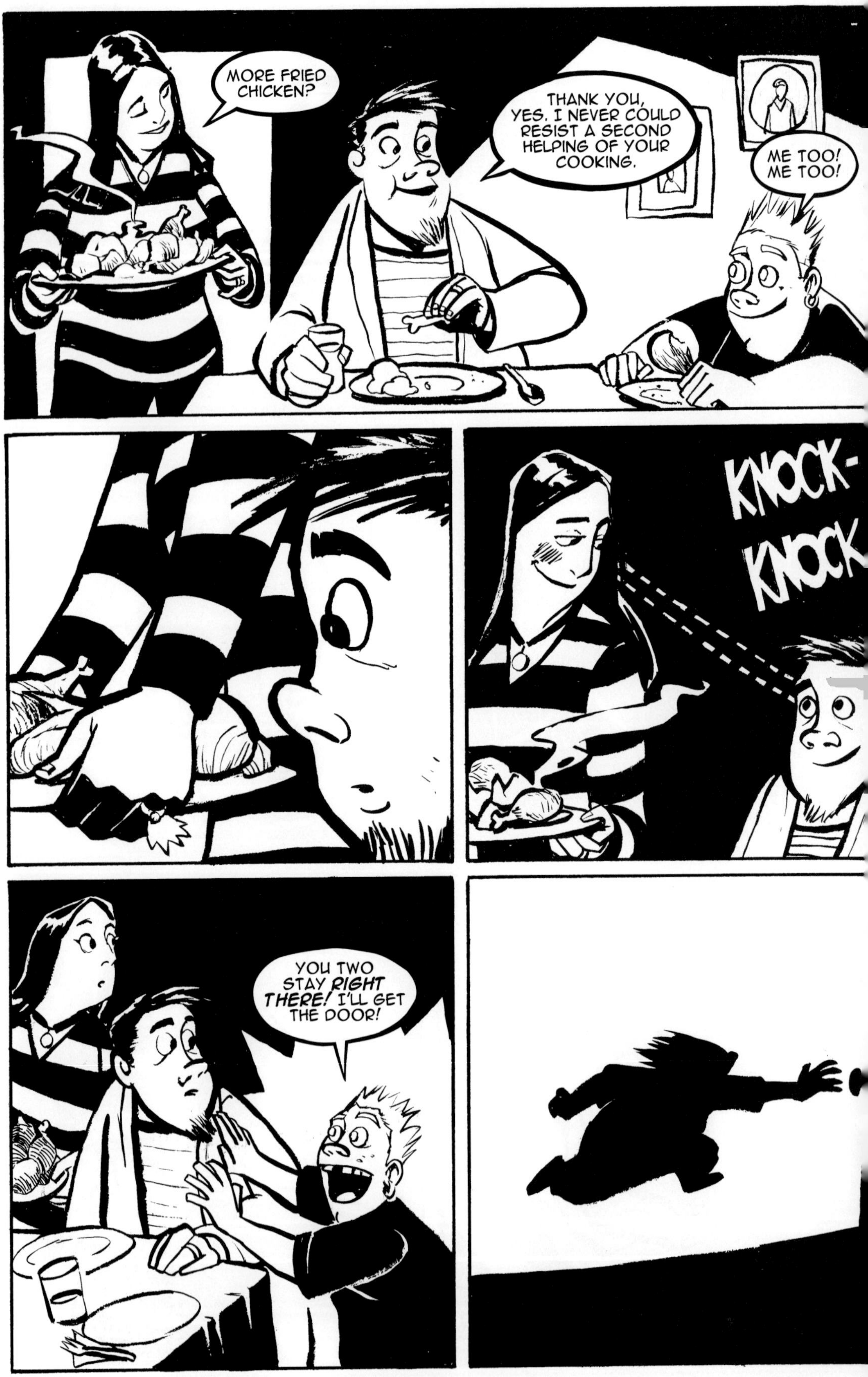
MORE FRIED CHICKEN?
THANK YOU, YES. I NEVER COULD RESIST A SECOND HELPING OF YOUR COOKING.
ME TOO! ME TOO!
KNOCK-KNOCK
YOU TWO STAY RIGHT THERE! I'LL GET THE DOOR!

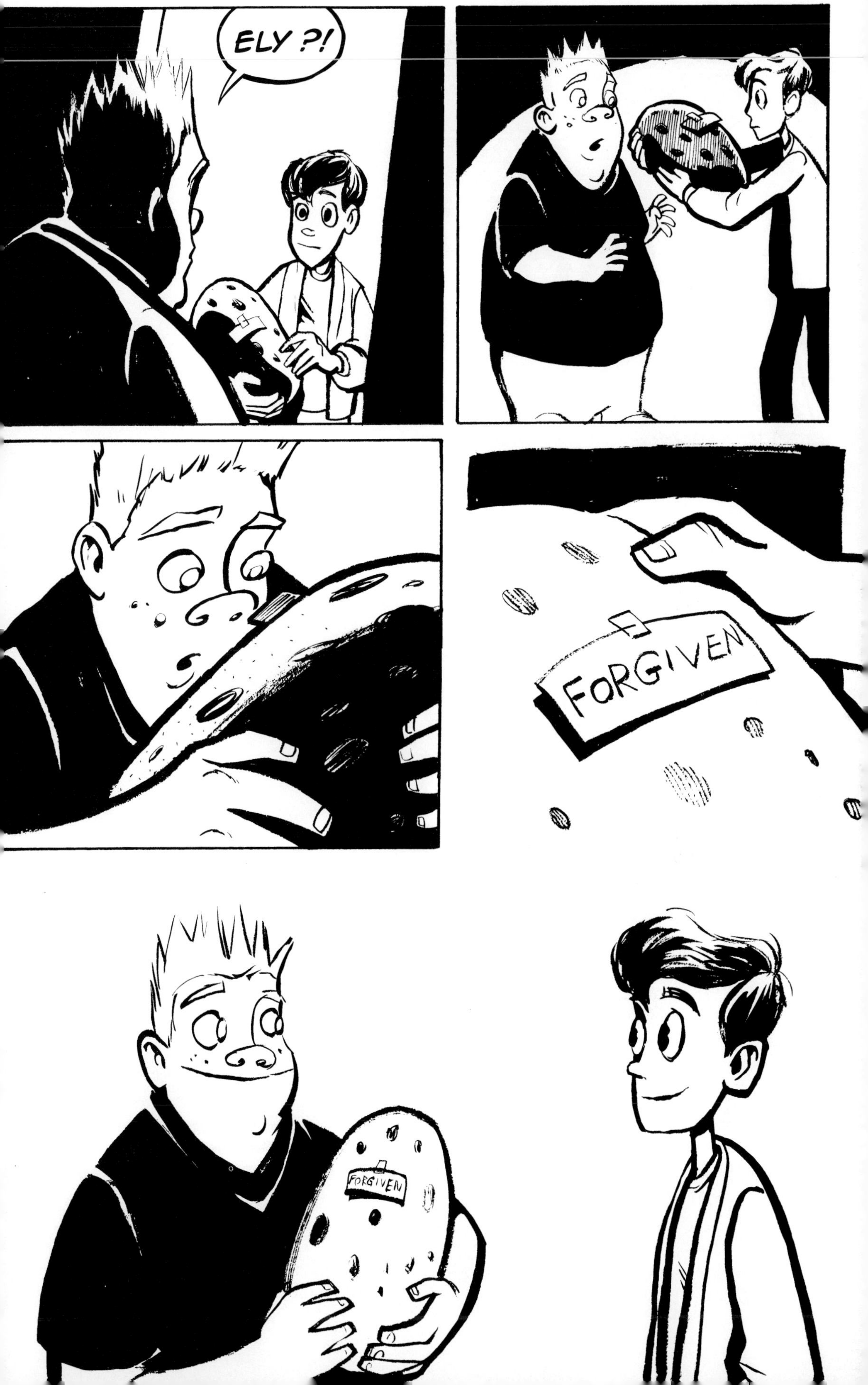
ELY ?!
FORGIVEN
FORGIVEN

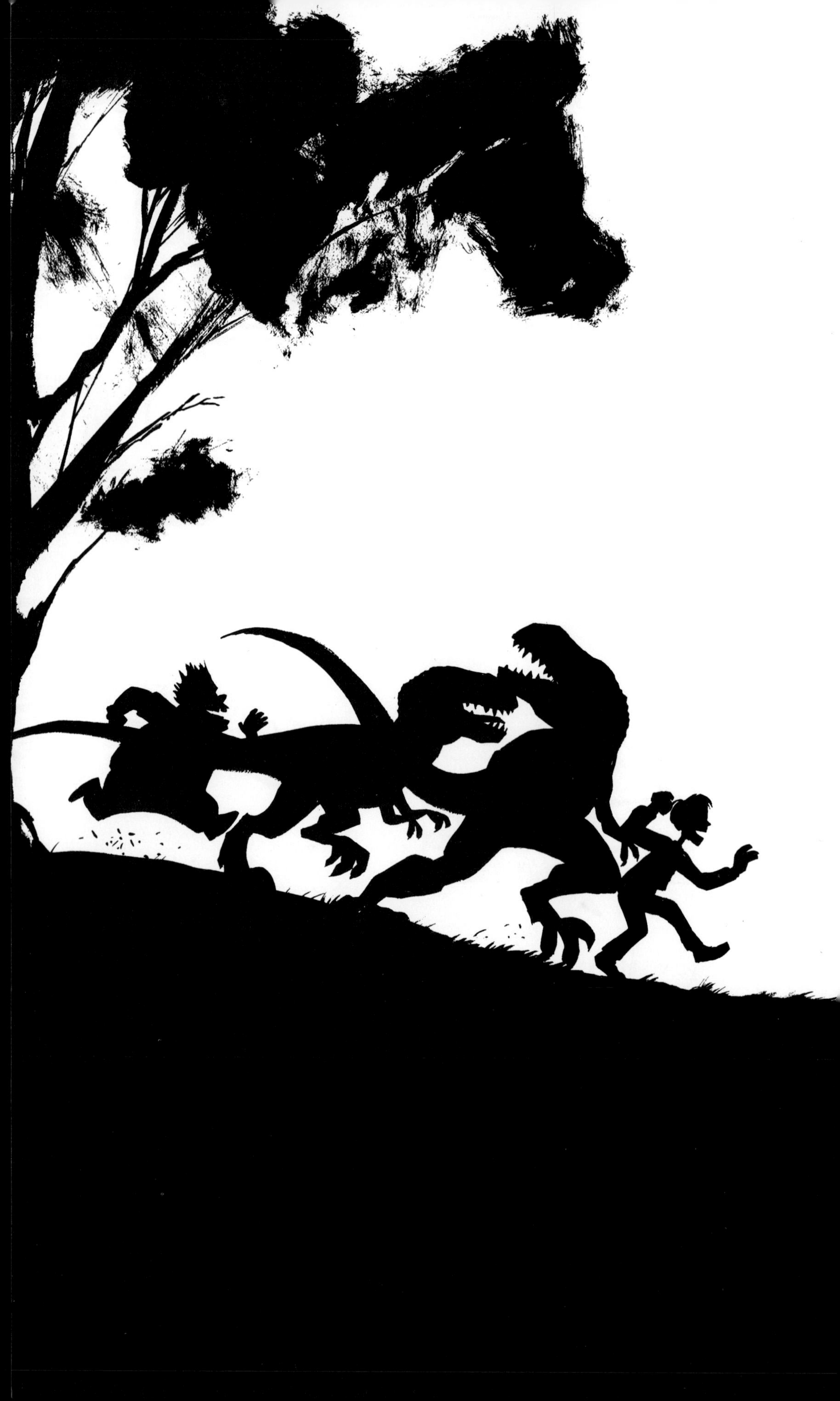

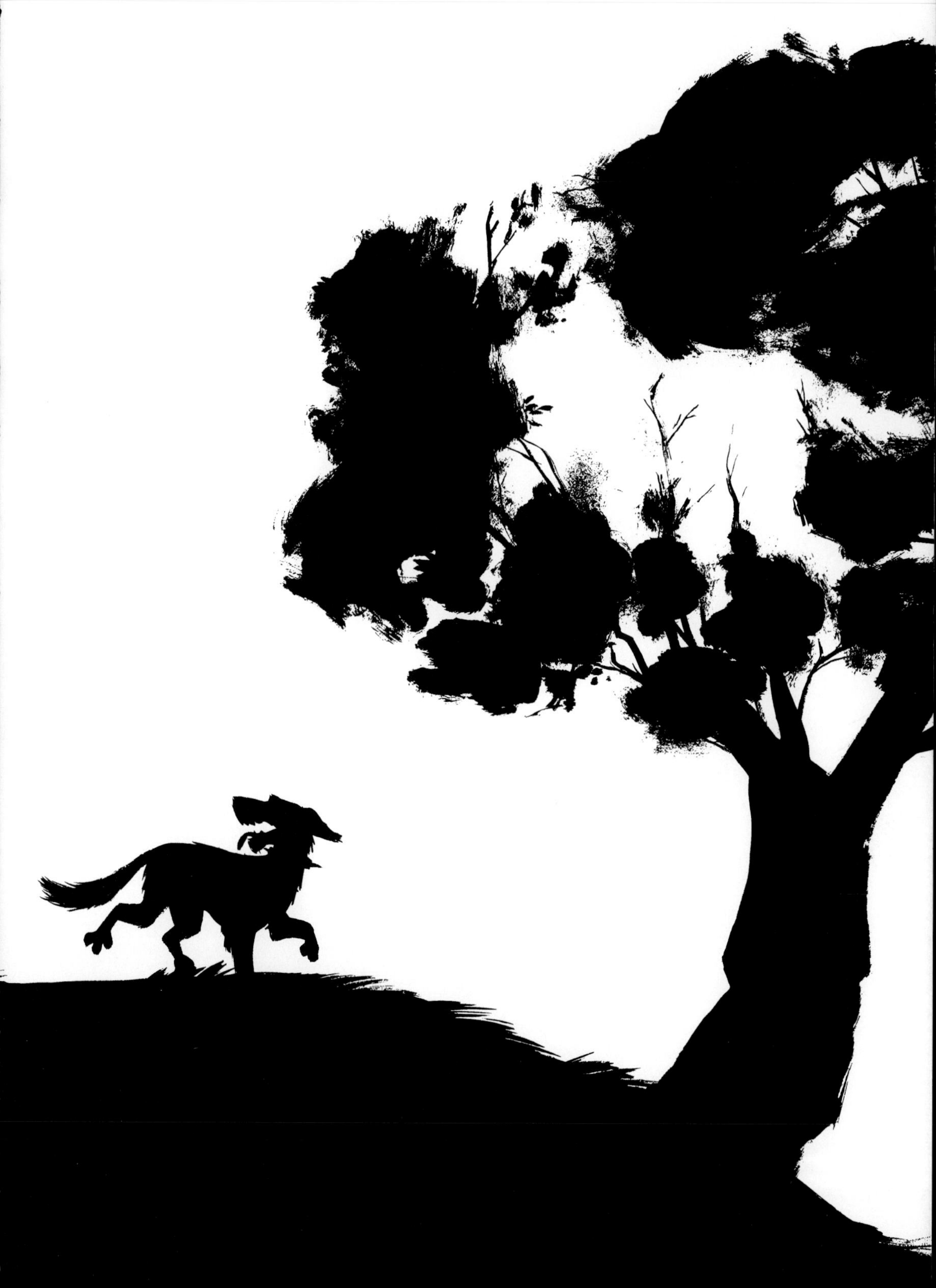